AN ORCHARD IN THE APPLE

A Memoir

Barbara L. Reid

LIGHT
MESSENGER
PUBLISHING

For John
& Bonnie —
I'm lucky to know
a pair of such
generous,
kind people.
Be well!
Barbara L Reid

An Orchard in the Apple

LIGHT
MESSENGER
PUBLISHING

LightMessengerPublishing@gmail.com

Cover design by
Heidi Favour
heidifavour@gmail.com

············

Book interior design by
Robert Lanphear
www.LanphearDesign.com

Reid, Barbara L.
An orchard in the apple/a memoir
ISBN: 978 0-692-93019-9

To my mother, Jacqueline Burd Reid,
a formidable woman and a far-out lady.

Contents

To the Reader vii

We know we belong to the land, and the land we belong to is grand 1

Our dreams are more romantic than the world we see 7

Don't carry the world upon your shoulders 15

Write me a letter containing these lines:
    Answer me quickly, will you be mine? 23

We are family 35

Away out west they have a name 39

[The House, part 1] Build me a castle forty feet high 45

[The House, part 2] Bless these walls so firm and stout,
    keeping want and trouble out 53

[The House, part 3] We climb the stair 63

[The House, part 4] Everybody eats when they come to my house 69

[The House, part 5] Country roads, take me home 77

Bring in the dog and put out the cat 89

He's gone away, for to stay 97

Mama said 105

It's time we hung some tinsel on that evergreen bough 115

Don't you ever ask them why 121

Troll the ancient Yuletide carol 125

Food, glorious food 129

The line is thinly drawn 'tween joy and sorrow 139

On the bonnie, bonnie banks 151

The sweetest days I've found, I've found with you 157

Let's see that dust fly with that broom! 165

The seasons are passing one by one 171

I've loved you since heaven knows when 185

Every summer we can rent a cottage in the Isle of Wight 197

Take me riding in your car, car 213

What else can I be but what I am? 219

Ch-ch-ch-ch-changes, turn and face the strange 227

Some think it well to be all melancholic 235

All I really want to do is, baby, be friends with you 239

No flounces, no feathers, no frills and furbelows 243

Don't know much about algebra 251

Pray that there's intelligent life 259

Afterword 263

Acknowledgments 265

To the Reader

I have written this collection of stories in the spirit of nonfiction, but it is not a historical record. Each chapter has grown organically from its own root to the tips of its leaves. The arrangement of chapters is just short of random, so you can start in the middle and swing from branch to branch if you're so inclined.

Telling my truth is very important to me. Whether or not these stories are accurate in a measurable or observable sense, they are true to my memory and my understanding. Where specific objective data is included, I have tried to fact-check as much as possible. If there are errors in dates or locations, or if I've left out details some might consider essential, I beg forgiveness. Some names have been changed to protect individual privacy, and there is one instance of a composite event – it all happened, but it didn't all happen on the same day.

A word about the chapter titles. A good portion of my youth was squandered in memorizing songs, and I'm desperate to get some marginal use out of the lyrics that continue to flavor my days. Hopefully the reader will see some sort of connection between the stories themselves and the musical phrases which, jostling one another in the dim root cellar of my mind, have risen to the top of the page.

My life has been ordinary and privileged, and I'm eternally grateful. The overarching theme, if there were one, could be called self-to-Self combat. I battle my "little self" – the one that likes to gossip, blame others, cast myself as a hapless victim – while my "big Self" calls me to look beneath the surface, be compassionate, and accept responsibility for my decisions. Each time I act on one of these impulses, toward the small or toward the expansive, I plant a seed in the world, and that seed has the capacity to grow and produce effects according to its nature, sweet or sour. This struggle makes my memoir, I propose, no more than a tiny slice of the human condition.

My family grew me from seed, and they will always remain central to who I am. I'm lucky enough to spend time with several dear relatives in our regular activities. Beyond that joyful present-time reality, I see that everything, known and unknown, that happened to my forebears is part of me, and is part of everything I produce or create. As an apple grows in the orchard, the orchard lives in the apple.

We know we belong
to the land, and the land
we belong to is grand*

I stepped into my shoes to take the compost out past the garage in the dark after dinner. Every day or two, we tossed our food scraps and plant trimmings over the bank at the edge of the woods. This was a normal part of our routine, and it was a long time before I realized that not everyone made compost. (In later years I learned that this was far from the best way to make compost! But at least we were careful to throw only decomposable food, leaves and grass clippings there. Left to its own devices, the pile did gradually turn into dirt.)

As chores went, this wasn't the worst, because you could sometimes accomplish a surreptitious goal at the same time. When the stray calico showed up, and Mother said, "Do *not* feed that cat," my sister and I snatched a couple of Mom's fluffy rice pancakes off the top of the compost and broke them up for the cat to nibble. She seemed very grateful, and decided to stick around to have two litters of kittens in our garage. Threats aside, in the end Mother let us keep them all.

In the semi-rural countryside just north of Edmonds, Washington, we lived frugally, although that term was never used. We turned off lights, wore homemade or hand-me-down clothes, and kept the temperature low, really low. There was a period when we did not have garbage pick-up service, and during that time anything flammable was collected in paper bags and burned in one of the fireplaces. Everything compostable went back to nature. Meat scraps and most

*Lyric from "Oklahoma," Richard Rodgers and Oscar Hammerstein, 1943

bones went to the dog. At the time, of course, the milkman traded full pint and quart bottles for the empty ones we left on the porch. Plastic wrap, bags and containers weren't yet commonly available – instead, Mother had a set of reusable, shower-cap-like covers, in six sizes, to stretch over bowls to keep food somewhat fresh in the refrigerator. And our household didn't use wine, liquor or soda, so we only needed to dispose of tin cans and chicken bones, and an occasional glass jar from mayonnaise or peanut butter. We saved up those things until Dad took them somewhere – perhaps to his office in downtown Edmonds, where garbage was always picked up. There were obvious flaws in this system, but I did develop a lifelong habit of thinking about what becomes of the things that we throw away.

Mom's parents lived at the end of a steep, winding dirt path down through the orchard. The apple trees – perhaps 30 of them – and the huge vegetable garden beyond Granddad's house were central to our lives. They were food sources, but also fields of learning.

In winter, when Granddad pruned the fruit trees, Mother and the three of us helped. While Grandma weeded her yard and prepared a picnic

Barbie (me) standing by the early version of our house, 1947. Right: our grandparents' home. Path to their house is out of sight, beginning on far side of our yard. Upper portion of orchard is on slope in center.

lunch for us all, Granddad wielded clippers, long-handled loppers, and the tall pole pruner with the hook and blade at the end. We clambered along behind him, up and down the damp, grassy slope, to gather the cut branches. My job was to pick up the last of the twigs that everyone else missed. (Anything left behind might later foul the mower.) Without realizing it, I absorbed Granddad's methods, and today, pruning fruit trees is one of my favorite activities. I even like collecting the twigs afterward! At the end of a day or two of pruning, our great reward – and certainly my brother's favorite part of the project – was roasting wieners over a bonfire of the branches.

My parents shared with Mother's parents a certain farming mentality, and this meant that we did not waste food, because someone had worked hard to grow it. The evidence was right before our eyes. If the land provided abundantly for us, it was because we acknowledged our responsibility to the land.

We didn't have a washing machine when I was small because Grandma had one, and as long as Mom could navigate her way up and down the narrow, crooked path with a full laundry basket, why waste resources on a second machine? On wash day I usually spent the afternoon with the two of them, playing quietly while they worked and talked. One of my favorite pastimes there was arranging and rearranging buttons from Grandma's button box, creating symmetrical designs and entire flower gardens on the tabletop.

The agitator was on wheels, and they pushed it close to one of the sinks to fill it through a detachable black rubber hose. When the machine was working, its labored sound was faintly troubling, as though it were struggling to do its job. They set it over a floor drain, where, after a certain span of huffing and panting, the agitator's stopper was removed so that it could be emptied and refilled with rinse water. I was proud and excited when the two women declared me old enough to put the clothes through the wringer and crank the handle myself. But first, my waist-length braids must be secured at the back of my head, and I had to be cautioned again to keep my hands away from the rollers. There was no dryer, and I loved helping hang the sheets on the clothesline, backlighted by the late morning sun.

At home, the hum and "tic-t-tic-t-tic" of the sewing machine was the soundtrack of my childhood. Mother had been wardrobe mistress in the drama department during her university years, and now she made nearly all our clothes. She even sewed beautiful, closely fitted slip covers for the furniture. The family's norm was that we saved money by staying away from stores.

My dad was largely separate from our day-to-day frugality, only because he was usually not at home. But he was far from a spendthrift. He bought his shirts and shoes from Sears Roebuck, and his workday lunch, at the counter of the village café around the corner from his office, was a simple sandwich. The truth is, he probably had no time to consider shopping or eating expensively. Once he started his engineering firm, his focus was almost entirely on his professional life. He worked long hours at the office, and although more often than not he came home for dinner, evenings were spent either back at the office writing reports, or attending a huge variety of meetings in the five cities where his business operated – Chambers of Commerce, Port Commissions, Utility Districts, School Boards, Rotary – all in his Sears suits.

None of us would say we had a miserly existence. At home, we had lighthearted free entertainment. While Mother was a dyed-in-the-wool teacher, and insisted on correct enunciation of every sound in the English lexicon (we all knew that "wear" and "where" are meant to be pronounced differently), we also had the option of playing with words. Spoonerisms such as "flutterby" and "one swell foop" showed up regularly in our language together. My mother and aunt taught us the special terms they had invented when studying French in school: *Merci beaucoup* became "murky buckets," and even today, my siblings and I check our watches whenever one of us says, "Kill a rat-tail?" (*Quelle heure est-il?*)

Before being blessed and cursed by the mesmerizing cathode ray tube, we played board games. Parcheesi and Clue were simple enough for me to enjoy, and the risk of hitting the slide in Chutes and Ladders felt rather exciting. Our card games included two with special decks of cards. All I remember about the first game is that every player's goal was to avoid ending up in the dreaded role of Old Maid – a premise which is quite an affront to today's feminist perspective. The most educational game was called Authors. Each card in the pack had a picture of a famous author along with his name and the title of one of his works. This is the only place I was exposed to the names of James Fenimore Cooper or Sir Walter Scott, or titles such as "The Charge of the Light Brigade," "A Tale of Two Cities," or "The House of the Seven Gables." We children studied to do well in school, but despite Granddad's Ph.D. in English, in our family we weren't exposed to literature.

We had art projects. With Mom's guidance, we used long-bladed tinsnips and needle-nose pliers to cut and curl the lids of empty food cans into three-dimensional metal stars, flowers and other shapes for the winter holidays. Mother told us later that other parents disapproved of her leading us in such a dangerous activity. Why, we could slice ourselves open with the metal edges! She scoffed, knowing how closely she always supervised us. We embellished these tin creations with bright nail polish and airplane-model paint, then suspended the weatherproof ornaments from the branches of one of the trees near the front yard. They flashed and twinkled in the breezes there at the top of the hill. There were also year-round papier-mâché animals and tissue-paper stained glass windows and melted-crayon pictures.

Our parents generously provided their time and resources to round out our education. (Truthfully, time on Mother's part and resources from Dad, at least in the early years.) There was always plenty to eat. We learned the names of all the plants in the woods and picked apples, blackberries and huckleberries. We tramped a half-mile down the hill to the rocky edge of Puget Sound for clamming or beachcombing. Mother made sure we were involved in the preschool co-op, Scouts and PTA. We had music lessons and coaching in athletics or art, and our parents didn't skimp if supplies or equipment were needed for our activities. The whole truth about any family is always complicated, but there's no doubt we were gifted with an abundant upbringing, springing from strong roots of conservation and simplicity.

Our dreams are more romantic than the world we see*

They came from different worlds and they lived in different worlds. They married, and that made all the difference.

Jacqui was a golden girl at university – professor's daughter, bright on her own merits, and artistically gifted. Her father insisted on fully funding college educations for all three of his children, and she was the first beneficiary. For a woman to develop her mind for the mind's sake was still unusual, and she thrived in the academic world. She and her friends had lively fun in Seattle's University District, with an occasional outing to Portland, OR or Vancouver, BC. Bachelor's degree, responsible work in the drama department, Master of Fine Arts, all while living in her parents' home as most unmarried women did.

Jim, on the other hand, fought his father to be allowed a university education. At his dad's insistence, he worked the family farm full time for two years after high school, then escaped with a small stake for tuition. After the first year or so of college, his father refused to send him the rest of the salary he had been promised as a farmhand, accusing him of "wasting money on wine and women." Jim, already frugally sharing a boarding-house room in Seattle, didn't speak to his father for years. He quit school to work entry-level jobs, until he accumulated enough funds to continue his education. Intelligent but not privileged, he finished by dint of single-mindedness and perseverance. Casting off earlier feelings of indebtedness to his father, he even found time to participate in varsity sports, applying earnest

* Lyric from "Make Believe," from Showboat, Jerome Kern and Oscar Hammerstein, 1927

effort to both work and play. With his new degree, he eventually won a government job in the Territory of Hawaii.

From rare conversations over the years and some old photos, plus, no doubt, liberal doses of my own imagination, I've put together a picture of their early marriage.

In the late 1930s on Oahu, Jim experienced an unfamiliar liberty. He worked hard at his job there, but the pay was adequate, there was time off and co-workers to enjoy it with, and they were surrounded by sunshine, beaches and coral reefs. They organized light-hearted competitive distance swims and spear-fishing dives, sand picnics, and songs and stories around campfires. They were clever and funny, and learned to count on each other.

Jim with fish on spear, 1938

When he brought Jac back after his nuptial trip to Seattle, his friends welcomed her with "aloha" cordiality, took her home to dinner, showed her around the island.

The gorgeous flowers everywhere thrilled her. But there was a worm in the apple – the climate. In her high school years she had been somewhat of an outdoor enthusiast in the forests and mountains of Washington State, but she had never been comfortable in hot weather. The unrelenting humid heat of Hawaii was oppressive. She was a Northern Star apple tree transplanted into coconut country. She wore wide hats and sought out shade and breezes. Worse, she had never learned to swim, so beyond ankle depth, she couldn't join the gang jumping into the ocean to cool off.

Photos show Jim clowning around on the shore with the group. I don't know if all the snapshots were taken before Jac arrived, or if she never did put on a bathing suit and participate in the beach parties. Either way, fitting

Newlyweds arrive on Oahu, January, 1940

into Jim's social world was anything but natural for her. The urban entertainments that had livened her days were conspicuously absent. The house was small with thin walls, providing little privacy for newlyweds and no place to host supper for a crowd. She had left her beloved family and her cosmopolitan friends twenty-five hundred miles away, and she wasn't one to instantly bond with new acquaintances. She must have been terribly homesick, but wouldn't want to dishearten Jim by exposing her distress, so she had no one to turn to with her confusing emotions.

Another development compounded her physical discomfort. Before she could say *humu-humu nuku-nuku apua'a*, she was pregnant.

As a child I noticed that Dad seemed always to be angry at both Mother and Carolyn. With Mom, I felt he was just returning like for like. They were stuck in a sort of involuntary boxing match in an unbreakable clinch. But why Carolyn?

At age thirteen, I noted in my diary that even if she and I were doing exactly the same thing – reading magazines, for example – he would shout at her and pat me on the head. She was always doing something wrong. Applying my youthful brain to this puzzle, I compared the wedding date – December 25, 1939 – and my sister's birthday – September 13, 1940. Although thirty-seven weeks is within the normal human gestation timeframe, it's on the short end. She was a big baby. I concluded that she must have been conceived out of wedlock.

First I hypothesized that she was some other man's daughter and our father had been tricked into raising her. That might explain his hostility. I asked Mother, in some oblique but probably obvious way, if there was another man in her life just before she married – a tall man. She laughed, "No."

"What about 'Uncle' George Teufel?"

"He was in Hawaii. I was in Seattle. I never met him before I married your father. Don't be silly, now."

Before long, I was forced to recognize how much Carolyn resembled our father physically, and it became apparent that my theory was fatally flawed.

Naturally, my next question was whether Mom and Dad had a premarital tryst. I was told that Jim didn't show up for the wedding until the last minute, and therefore, they could not have had any contact. Even when I first saw the proposed timeline leading up to the nuptials – his planned five-day pause in Seattle before driving to Oregon to pick up his folks – I assumed that short week was crammed full of celebratory parties and open houses. But considering both the open and veiled sexual references in her letters, and the passionate vows of fidelity on both sides, it seems possible that the couple was primed to seek an opportunity for a thrilling illicit assignation. They could rationalize that they were on the threshold, after all.

My current thought is that – regardless of the exact day of conception – when Jacqui became great with child, lonely and ill at ease in every way, Jim's fun on the beach came to an end. She took her parental role very seriously from the start, and as soon as the baby was born, her attention was focused on motherhood. Jim still had the comradeship of colleagues at work, but unspoken expectations were imposed at home, and freedom was severely curtailed. His frustration, held back as much as he could restrain it, may have emerged later in the form of resentment toward that baby who unwittingly and innocently initiated a permanent change in life as he had known it. Whatever the cause, he treated Carolyn unfairly, and it's always made me feel sad for her.

Years later, when we lived in Edmonds, two of the couples from Hawaiian days also relocated to the Northwest and remained friends – George and Helen Teufel, and Norm and Jan Jacobsen. We kids loved these warm and cheerful people. One night, in Edmonds in the 1950s, Dad came home from work, gleefully bringing Norm along. "Look who's here! He had an assignment out this way, and I couldn't leave him to find supper on his own," Dad crowed, knowing how much fun we had with Norm in the house. Mother was absolutely livid. Pots and pans clanged like alarm bells. I was so astonished by this that, against all my training, I asked her why she was mad.

That's when I heard an early verse in the "Your father is so selfish and inconsiderate" litany. In Hawaii, some fifteen years earlier, one night he had unexpectedly brought home a visitor at supper time. They were so poor, and food storage in their tiny house was so limited, that she didn't have enough supper to feed a third person. "I had to *secretly* run out the back door to the neighbor and *borrow a potato!*" she stage-whispered to me. She reddened just telling it, she had been so humiliated. Afterward, she read him the riot act. But here he was, doing the *same thing!*

Of course, it wasn't the same. By this time they had adequate resources to feed us well, and she always prepared more than enough food for our meals. She had a well-equipped kitchen with plenty of backup supplies in the refrigerator and the canned-goods cupboards. What *was* the same was that she felt subservient – *she* was required to adjust to whatever choices *he* made. Her anger at this powerlessness, once triggered, festered and metastasized. Dad was, and remained, the villain of the piece.

When I was twelve, I became aware that a couple of my classmates lived with their mothers who were divorced. This was honestly my first personal exposure to "broken marriages," as they were called. The next time Mom made one of her familiar comments about Dad, I blurted, "Have you ever thought about getting a divorce?"

She breathed out a voluminous sigh which carried this answer: "If it weren't for you kids, I think I might."

If she thought about this statement at all, she probably meant it as an expression of appreciation for her children, and was oblivious to the implications. But the sticky, malodorous fallout from this remark adhered to me for years. If I hadn't been born, my mother could be free. As long as I – the youngest – depended on her, she had to stay in a wretched situation. It was, therefore, my job to rescue her emotionally in whatever ways I could. How many long strings of complaints did I listen to, and agree with, to make her feel better? How many times did I try to cheer Dad up so he wouldn't be so difficult for her?

When, at last, I went to college, I fully expected Mom to get some relief by acting on her earlier threat. Instead, she persuaded Dad to join her in signing up with the county court to become foster parents to teenage girls. I was astounded and outraged. I had staggered under the burden of being a burden all those years, and she decided to bring more dependents into the house instead of escaping? Besides that, she'd been so blind to my needs in the teen years that I couldn't see how she was the right person to help adolescents in this way.

One time I called her from my VISTA assignment in Pennsylvania, just to say hello. We chatted as usual. After about a minute, I heard ear-shattering screams in the background. These sounds were straight out of a horror film, and they didn't stop. Mother, to my astonishment, tried to continue our conversation. I interrupted, shouting: "Maybe you'd better go!"

"Oh, it's just the girls."

"Girls? I thought you were supposed to be assigned one girl at a time."

"Well, there were three that needed a place, so I volunteered."

"*Three* screaming teenage girls? What are they doing right now?"

At this point I heard one of the voices shrieking, "My hair! You pulled out my hair, you God-damn bitch!"

"I think you'd better go, Mom."

"I guess you're right."

Those girls, and several others, came and went. Eventually one, who I'll call Lena, stayed and became a surrogate daughter. My background was so vastly unlike hers that I didn't find much in common with her, and felt more like an interested observer as I saw the three of them bond into a fa1mily unit. Dad interacted with Lena in a different way than he had with us – less defensive and critical, I'd say. I'm sure I must have been jealous at times, but I was no longer interested in living in that house with those parents, and the main emotion I remember is a long-lasting anger at Mother for sighing so many times over the years about being trapped by her parental duties, then turning around and purposely choosing to extend those alleged afflictions.

Don't carry the world
upon your shoulders*

The first photo shows him lounging on a bench in a granite alcove on the University of Washington campus, a come-hither look communicated by the somewhat sidewise, upward gaze of his dark eyes. He appears to be leaning on one elbow, but on closer examination, more likely that hand has been brought to his cheek to enhance his allure. A half-smile plays at his lips. This picture is so reminiscent of Rudolph Valentino that one half expects the stone slab to transmute to the silken cushions and drapes of a sheikh's chamber.

In the second photo, a few years later, he reclines on a Hawaiian beach wearing only a swimsuit and a skullcap. The pose, with knees jutting upward and feet flat on the cloth, illustrates that this man is much too

Jim Reid, University of Washington, 1933

long and tall to fit on any standard beach towel. This time he actually is leaning on one elbow, but the fact that his hands are clasped at his side assures us that he's consciously displaying his biceps for the camera. His physique is that of a healthy, active fellow at the height

* Lyric from "Hey Jude," John Lennon and possibly Paul McCartney, 1968

of his youth. It's impossible to say why a white beanie is part of his costume – is it a joke, or was it a style of the day? The final accessory, also somewhat out of place at the seashore, is a pipe clenched in his mouth, implying a sophistication in contrast to the little hat. The earlier half-smile is replaced by a sort of giggling smirk, as though life is so comical you have to bite down on your pipe to keep from laughing out loud.

I doubt that my mom ever saw these photos of Dad before she married him. To me, they reveal a carefree and seductive self-centeredness that doesn't seem as if it would appeal to a serious woman seeking the father

Jim Reid, Oahu, 1939

of her future children. On the other hand, she was young, and he definitely had sex appeal!

Dad had left his family's farm as a skinny, hard-working 18-year-old. At the boarding house near the university, suddenly getting the nutrition he needed, he grew muscular enough to play on the football team. For some years after that, fitness and fun were part of his life. When he started his engineering job in Honolulu, he and his buddies swam and dived in the surf every day. In the 1930's there were no regulations prohibiting the destruction of sea creatures, and the young men's main entertainment was to swim out to a reef and spear exotic fishes. They operated on a shoestring, making their own metal or hardwood spears and throwing them by hand. Having no access to diving equipment, they had contests to see how long they could hold their breath, and Jim boasted that he normally surpassed three and a half minutes.

When I was little I generally liked being with Dad. Besides being fit and good-looking, he was gentle and laughed easily. If our family got separated in a public place, I didn't worry, since at 6'4" he was easy to find in a crowd. He attributed his straight black hair and prominent nose to a fictional Cherokee or Navaho ancestor – implicating different tribes at different times. As I grew older, I found this reference bizarre, since he was known to make derogatory comments, and at least once when we were driving through a Native American reservation, he uttered a trite but vicious remark about all Indians. In any case, as far as genealogical research has established, his heritage was limited to England and Scotland.

As long as I knew him, Dad had a hearing impairment. He attributed his ear problems to flying in the unpressurized cabins of Army transport planes during the Second World War. His use of hearing aids was erratic, and some of the devices were of poor quality, so we children grew accustomed to raising our voices if we actively wanted his attention. We also grew accustomed to talking to one another in normal tones, knowing we were leaving our father out of the conversation. Once in a while he would acquire a good hearing aid and surprise us by jumping into a discussion, but for the most part, there were two separate worlds at the dinner table – the family's world and Dad's isolation. Mother, as a drama student, had learned to "project the voice from the diaphragm," and she could increase her volume without shouting. She sometimes made ill-fated attempts to bridge the generation gap, encouraging us all to speak up in the same way. We didn't follow through. But eventually, as we youngsters moved into adulthood, technological advances brought more effective devices, and late in his life it was easier to communicate with him.

My father's physical appearance in middle age and beyond bore little resemblance to the somewhat devilish athlete of his younger days. As with most Americans, his waistline expanded, although not quite to the point of being described as obese. The most notable change was an inexorable sagging of the shoulders. This increased year by year, and Mother half-jokingly commented that it was because he carried the world on his shoulders. I think it was true. Once he became a husband and father at the age of thirty, he took very seriously the responsibility of supporting his family. While he thrived on creating and growing his civil engineering company, the work was demanding and financially risky. Marriage and parenthood were difficult for him. He worked all day, every evening and most weekends.

He was diagnosed with a heart attack in his fifties, and developed a stomach ulcer around that same time. After that, he never seemed really healthy – his physique was characterized by his heavy tread and slumped shoulders, and ongoing heart problems led to hospitalizations and implanted pacemakers.

By those middle years, Dad did not value exercise. Once he finished his duty in Newfoundland and Greenland during the Korean War and started his company, daily activity consisted of walks to the car and perhaps a one-block stroll from the office to the café or bakery.

Edmonds Annual Hiking Club,
circa 1980. Jim Reid at left with camera.

The exception was the Edmonds Annual Hiking Club. With a few fellow businessmen in town, Dad participated in a hike once a year. He had a strong constitution and an incomparable belief in mind over matter, and early on, he kept up with the best. But as time went on, and his health and fitness gradually waned, the others sometimes found themselves waiting for Jim on the trail. His response to this problem was typical of his problem-solving approach: Every year, two weeks before the annual hike, Dad would dig out his old Army knapsack, fill it with rocks, strap it on and walk up and down the hills around our house. Within the two weeks he might make this trek twice or as many as five times, whereupon he declared himself in great shape for the hike. Today, my siblings and I need only say "rocks in my backpack" to spur instant amusement.

His friends were very kind, and they only razzed him lightheartedly as they slowed their pace year by year, then planned shorter and shorter hikes to accommodate "the old man." The loyalty and affection of those friends proved that, even though we youngsters found him hard to connect with, he had lovable qualities. At his request, upon his death the Edmonds Annual Hiking Club scattered some of his ashes at a favorite site on one of their hikes, a very touching gesture.

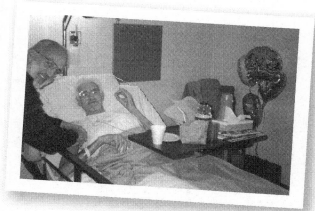

With all his health issues, Dad lived to 84, which he seemed to accomplish almost entirely through a powerful will to stay alive. When the doctor phoned my brother

Ken with Dad, victorious on his 84th birthday, 1993. This was four days after doctors had predicted he'd live only three days.

to say Jim's kidneys were failing, we all traveled to the town where he lived in Montana, thinking this was the end. Under the attention of all his children, he rallied. On his birthday that week, we brought balloons and a cake to his hospital room. In a slightly wavering voice he asked, "Are you sure this is the 27th?"

"Yes, Dad," we replied, thinking maybe his sharp mind was starting to fade.

With a pre-loaded, victorious grin, he declaimed in a stronger voice, "That's funny, the doctor said I wouldn't be here by the 27th. Didn't I show him!"

After a week in Montana, my siblings and I needed to return to our jobs. In the hospital hallway, I asked the doctor for a prognosis. The doctor, who had a very direct communication style, replied with an admiring smile and a shrug, "Your father has no kidney function. I have no idea why he is still alive. It's my guess that as long as you all are here, he's not going anywhere." With that, we explained to Dad that we had to come home to resume our daily routines, and he lived an astonishing five weeks longer. Thankfully, my brother was able to be with him at the very end.

How did Dad get to be the way he was? Thanks to my sister's initiative, we have some remembrances he recorded in his late 70's. The one that comes to my mind most often is the Christmas story. This is one of the saddest of Dad's memories, and it touches me deeply with compassion for that little boy.

Dad's father, our Granddad Reid, was a harsh, unbending man. He had been the president of a small-town bank which had to default on some loans during an economic downturn. He owned a small farm and decided that, to the maximum degree possible, everything they earned on the farm would go to pay off the loans. It seems he made this decision on his own, as outsiders agreed there was no such legal or ethical requirement. The family was plunged into miserable poverty by his so-called principled decision.

One Christmas, the only gift for each child was a single small, cheap toy. In his stocking, my dad found a tin horn. He was thrilled to have it and wanted to start blowing on it right away. But in the way of little children, he jumped up to play with his siblings, and when he sat down, oh dear! He sat on the horn. Tin is a very soft metal, and the horn was flattened beyond repair. The boy was as flattened as the toy. "Do you think," he asked his parents tentatively, "do you think maybe Santa would bring me something else?"

Instead of simply telling him Santa doesn't come back after Christmas, his parents said, "I don't know, why don't you hang up your stocking tonight and find out?" The next morning he could see there was something in his sock! Reaching in excitedly, what did he find? A lump of coal.

Now, in case the symbolism has changed by the time you read this, I'll explain that coal is what Santa puts in the stockings of children who have been very, very bad. This cruel trick is especially heartbreaking because when he told it to us, his own adult children, the memory had been held in his heart for seven decades and its hurtful power was undimmed.

Dad grew up to express some of his own father's desirable qualities, including honest business practices, an iron will, and a commitment to working hard and doing his best. To a degree he followed in his father's unfortunate example of being a relatively uninvolved, emotionally non-supportive parent. But there were a couple of patterns he overturned. First, when I think of all Dad told us about his father, I'm impressed that he himself never deprived us of anything material. He and Mother taught us to live simply and not waste anything, but at the same time they shared an admirable generosity with their resources where the children were concerned, and I have to credit Dad with achieving this significant distinction from his father.

Another accomplishment was his willingness, late in life, to look back and say to his offspring, "I'm sorry I wasn't a better father." It's certain that he never heard anything of that kind from his father, and for someone of my dad's generation – born in 1909 – that's a rare awareness and a rarer utterance. In the end, there are no perfect parents, and I'm grateful that I lived long enough, and was given a strong enough foundation, to appreciate those precious aspects of my father that became apparent to me later, as well as the unwanted aspects that seemed obvious earlier.

Write me a letter
containing these lines:
answer me quickly,
will you be mine?*

9/19/1938: *"Dear Jim, That last letter of yours was practically perfect, my dear! And it arrived when I needed it more desperately than I've needed anything in a long while. I'm feeling awfully blue these days, at best, and was at my lowest ebb just then. I suppose maybe a wedding gets under anyone's skin, and just now I'm feeling very useless and unwanted and unnecessary anyhow. It's hard to see everyone else finding and filling his niche, and to be jobless myself, and without prospects. You see, the Hollywood thing rather went sour – I had a terribly disturbing letter from Morgan Padelford last week, which put a new face on things. I don't know what I'll do now, or where I'll turn. Frankly, I'm stumped. And let me warn you, young man, about writing so enticingly of yourself and the Islands – I'm tempted to take your* warning *about marrying you as an* offer, *and arrive on your doorstep with a wedding veil in one hand and a dress in the other! Seriously, my dear – I'm growing up at last, and I'd like to be near you in the process, to keep friends with you, and for your help and advice. That would be wonderful."*

Who wrote those lines? Could it have been Jacqueline Burd, the confident, competent, authoritative woman I later called Mother? How many years did it take her to manufacture the impervious emotion-proof shield that defined her later persona – the counselor who listened, sympathized, and advised but never revealed her own

---

* Lyric from "Down in the Valley," traditional American folk song

feelings? Or was the earlier self-deprecating, needy girl the actual disguise? Will the real Jacqui please stand up?

We found twenty letters in a trunk in Mother's apartment after her death. Strangely, only the messages *she* had written — some addressed to Jim, and others to her parents — were in the trunk, and it's a mystery why she had them. All the letters are hand-written and in their original envelopes. Did Dad save them and return them to her when they were married? Did her parents do the same? We never found any of *his* early letters, suggesting that, early or late, she disposed of them.

I have strong reservations about sharing these papers. They were intensely private and personal. I question my motives. As far as I can discern, my aims are dual: to provide the reader with a particular view of a historical time; and to expand my own understanding of the complexities of my family by reflecting on some of its origins. I'll never know what Mother and Dad would think of their early days being exposed in this way. For better or worse, I now set my qualms aside and write.

In 1938, Jac had just collected her Master of Fine Arts degree and celebrated an unwelcome milestone — her twenty-fifth birthday. She lived with her parents. Her sister, three years younger, was about to be married, in defiance of a cultural expectation — left over from earlier eras, but still packing some power — that older daughters marry first. Although Jacqui was busy sewing Peg's wedding dress, as well as outfits for herself and their mother, and attending parties and moving furniture to accommodate numerous visiting relatives, her life was frighteningly empty. Beneath what she called *"the usual rush and scurry,"* she lacked an identity.

For a woman in those times, an identity could be acquired in only one of two ways. Having received no viable marriage proposals (the preferred option), she decided to be a career girl, and the first exciting job in her field of theatrical costuming was tucked in her well-designed pocket.

Morgan Padelford was the son of Frederick Padelford, Dean of the Graduate School of the University of Washington and a friend of Jac's father. According to official records, Morgan was Associate Color Director (for the new invention called Technicolor) on four movies in that year of 1938, including Warner Brothers' Oscar-winning "Adventures of Robin Hood" starring Errol Flynn. It's likely that he had offered Jac a position in the wardrobe department of the WB film studio in Hollywood, an exhilarating opportunity for her. She did not recount exactly what Morgan wrote that caused her to cancel her Hollywood plans – could he have described the common Hollywood phenomenon of the "casting couch"? Whatever his "*terribly disturbing*" news was, suddenly that job became untenable.

Jac, University of Washington, 1936.

Plan B followed Plan A, tumbling away into deep space like a meteorite flaming out, scattering debris everywhere but nothing salvageable. Except – maybe, just maybe, an eligible fellow far away, who joked about marrying her. A distant figure in hazy focus, winking enigmatically, and perhaps ready to be enticed.

They had met when Jim, a good-looking football player, took a role in a campus play. Jac was the university's Wardrobe Mistress, designing costumes for entire productions and carrying out related tasks, right down to taking the actors' measurements and helping with quick changes. They got to know each other backstage, and as was the custom, became friends in an informal social group. Since her family's home was just off campus, it's likely that Jim joined the crowd for gatherings at her place before a concert or after a game. In return, as long as he was on the team, she became quite a fan of Husky football.

By 1938, Jim had earned his engineering degree and was working for the Corps of Engineers in Honolulu. As campus friends, they wrote to one another.

There's a gap in the extant correspondence after the September letter (above) until the following spring. By April, Jac had found a WPA** job working on Treasure Island, off San Francisco, for the Golden Gate International Exposition. In the holiday atmosphere, it was easy to meet young men, but she found herself propositioned rather than romanced. And who did she turn to, to process her puzzlement at this situation? The young man across the ocean. There must have been some very cordial correspondence between autumn and spring. To me, looking back from three quarters of a century later, the next letter seems to overreach all social boundaries.

4/1/1939: *"May I write as I'd like to have the opportunity of talking with you, not because I want to influence you or embarrass you or encourage you, but because I truly want to share with you some of the things that are happening to me, and so perhaps solve some of them in the telling. You're wise, and clean, and American, and masculine – and so much more mature than I in so many ways. Probably none of this will be new to you – I'm just young and stupid and slow, I suppose.... Lord, Jim, isn't there anything interesting or worthwhile about me but body – or about life but sex? ... Am I just horribly provincial, or is it really a strange streak in me? I know I must be friends first, before I could even imagine being lovers – but is that too much to expect?... I never really appreciated you, you see, having no mature standard of comparison.... I've been a bit confused myself – have been busy trying to analyze myself, deciding what I'd been doing to give men the impression they could treat me like a girl from the streets and expect me to enjoy it. Darn it all, Jim, what is wrong with me? Wish you were here to talk – or shake – some sense into me!"*

** WPA: Works Progress Administration, one of the New Deal programs initiated by Franklin D Roosevelt to provide employment and help lift the US out of the Great Depression of the 1930s.

I can't believe she used the words "sex" and "lovers" with such apparent ease. In my adolescence, I could have benefited from some conversations along these lines, but the woman I knew was completely walled off from anything to do with male-female relations. In fact, I had always assumed that my parents had sex exactly three times in their lives, and probably without ever saying a word.

Beyond that issue, the idea of my mother asking to be *shaken* is unthinkable. Yet she wrote the same words again in a second letter. In my lifetime, any interpersonal violence was anathema to her, particularly if men ever used force against women. I still can't reconcile her suggesting that a young man take her by the shoulders and teach her a lesson in this way, unless this phrase was the closest she could get to saying, "I want you to touch me."

In reply to this startling directness, it looks very much as if he proposed – wouldn't we love to have a record of his message! She wrote:

4/12/1939: *"Jim – Jim – Jim! You are a dear, dear person! Found your wire under the door when I got home from 'The Castles'… truly, I didn't sleep much! But I feel super wonderful this morning! My dear, what am I to say to you? You're the grandest person in all the world. Oh, why can't we be living & working somewhere near one another – I think we need that! I want quite dreadfully to be near you – but can we be sure we're not both doing a wee bit of wishful thinking?… And, incidentally, I can't come to you without a cent to my name or clothes on my back, or anything at all to contribute. Anyway, dearest – the folks will be here by next Sun. and I'll talk with them, and you'll write me again, and I'll write you! And I'm counting rather desperately on seeing you in Sept. – though I suppose maybe I could live till Dec. if you can't possibly get over before then…. By then I'll have saved enough to come over there – think of Christmas there with you!… My heart is very full today, and singing with joy, and yet so very humble and grateful for your love and tenderness…. I humbly hope that I may contribute in some tiny way to the fulfillment of your dreams."*

The next three weeks, more frank talk:

4/18/1939: *"I'm so honored that you feel free to write me as you do, and to let me write as I do. I need your ideas and advice — I need terribly to know that someone still holds himself to certain standards, still believes his own self-respect is important. Of course, I knew without your telling me that your own conduct had been controlled by your firm mind rather than your powerful body. I am so glad, my dear!... I agree that sex morality is only a small part of morality as a whole, and that it is a personal or at least a dual matter, largely.... Your standards in all things about yourself are so gloriously high."*

Tue. April 25: *"I think I'll follow your instructions... and 'postpone certain phases of my life till after marriage.'... Do you know, Jim, that I'm so Victorian that I've always hoped and expected to enter marriage a virgin, and to find there the highest ecstasy and the deepest joy...."*

May 4: *"... And I believe in the double bed and the single standard for married people!"*

Throughout their marriage they always shared a bed. As their daughter, I would be happy to think that Jac's hopes and expectations of ecstasy and joy came true, even briefly. I have no way of knowing, as it's not the sort of thing either of them would ever have recounted to their children.

Her letter from Treasure Island on April 11, 1939, expresses nostalgia for a world in which she delighted: *"Mother and Dad are coming down this week... gee, won't it be fun to see them! I really miss them lots — and especially the grand groups that gathered so often at home. I miss those groups more than anything. How I long to gather you and my folks and other dear friends around the piano, and sing at the top of my lungs!"*

On a practical note, mail delivery was hard to predict. For a 3-cent stamp, they sent their early letters by steamer; then, with rising eagerness and impatience, they paid an exorbitant 20 cents to use the new Clipper air service. Her first paragraph on April 25:

"*I suppose maybe it's foolish to try to send this by Clipper – they've been so unreliable lately, that I'm sure boat mail gets to you quicker! [But I] Watched the darn thing fussing around in the bay all last week, each day thinking "Now it will really go – today it will start!" And then seeing it there again the next day! I nearly went crazy! Because there was mail on her that was most terribly important to me.*"

In praise of air mail, the following week she wrote, "*Just got your Clipper letter of yesterday – isn't science & navigation wonderful?*"

The exchange continued with regularity. She kept writing, elaborating on the theme of appreciation, along with several detailed narratives about her activities. Her California job was much less than she had hoped: assistant-of-all-trades and supervisor of a rapidly rotating staff of young people whose duties amounted to the daily maintenance of old, overused costumes for the shows. Living in the middle of a festival in the middle of San Francisco Bay ("*the bridges reaching out to the world, and Treasure Island like a gorgeous vision from a Walt Disney fairy tale*"), there was lots of fun to be had, but the work was unchallenging and unsatisfying, and she and her boss began to have differences.

The question ping-ponged over the Pacific: "*When will you know for certain whether you can come over?... And if you can't come, I... will find some excuse for [a] trip.*" Disappointingly, every indication is that neither of them was able to accomplish that.

In September she abruptly left her job, long before the exposition closed for the winter, and moved back to her parents' home in Seattle. Plan C had worked! This was even better than the *mele kalikimaka* in Hawaii that she had fantasized – preparations for a Christmas Day wedding were soon underway in Seattle.

Jim wasn't able to cross the ocean to introduce his betrothed to his parents, so in late September she boldly made a trek alone to eastern Oregon, to meet them and see their farm. It's hard to imagine the emotions that must have flowed underground on all sides, but her report, both to her fiancé and to her folks, focused on acreage, livestock, crops, and equipment.

She restricted herself almost entirely to surface comments. To her parents, she described her future father-in-law as a farmer, *"director of the irrigation district, the REA [rural electrification] district, the school board, and the co-op... So you see he's really a rather important man!"* And *"Mrs. Reid is very nice, an excellent cook and housekeeper."* She also briefly remarked that neither of them was in good health. But there was no mention of their personal interactions with her. In the long run, her relations with Jim's family were civil, but never warm.

In the letter to her mother and father, she did include a special note to her single, 20-year-old brother: *"Barbara, the 'little sister,' is 21, just about my height, built somewhat as I am but somewhat smaller, dark and pretty and heaps of fun! Sherm, I think you'll like her lots! And I've nearly convinced her she'll like you, though she holds out for a tall dark engineer from Washington! Seems Jim is the pattern for her ideal man!"* Marrying was the thing to do, and brazen matchmaking was part of the equation.

From September to November, Jac's parents stayed at her uncle's Illinois farm, and she stayed in their Seattle home. Because it was improper for a single young woman to live alone, *"Regina D, a Portland girl, Drama grad, is going to school to finish her M.A. and get her teaching diploma, and will be sharing the house with me."*

She wrote one long letter using carbon paper, *"original to Jim, copy to the migratory Burds."* We have the carbon copy – this may have been one letter that Jim did not see fit to keep and return to her. Six of the eight pages are devoted to a breezy description of a whirlwind week initiated by a man she had met on Treasure Island.

Oct. 23, 1939: *"The Russians have been in town! Meaning the 'General Plattoff's Don Cossack Choir'! Jim – remember I told you about my Russian friend at the Fair – Tannga? You met him, Mom. Well, he's been with the Choir since Sept. 1. So – they came into town Wed night, about 11, and Tannga called me at once. We had him to dinner on Thur. evening, after numerous almost incomprehensible telephone conversations, during the course of which I agreed to make him a pair of trousers!... He brought his old ones and the new material....*

"Well, after a good bit of conversation, we persuaded Tannga to bring two of his friends to dinner on Fri. He warned us, however, continually and with great emphasis, that they were romantic – oh, terribly romantic! 'But then, they are Cossacks, and officers – so what can you expect?' (Quoted directly!) We invited Beth L as the third girl, and cleaned the place up in their honor! I made the trousers, except finishing the waist, and we were ready for them at 6:30.... Well, they finally arrived about 8 – one of them has a balalaika presented him by the Tsar after a concert he gave.... All three are quite charming – Tannga himself, Vladimir F, and Georj S. Georj is the youngest in the Choir – 24 – blond and handsome, but all too well aware of it! Of course he chose Beth – and immediately noticed her excitement, which was so great that her hands shook so she could hardly eat! Well, he flirted with her, and she led him on – quite innocently, but oh so thoroughly – until he got almost out of hand!

"Mr. F is a most amazing and charming person – seems a bit older than the other two but says he is 53, and must really be, to have done all he has in one lifetime.... Sherm, I do wish you could have met them – I know you'd have enjoyed it all.

"Dinner was over about 10 – and the men had a rehearsal at the Meany at 10:40, so we took them over. They were through at 12:30 and we went back to get them – and almost got dragged into a 'party'! In fact Georj left rather under protest, but apparently Beth's charms won out! Well, the two of them played games – Beth leading him on and retreating at the same time, and he pursuing and being constantly frustrated – while the rest of us played Chinese Checkers.... [They] finally left about 3, and Regina & I staggered up to bed.

"Sat. I rose at 8 and went to work on Tannga's pants, which I had fitted the night before. Finished them about noon, & we took bus & streetcar to town to leave them at the hotel for him, then dashed back to the stadium in time for a little more than ½ the game!... We pieced out a dinner of leftovers, rested a bit, and after bathing and dressing felt much better. We got all done up fit to kill, for the concert, and went down by bus, streetcar and foot, much to the amazed amusement of the populace! I wore my white chiffon, Mom's white wrap, my big pearls in my hair, and

*a white sequin kerchief over that, while Regina wore a slinky black coat
& dress & a black veil! No one else in the balcony was nearly so gorgeous!
The music was simply exquisite....*

*"Met Tom & Peggy H. downstairs when we were trying to get
backstage, & took them with us. Oh, yes, I forgot to say Tannga's dancing
simply brought down the house! Everyone was crazy about him – and I
had no idea he was so good! We could hardly get near him afterwards!
Tannga... got me a gift he had ready (a beautiful box of chocolates) and
a souvenir program signed for me by every member of the Choir!... He
departed for a supper party... and Tom brought us home.*

*"We had hardly gotten settled when the phone rang – Tannga! They
were through – and lonesome. So... Tom went down and brought them
back. We had some wine (Tom's contribution) ice cream, cake, & coffee,
talked, had several balalaika solos, songs, and then all sang.... Finally had
to about throw them out, at 5! We all rode downtown, dropped them then
Peggy, and Tom brought us back. We got to sleep about 6 – and at 10:45
Tannga phoned! Yesterday passed in a fog...*

*"Oh yes – it appears that Tannga was under the impression that he
had proposed to me in S.F., tho' I'm afraid I didn't quite take it that
way! Anyhow, I told him about Christmas, just to avoid hurting him
later if he should be serious. He wished us great happiness,.... thinks
it's the most wonderful thing in the world.... Anyhow, the final note
was struck when he wrote a card & handed it to Regina, asking her to
correct his English. It said that he liked her very much, & me too, but
as I was busy he'd like to be her friend – and if she was busy too he'd
be entirely lost! But maybe this would hurt 'Jaky's' feelings – he'd not
want to do that – but could he have her address! That's the Russian
acceptance of fate, Regina says!"*

Pearls in her hair for another man – what could have been better
planned to stir Jim's jealousy and his desire? I can't help thinking that
Jac was not above playing the same flirtatious game she attributed to
Beth. How could her distant husband-to-be receive such an obviously
enthusiastic account of another man who had, at the very least,
romantic feelings toward her – especially when he read that she had

tailored Tannga's pants during a midnight party? She wasn't just a clothing designer, she was a designing woman.

The letter below was written to her parents when her family and bridesmaids (friend Lou and sister Peg) had been notified, but before the pending marriage was announced to others, so none of the social whirl was directly related to her engagement. This diary-like listing further illuminates the level of activity she was accustomed to:

Nov. 9, 1939: *"Dear Folksies! ....Our social life has not been too gay of late, but it does seem we're always busy! Regina went with Lou & me to the game last Sat. (we won – 9-0!) as H had to work. Afterwards we met H & all went to a Smorgasbord put on by the Central Lutheran Church. It was much fun, and wonderful food – all you could eat, & only 50 cents! MK & Mrs C were there, as well as Ted with Bill & Betsy, and Mrs O & Lloyd. We finished off the evening at the Neptune seeing Irene Dunne & Charles Boyer in "When Tomorrow Comes" – a swell show, but sad. Came home to find Peg, Van, & Snuffy here making Xmas presents...*

"Mon. morning Sally called to invite me to see "Our Town" at the Repertory with her that night. Later Beth called & gave Regina tickets, so we both got to see it, free, & on the same night! ... Tue. night we went to see Lunt & Fontanne in "The Shrew," preceded by dinner here for our party of 6 – Lou, H, M, JA, Regina & I. The show was simply wonderful – we had a marvelous time! Yesterday.... went to see "Bachelor Mother" with Ginger Rogers & David Niven, at the Egyptian at 7, and left Regina (at 8:30) to see "On Borrowed Time," as I'd already seen it twice! Peg and Van were here when I returned, so she marked the hem in my white nightgown. Then I cut out my coat & lining.

"Tomorrow night Ted, Bill & Betsy, Lou, 2 of Regina's young men are coming for dinner. Lou doesn't work Sat. so she's spending the weekend here to work on her dress... Hope to get down to Portland after Thanksgiving, to see Janie & the baby!"

Did she have any way to foresee that soon enough, church smorgasbords, concerts, theatre, movies, friends and relatives dropping in, and city life in general would be only fond memories, and that she'd have little use for the stylish new dresses, coat, hat and gloves in her carefully assembled trousseau?

Elegant newlyweds in Seattle, December 1939.

The last letter before the wedding outlines Jim's travel plans. His trans-Pacific ship was to dock in Vancouver, B.C., on December 15. He would spend five or six days in Seattle, pick up a car, and drive to Hermiston, Oregon, where his parents would join him for the ride back. They would pull into town on December 24, just in time for the wedding the next day. If, as we assume, that plan was followed, they were face to face only for a few hours during the handful of winter days between his Seattle arrival and departure.

In short, the entire courtship, from friendship to flirtation to mutual admiration to proposal and acceptance, appears to have been by mail.

Did they know each other at all?

We are family*

When my dad was in his seventies, I posed a question. "Why did you decide to get married when you did?"

His reply mentioned nothing about love. He said very calmly, "Well, I guess it was what men did – marry, settle down, raise a family. I was almost thirty, and it seemed like it was time."

If Mother had answered the same question honestly, her words might have echoed his. For one thing, according to the mores of the day and their own personal standards, neither of them could freely enjoy sex outside of marriage. One would think they were more than ready. Further, on May 4, 1939, she had written that she wanted marriage and *"after a year or so, children, and the chance to raise them cleanly and decently."* Options were limited for each of them, and no doubt matrimony looked like the best available choice.

The children began arriving before the first year was up. Mother very rarely talked about the process of giving birth, but once she did say that Carolyn came fast – so fast that Jim wasn't able to get home quickly enough. His co-worker George Teufel drove her to the hospital. The nurses were in no hurry checking her in, until George bellowed, "If you don't get this woman admitted, she's going to have this baby right here in the lobby!" She was whisked off to a room, and sure enough, in minutes it was all over. This was probably the action that transformed Mr. Teufel from a young friend of the couple into our "Uncle George."

Nearly four years later, Kenneth was born in the same US Army hospital in Honolulu. By contrast, he must have struggled to come into the world. Only years later did we learn anything about his birth,

* Lyric from "We Are Family," Bernard Edwards and Nile Rodgers, 1979

and that was due to a mere question of teenage fashion. When he was playing high school basketball, Ken always trotted down the court brushing one drooping lock of brown hair off his forehead. Most of the boys on the team had crew cuts. Needing to fit in, Ken told Mom he wanted a haircut. "Your Aunt Peggy can do that, she cuts both her boys' hair."

During the next Sunday afternoon gathering at Grandma's, Ken was draped with a towel. Mom's sister complained that his head was too bumpy to look good in a close-cropped style, but it's what he wanted, and she wielded the clippers. Afterward, I was nostalgic for that endearing swipe of the hand across the forelock, but one of his friends emphatically declared that he looked "One Hundred Percent Better!" He came home that day reporting his pal's comment, with the rhetorical question, "How bad *did* I look???"

A break from Honolulu in Seattle, 1943. Grandma, Mom with Carolyn, and other close relatives.

Now that we could see the shape of his head, we had to ask Mother about her knobby-skulled son. She reluctantly told us that the doctor had used forceps during the birth. She seemed to regret that fact, and never had a good word for the quality of military medical care. I find myself wondering if the forceps were also implicated in Kenneth's terrible childhood ear aches that often woke us at night, or his deviated nasal septum that caused him to be a mouth-breather for many years. (I still hear the voice of my mother, that erstwhile sweet young bride, fifteen years later, commanding,

"That slack jaw makes you look stupid, and you're not stupid! Close your mouth and breathe through your nose!" Nobody knew it was just about impossible for him.)

When the first baby came, Dad was a civilian employee of the US Army. The morning after the tragic Pearl Harbor attack, the major who was his boss made him an offer he couldn't refuse. Along with all other members of the reserves, he was called up, and was in uniform by afternoon. He continued at the same engineering job, with a new national-defense emphasis to their projects.

And Granddad pops up!

During the war, Mom crossed the Pacific at least twice – once with Carolyn, once with both children. The military transport ships, crowded with soldiers and sailors, were in no way suitable for a lone mother with one or two little ones. But she later told us how grateful she was that some of the young soldiers offered strong arms or encouraging words in support of the army bride among them. And at the distant end of each voyage she was revived by the embrace of her parents and siblings.

Mother's parents had moved out of Seattle to north Edmonds, where they tore down an old farmhouse and built a new home on the foundation. Over the garage they built a guest apartment, and it was here that Jac and her babies slept. During the days, I doubt that they spent more than a few minutes away from Grandma, who was all too happy to prepare meals and help care for the tots.

At last in 1945 the Reid family of four permanently relocated to the Seattle area. Mother and Dad acquired from Granddad an acre at the upper edge of his property. The next few years must have been a blur of raising the children, building the house, and getting situated as community members. Dad had a job in a Seattle firm, while through word of mouth he became known locally as a well-qualified civil engineer. This reputation was to serve him well later, when he would establish his own business. I made my entrance on the scene, and as soon as our new house was livable, Mom initiated her own community presence by founding the area's first cooperative preschool, joining the governing board of the Maplewood Community Center, and becoming active in the PTA. For strength, she had her parents "within spittin' distance," and Dad began learning how to live in close proximity to a flock of in-laws.

In alignment with their original goals, they married, settled down, and began raising children – *"cleanly and decently,"* as planned.

Away out west,
they have a name*

Carolyn was almost named Rosemary. Once when we were kids, she told me she thought our folks had made the right choice, because in the 1950s a swim suit designer named Rosemarie Reid became well-known, and my sister didn't like the idea of being confused with someone famous. She was not given a middle name because, as our parents – and their entire generation – knew for certain, a girl's maiden name just becomes her middle name when she marries, so there's no point to anything extra. How our culture has changed! Not only Carolyn, but our brother's three daughters – all married with families – use their original last name of Reid, as I always have, married or single.

Six years later, either societal thinking had changed or our parents had a greater vested interest in bestowing an extra name, since I was the last child. My name exemplifies the ongoing tug-of-war that was my parents' marriage. Dad told me I was named after his sister, Barbara. Mother told me I was named for one of her two best college chums, and to seal her claim, she gave me a middle name in honor of the other, Lou. Aunt Barbara lived in California and our families exchanged visits rarely. As for Mom's friends, I only met Barbara a few times, briefly. But after Mother's death I got better acquainted with Lucy – known as Lou – a beautiful, kind and brilliant woman who, after standing up at Mother's wedding, had remained single, and spent the greatest part of her highly accomplished career as an editor at Sunset Magazine.

* Lyric from "They Call the Wind Maria," Alan Jay Lerner and Frederick Loewe, 1951

By contrast, I don't recall any discussion of Ken's naming. His middle name, Burd, is in a long-standing American tradition of plunking the mother's maiden name between the beginning and the end. But he somehow escaped the generations-long paternal tradition by which first and second sons were dubbed either William Wallace Reid or James Howard Reid. Dad was Junior, after his father, James Howard. Dad's older brother was Wally, after his uncle, William Wallace, and Wally passed the name to his own son, but always called him Rocky. Today he's known as Clyde. Where Kenneth's moniker came from I don't know, although it's likely that the choice involved Mother's independent streak.

As young children, we were all given nicknames. Carolyn, the first-born, was tall and active from the start. She was a doer, not a cuddler, all elbows and leg-bones, and was dubbed Cricket. The name stuck with her into early adulthood, and remains descriptive of this lively woman in almost perpetual motion.

When Kenneth, as a baby, first started eating solid food, Grandma came to help Mother feed him. The two women alternated rapidly scooping food into his mouth because otherwise he would start wailing in panic between spoonfuls. (Today I wonder if he cried due to ongoing pain from his structural sinus problems. Food may have been quite comforting.) In any case, with this feeding regimen he grew so fat that they called him their little Buddha. By the time he could run around a baseball diamond, this body image was long outgrown, and the name with it.

As for me, I was simply "our baby." This phrase, in the mouths of my siblings, was ammunition. But for Mother, it was a term of endearment, which she continued to apply into my thirties. Although I appreciated the fondness behind the word, eventually, with a hug, I asked her to desist. She did.

We never called Carolyn "Carrie" nor Kenneth "Kenny" – these diminutives did not suit Mother. However, in the family I was always called Barbie. Youngest child syndrome. I can still hear Mother's voice at lunchtime, as she leaned forward to call out musically through the open living-room window, with an upswing: "Caro-*lyn*! Ken-*neth*! Barbie *Lou*!" or sometimes with the opposite inflection: "*Car*-olyn! *Ken*-neth! *Bar*-bie Lou!"

A few years ago, a twenty-year-old co-worker asked if I had been named after the Barbie doll. "Nope. There was no Barbie doll when I was named."

"Sure there was, she was created in the late fifties."

"Yes, when I was about ten."

"Uh-uh. No. *Really*??" That was worth a big smile!

In my youth I hated being called Barb, because a barb is sharp and prickly. Then as an adult I decided I didn't want to be introduced to strangers as Barbie, so I asked my relatives to use Barbara. But they proved unable to call me Barbara without putting it in quotation marks, so I became Barb to them, and I've come to accept, if not embrace, the pointed side of my personality. Later, when my dear aunt and uncle were in their dotage, they couldn't remember not to use my childhood nickname, so these days I've softened to the use of the "ie" form again, with family. I've just about evolved to accept the old adage – call me what you want, just don't call me late for dinner.

Mother had pet names that applied to all three of us. The first one I recall was "Snicklefritz," which she used as other mothers might use "sweetie pie" or "darling." Since we have no German heritage, I'll always wonder how this term came to be a favorite of hers, but I loved the ticklish sound of it. Another affectionate word came out when one of us was mischievous, especially if we played a trick on *her*. She would laugh, possibly even in admiration of our inventiveness, and call us "scalawags." Merriam-Webster defines this just as Mother used it: "a usually young person who causes trouble." I always felt warmly embraced when Mom used these unique expressions.

In keeping with her personality, our mother knew what she wanted her children to call her. When we were young, "Mommy" was the preferred term. Acceptable alternatives were "Mother" or "Mom." The one name we were not to use was "Mama." I don't remember any direct instruction on this rule, and it's possible that as the third child,

I picked it up by osmosis. Traditionally "Mama" is a baby's first word, and may have had infantile connotations for Mother.

By contrast, nobody seemed particular about what we called our father. "Daddy" sufficed for childhood, and morphed naturally into "Dad" at a certain age. We children didn't call him "Father," but when he wasn't present, Mom not infrequently referred to him as "your father." They called each other Jim and Jacqui, and on occasion, "Honey." When they used the word "Dear," there was often a whiff of sarcasm, masking something that would never be directly expressed. "Will you be able to meet us at the park for the Cub Scout games, *Dear?*" contained the pointed reminder that he had missed the last three Scout events.

My mother was named Jacqueline but her father always called her Jac. I used to wonder if he had wished his first-born was a boy, especially since he also pushed her to learn to manipulate tools, do physical work, and use her brain to the utmost – not considered traditional feminine qualities at the time. Her mom and most others called her Jackie. After years of indecision, in her fifties, she settled on spelling her nickname "Jacqui."

We grew up with our maternal aunt and uncle nearby, and learned a little about their history. The middle sibling was named Miriam, and she was born with a hip misalignment. Because of her limp, my granddad nicknamed her "Peg-leg" right away, and despite the disappearance of this imbalance before long, she spent the rest of her life as Peg or Peggy. Although I saw her often, I never knew that wasn't her given name until, as a teenager, I heard members of the older generation mention it. After that, some of us tried to switch over to her original appellation, but she absolutely refused to answer to Miriam. Peggy she was, and Peggy she remained. There was just one relic of her very early youth when she had been called Mimi. Whenever someone in the family complained that their own derriere needed slimming, we'd hear the old quote, "Well, you know what Peggy said, 'Too big boppoo Mimi got.' That's the Burd bottom."

My uncle, the youngest child, was Sherman, (or Sherm). Nobody nicknamed him. There were other Shermans in the extended Burd family, although the name didn't permeate like the male titles of the Reid clan.

Do our names have meaning? As the namesake of three women and the heir to entire dynasties of Reids and Burds, I don't know. "Barbara" derives from a Greek word meaning *foreigner or stranger*, and certainly, I have very often felt like an outsider from a far-away land. My Buddhist teacher, Djwhal Khul, went by the nickname "DK," and he told me more than once that this could be taken as a reminder that change is constant and everything is subject to *decay*. It seems to me we're free to imbue names with various meanings, if only for the fun of it!

The House: Part One

Build me a castle,
forty feet high*

The way the land tilted down and down toward Puget Sound, the major feature of the house was the view. Sunsets were breathtaking, setting fire to the sky and water, and even though the morning sun rose *behind* our property, dawn sometimes reached westward to paint the snowy Olympic Mountains in delicate pink.

Except for the year we spent in Missouri and Florida when war separated us from Dad, I lived there from 1949 until 1965. My folks stayed seventeen or eighteen years longer.

Because of the particular configuration of the slope, Dad had been able to plan the site so that the building was nestled into the hill on a true north-south axis. As an engineer, he was very proud to tell me that we faced due west. I became so accustomed to this that when I first started visiting other towns, and even other countries, I had an intuitive "sense of direction" in which I had great confidence, but which was usually wrong. A few people had a hearty laugh at my expense before I realized, upon inspection, that this "sense" told me that uphill was always east!

The location was idyllic. But oh, dear, the house itself.

When construction began, we lived a couple of miles away at Five Corners in a big old farmhouse we rented. That's the home I was brought to, after my birth at Swedish Hospital in Seattle. It was 1946.

What I remember about that old place was a cherry tree taller than the house and wider than the yard. Because no human could keep the

* Lyric from "Down in the Valley," traditional American folk song

45

cherries picked, the lawn underneath was squishy with juice and pulp, giving Mother fits as she constantly cleaned sticky layers of dirt from the floor and the children. Once I was able to walk, I already sensed that I shouldn't go out into the yard because, coming back in, I would cause more work for her.

Before the framing was up for our new dwelling, the farmhouse owners decided to live in the place themselves instead of continuing to rent it out. Their decision caused us more trauma than anyone anticipated.

That winter we moved to a cottage, in the woods next to Miss Ward's and Mrs. Bowden's place. Miss Ward, a thin lady, was the classic type of a dear old spinster, and Mrs. Bowden was a softer, kindly widow. They lived just down the hill from our building site, and were later to be our nearest neighbors.

In this move Carolyn was uprooted from her beloved first-grade class and sent to Edmonds Elementary School to survive the semester with a teacher who was dour and critical. Kenneth and I were both in diapers, and I was colicky. Unexpectedly, Dad was diagnosed with mononucleosis, which at the time was treated with lengthy bed rest, and he was not a cheerful invalid. The cottage was tiny and un-insulated. It was winter. A truly miserable time for everyone. Mother was the center pole in the shaky tent of our daily life, and although she was a phenomenally strong woman, I wonder whether she could have supported the family structure without the nearby help of her mother and father.

For me too, the best asset of our new location was Grandma and Granddad's house, only about a hundred yards from our cottage. I don't know how young I was when I started spending large parts of many days with Grandma, but she was as close and dear to me as my parents.

The new house must have lain untouched for some time until Dad was back on his feet. At two and three years old, what I noticed of the construction was mud everywhere, outdoors and in. Even as a little child, I was very attuned to Mother's burdens and wanted to avoid adding to them. I did what I could to stay clean, although it was a losing battle.

Our landlords, Miss Ward and Mrs. Bowden, kindly welcomed me to spend time in their pleasant home. I remember Mrs. Bowden, apparently hopeful of becoming a surrogate relative, saying gently, "You can call me Grandma Bowden if you want." The idea repelled me! I liked her well enough, but in my book, "Grandma" was not a title like "Aunt." After all, I had two or three aunts, but there was only one Grandma. Without directly answering, I continued to call her Mrs. Bowden.

First floor, fireplace room windows, 1947 (left).

October 1949

Second floor under construction, 1949(right).

My parents came up with the money-saving plan to live in the lower floor of the new house while the top story was being added. The site was steep, so the back of the building was designed to be sunk into the hill. The finished house, when seen from below, would resemble a shoebox: long, rectangular, flat-roofed, with wide overhanging eaves, the lid a little oversized for the box. The driveway, and eventually the main entry, were at second-floor level, so that's where the shared spaces were, laid out atop the bedrooms. When completed and viewed from the front, it appeared to be a one-story structure with some interesting features such as a wide chimney of golden brick, a partially recessed front door, and a breezeway connecting to the garage, which was set at a 45-degree angle to the house. But that was a long way from the early concrete pad with sticks gradually rising from it.

When he was on the job site, Dad was full of optimism and enthusiasm. He was interested in new technologies, and was always looking for something novel that could be incorporated at low cost. He eagerly signed up for experimental options, most of which never gained general acceptance – because the average homeowner wanted things to work reliably. There were a number of unusual materials and systems.

You couldn't count on good water pressure. I heard this blamed on the local water pipes. Two miles out of town, we were beyond the reach of the city water system, so our connection was through old, privately owned networks of conduits, many of which were actually made of wood. One time Dad took Ken and me to the main road to show us a section that had been dug out for repair. The pipes were made like long barrels, a square or circle of maple or fir staves bound together with bands. Naturally, over time the wood rotted and the water mains leaked.

Or perhaps our plumbing was installed on a bargain basis, like the electricity. As far as I know, the wiring never caused any fires or total outages, but upstairs, various light switches randomly stopped working. We had "low-voltage wiring" with unique silent wall switches that, instead of staying in the On or Off position, were designed to bounce back to center. You pressed the switch to the right to turn it on, left to turn it off. Several of the rooms had two switches for the same overhead lights – one at each entry to the room. We developed a game of "dueling switches," where one child stood at each door, testing how quickly we could turn the light on and off. Before long one of us would be holding our switch steadily in the On or Off position to foil our opponent. You could almost feel the current trying to decide which way to flow. I'm pretty sure this didn't contribute to the longevity of the system.

Pocket doors were included in the innovations installed in the house. There were three of them upstairs. They were real space-savers compared to traditional doors, but solid and very heavy to open and shut, and they rumbled like thunder. It was rare that any of us closed those sliding doors.

I had a special antipathy to the lower floor, where the bedrooms were. The oil furnace pumped warmth through ducts in the diaphragm between the bottom and top floors. This sounds very efficient until you realize that the downstairs level, set into the hill, was always cooled by the steady temperature of the surrounding clay soil. Underfoot were black asphalt tiles laid on the foundational concrete slab – two more cost-saving features – keeping the floors at an ambient temperature in the low fifties. Each bedroom had a single heat vent in the ceiling, and as you may know, warm air rises and hardly ever sinks. In fall, winter and spring you were very lucky if your brain was kept warm enough to think – at the other extreme, you would sometimes lose all feeling in your feet. Doing homework in this atmosphere required superhuman concentration. (You couldn't snuggle in bed to do homework; you had to sit at your desk, because "handwriting counted." Remember handwriting?)

The lower floor of the house consisted of a long hall with a room at each end and three rooms opening off the west side. On the east side of the hall were the bathroom, stairs, and a row of closets, all backed into the hillside. Except for a couple of extra windows in the room at the south end, the only natural light came through two medium-sized windows in each of the three bedrooms. When bedroom doors were closed, natural light was eliminated and, perhaps for reasons of economy, the overhead hall lights were dim and far apart. I guess you'd call it a daylight basement, but daylight was at a premium. I remember it as a gloomy space.

There's a Christmas-card photo of us three youngsters, when Carolyn was seven and Ken and I were toddlers, in what we always called "the fireplace room," at the south end of the house. That was the early, downstairs living room, and a mighty small one, also

Christmas 1947, in the fireplace room.

serving as our parents' bedroom. The red-brick fireplace was on the east wall. There was a pretty bank of windows in the south wall, with the craggy "banana apple" tree seasonally changing outside the window. (Those crisp, yellow, speckled apples actually tasted a little like bananas!) An exterior door opened onto the flat patch of lawn to the west.

But my lasting impression of the room was darkness. Mother, of course, did all the decorating, and I'm pretty sure that room generally had dark wallpaper, leaves or flowers scattered on backgrounds of forest green or charcoal gray. I've sometimes wondered if I'd feel differently about the room if it had been painted ivory or sky blue. But perhaps the darkness also reflects my feeling about the family being cooped up in that little space, when there was so often so much tension among us.

When at last we acquired a television set, it was situated in the fireplace room. By then, we had a generous living room upstairs, but Mother had declared that she would *not* have her main floor dominated by that noisemaker. (Like most Americans, much later she changed her tune, for the sake of convenience.) Some evenings we children crowded onto the downstairs couch, parents in their chairs, to watch selected programs.

Mother disapproved of cartoons, and she had a firm unwritten rule banning daytime TV. We didn't come home from school and flip on the tube, and we didn't while away our Saturday mornings in front of the screen. Many of my little friends were on a first-name basis with Annette, Cubby, and Karen of *The Mickey Mouse Club*. But at our house, TV was for family viewing together, after dinner. The five of us watched weekly broadcasts of such classics as *The Lone Ranger*, *Perry Mason*, and *Wyatt Earp*. Sunday nights were for *Disneyland* (introduced each week by Walt himself). Two of my favorites were *Father Knows Best* and *The Rifleman*. What did those two have in common? The male protagonists were fathers who showed some interest in raising their children.

Dad drove us crazy with sidebar comments poking holes in the illusions of the shows: "That buckboard isn't moving, they're just rolling the pictures along in the background," or, "He'd never get away with that in a real courtroom." In the long run, these observations may have planted the first seeds of our critical thinking skills, but in our eyes at the time, he was just spoiling the mood. We wanted nothing so much as to suspend disbelief and immerse ourselves in the story.

Mother scorned slapstick and distrusted comedians for "*trying* to be funny." We never saw the classic variety shows, *I Love Lucy*, *Jack Benny*, or *Milton Berle*. The exception was *People Are Funny* with Art Linkletter, where, although situations were contrived, actual responses of real children were the focus. My grandparents saw *Lawrence Welk* every week, and since I spent a lot of time in their house, I was a regular viewer of that extremely clean-cut, white-bread musical revue.

An off-screen performance enacted in many homes at that time was the Antenna Drama. Fathers all over the country climbed onto roofs and waggled wire contraptions. Having the television set in the basement made it especially challenging to correctly adjust the antenna, way up on the flat roof. Dad's hearing loss intensified the communication difficulty. A lot of shouting and various amounts of frustration were involved.

"Is that good?"

Gray zigzags and crackling static. "No, not yet!"

"What?"

These exchanges were replayed until there was some improvement in the signal. Then Dad came inside, and the knobs on the back of the set had to be twiddled. Ken soon became our back-of-the-set adjuster. Our bane was the vertical roll – he would just barely finesse it to stop racing up the screen, then it would start a slow determined creep downward.

Granddad Reid, Hermiston, Oregon, with his roll-top desk, 1952, shortly before moving to our house in Edmonds.

When Dad's father moved in with us, his small roll-top desk came along. I understand this was the desk he had used as a banker before the bank "went bust," plunging his young family into poverty. At our house, after a time, Dad set up the desk in the fireplace room and dubbed that corner his "study." He may have used the space to make notes on a report once or twice, but the nomenclature didn't stick long, as he stopped bringing work home and just spent evenings at the office. The desk remained unnoticed in the corner for years. Despite its sad history, I like to think the old workhorse of a desk is now as happy in my condominium as I am.

The House: Part Two

Bless these walls so firm and stout, keep want and trouble out*

As the fireplace room was the southern terminus, the furnace room was its northern counterpart. It had no windows except for the top half of the exterior door in its north wall. That room was clearly intended to be used for laundry, but the wash was never done there. Grandma had a washing machine, and Mother did all our laundry down the hill at her parents' house until she started working. After that, our new washer-dryer was installed in the sewing room upstairs.

So the room held only the big, boxy oil furnace and three long parallel clotheslines in case Mother had to bring home the clean, wet clothes from washday at Grandma's and hang them to dry indoors on a rainy day. Wide shelves were added along the back wall, on which we stored the Christmas decorations. There was a deep double laundry sink, which went unused until the 1970s, when Mother tried experimenting with dyeing fabric. A pull-cord still hung from a single bulb in the middle of the ceiling, and the light was so weak that I could hardly believe she got an accurate view of the colors she created.

The concrete floor sloped toward a central drain, which unfortunately must have been just about level with the top of the septic tank outside. Periodically the gagging stench of fluids would rise through the grille on the floor drain. At least once, the smell was accompanied by the fluids themselves.

* Lyric from "Bless this House," May Brahe and Helen Taylor, 1927

I was horrified when I witnessed this revolting event. There were angry accusations between Mother and Dad. I assume, now, that one of them had failed to arrange to have the tank pumped out, but no one explained any of that at the time. As with all unpleasant occurrences, my folks operated on the understanding, "The less said to the children, the better." As a result, a worry took up residence in the back of my mind – would it happen again?

From a child's perspective, there were two other consequences. First, we were forbidden to play on the soggy north lawn (the drain field) for a few days. Second, we were lectured again on the eleventh commandment: use no more than three little squares of paper from the roll. I later learned that around the country, many children of my vintage lived by that same imperative. I can only imagine the relief my parents must have felt when, at last, our hilly neighborhood was included in the city sewer catchment area!

The three bedrooms were used in different ways over time. The first one, next to the furnace room, was the original kitchen/ dining room. I have no memory of that kitchen, but I found it significant that if anyone ever brought it up later, Mother winced and changed the subject. She did say that there were no built-in counters, making it seriously inconvenient to prepare meals for five people. In later years, with her big upstairs kitchen, she always insisted we keep the surfaces empty and clean in the "work triangle" between stove, fridge and sink: "Don't be bringing your books in here, I need my counter space!" It looks as though Carolyn and I have inherited this characteristic, as we are both still happiest in kitchens with plenty of counter space.

Once the upstairs was built, the former kitchen became – and remained – Ken's room. His was the only bedroom with hot and cold running water.

After we were all grown and out of the house, the north bedroom was outfitted as a place for the grandchildren when they came to stay. At the same time, Dad took up tomato-growing as a second hobby (in addition to photography), and the room that had been Ken's was the main locus of this activity. Dad's garden patch was just outside, and he would select the largest and juiciest tomatoes, save the seeds on strips of paper towel, and plant each in a tiny peat pot, upsizing the pots under grow-lights until the seedlings were big enough to transplant outdoors. On summer visits, we sometimes saw him in the back yard wielding a dainty artist's paint brush, like an enormous bumble bee, transferring pollen from blossom to blossom.

Barbie and Carolyn in Carolyn's bedroom, 1952

He gave away the tomatoes he grew. Sometimes there were accolades from colleagues and in-laws, but, accustomed as we were to disregarding him, those of us in the nuclear family expressed no appreciation for this venture. The grandchildren still recall the heavy scent of tomato leaves permeating the atmosphere of the guest bedroom.

The next room, at the bottom of the central stairs, was always Carolyn's. I believe this was the smallest of the bedrooms. Instead of a table or desk, there was a built-in counter with desk drawers beneath. She was enough older that I generally felt she had a life separate from mine, so I don't remember much about her room from the early days. She collected "storybook dolls," and two wall-hung, glass-fronted cabinets were built to display her dolls. Decades later, when Mother was preparing to move out of the house, I had the bright idea of giving Mom's collection of international dolls to the Edmonds Museum. Unfortunately I put the storybook dolls in the donation box, for which I'm not sure Carolyn has forgiven me yet!

When we were toddlers, Kenneth and I slept on bunk beds in the third bedroom. This was the room that had an extra door leading out onto the west lawn, overlooking our grandparents' house. Unbeknownst to me, Ken walked in his sleep. One winter night, during a rare Edmonds snowstorm, he woke me up and said, "We've got to go find Mother." Trusting my big brother implicitly, I placed my hand in his, and we left the house. In the pitch dark, the two of us walked through the snow, barefoot in our pajamas, down the long path to Grandma's place.

Grandma's house in snow. Part of the path is barely visible across center of photo.

We arrived, wet, cold and sobbing, to find Mother and Grandma in the warm, steamy utility room finishing up the laundry. All were comforted, and I suspect Granddad put us in his car and drove all the way around the hill to bring us home. (The walking path was about two blocks long, as a drunken crow flies, but we were probably a little more than a mile away by road.)

It's funny the moments that stick with us through the years. My other memory of sharing the room with Kenneth was one night when we were awakened by Dad's deep voice loudly demanding, "Did you brush your teeth?" Although it may not have been past ten o'clock, we were both little tykes and had been sound asleep.

Even after we dragged ourselves up from dreamland and he repeated the question, I couldn't fathom why he was asking at that moment. I'm not sure if I answered at all, but Kenneth replied, "Yes."

With a triumphant "Ha!" Dad boomed, "I caught you! You did not! Your toothbrushes are dry! Both of you get up and brush your teeth right now!" We stumbled into the bathroom and obeyed, alarmed and mystified.

I imagine that Mother had probably asked him to get more involved in raising us, and this was his way of helping out. Compared to how harshly he himself had been reared, this nighttime wakening may have seemed very appropriate to him. But I'm afraid the lesson he hoped to teach us – to brush our teeth – was subsumed, at least for me, by the frightening lesson that Dad might do anything at any moment, with little cause. Of course all he had done was speak to us, and to my knowledge no one in our family was ever physically touched in anger. But I came away with a new awareness – he was very powerful and unpredictable, and I was very small.

After the upper floor was finished and I was around five or six, perhaps because the two of us had reached the age when sleeping in the same room was inappropriate, this became my room when Ken moved to the former kitchen.

When Granddad Reid came to stay in 1953, I moved in with Carolyn, for the duration of his last four years of life. Of my dad and his two siblings, I think Dad was the one with both the stability and the space to have his father stay. Besides, of the three, Dad had always been the offspring with the extreme sense of responsibility. He felt a strong obligation to provide for his father in the declining years, despite the old man's cold, severe personality which had been so painful for him throughout his life.

Of course Dad, the workaholic, spent even less time with his father than he did with us, so the burden fell on Mom. Fortunately or unfortunately, she too had an extreme sense of responsibility. Granddad Reid was "bedridden" – my new vocabulary word whose definition became all too apparent. At first he was able to make his way down the hall to the bathroom. However, eventually I saw – but never had to deal with—a bedpan and a urinal, which Mother wielded without any help from the rest of us.

For every meal, Mother made a tray for Granddad Reid and either she or I delivered it to his bed. Bringing lunch or dinner to him also meant helping him sit up, bracing him with pillows, settling the tray on the bed so it wouldn't tip. He probably had some form of dementia. In my eyes he was just a grumpy, deaf, brittle old stick. He never thanked either of us, and usually had some complaint or other, to which we would respond at top volume but he couldn't (or wouldn't) hear us. Afterward, one of us had to retrieve the tray, and I always prayed he'd be asleep when I returned.

My dad James H. Reid, Jr., with his siblings and their father, James H. Reid, Sr., 1956.

I think Dad stopped by the bedside every day to say hello, but the only task I saw him handle was taking an occasional snapshot. When the old fellow was nearing the end, Dad contacted Uncle Wally and Aunt Barbara to come visit. By this time he wasn't well enough to get dressed, so his final portraits, in the sunshine outside his bedroom, were in pajamas and bathrobe.

I felt very little sadness when Granddad Reid died, because I'd felt very little connection while he lived. It was May, and I remember watching the black hearse drive away, the road flanked by blooming trees and daffodils, and pondering the irony of death in the midst of all the celebratory colors of nature.

I had my room again until I was fourteen, when we welcomed the delightful Bror, an exchange student from Norway. I moved into

Carolyn's room again. By then she was away at college, so we only had to share during vacations – but the nomenclature never changed, it was always Carolyn's room. Bror was an ideal brother (if only for a few months), kind and considerate to his core, polite and yet with lively interests and an upbeat sense of humor. He, Ken and I were in high school, which gave us something in common. Although my path rarely crossed either of theirs at school, the three of us did attend a few events together in the summer. Ken has stayed in regular contact ever since, thankfully, so we've seen Bror – now a doting grandfather in Norway – a number of times since 1960.

Bror, Carolyn and Barb on Edmonds-Kingston ferry, 1960.

When Bror returned to Norway, our parents transformed his room – formerly mine – into their bedroom, leaving the fireplace room rarely used. I stayed in Carolyn's room. She was in the Peace Corps in Colombia at that time, and was finished with living in the family home. It was in that place that I did a lot of journaling and poetry writing, and began yearning for more privacy.

At night, when the wind was right, I could hear the labored throbbing of tugboat engines as they returned northward to the Everett port. Peering out the window in the dark, between the tree trunks, I saw the white running lights of these sturdy boats, a line and dot like a staggered exclamation mark, somehow calling up a deep loneliness in me that I couldn't name.

Like most doors in the lower floor, my bedroom door didn't latch properly. I feel sad when I remember the day that Dad silently pushed my bedroom door wide open. I was sixteen, standing by the closet in my underwear. I was outraged that he didn't have the sense to knock, and I shouted at him. His feelings were hurt. "I only wanted to tell you something." This may have been the moment he began to notice I was growing up physically, but he never stopped expecting me to revert to his ideal image of who I was – four years old and sweet as pie.

During those periods when my room was next to Mom and Dad's, I sometimes heard them talking in bed. From the tones of voice and an occasional understandable phrase, it was clear to me that Mother was frustrated with Dad's distance from the family. Yet, in some way, they were both trapped in their roles, and they were both highly defensive. They never got the knack of communicating in a way that could bring about any change in their relationship.

At first we never locked our outside doors. Moreover, from the fireplace room (where the TV was) you couldn't hear someone walking into the house upstairs – a fact occasionally proven by a friend wandering in looking for us, calling until someone happened to hear the voice. This didn't seem to bother anyone except me. But at some point, we did start trying to remember to lock up at night. Maybe a neighbor had a break-in or a strange car was seen in the area. The exterior door to the furnace room, like the interior doors, didn't latch completely unless you leaned on it just right, and once in a while I'd wander to the bathroom in the night and see that door, at the end of a dark hall and a darker room, standing wide open. No matter how I tried to be sure that I was the last one to close it – and turn the lock in the knob – someone else was likely to use the door during the evening and casually swing it *almost* shut without latching it.

There were so many doors into the house – three on the bottom floor and two upstairs, as well as a wide-swinging window in the upstairs powder room – that I had frequent nightmares about someone silently sneaking in, or threatening to enter, with unspecified evil intentions. In the dreams I would race frantically from one door to another trying to lock them all before the intruder could find a way in. I never told anyone about these scary dreams. Now, having learned a bit about dream interpretation, I wonder if the nightmares were a reaction to the intrusiveness of my parents, striving to control everything about me and leaving me precious little physical, emotional or mental space for my own freedom and growth.

The House: Part Three

We climb the stair[*]

My legs still know the stairs. Four long strides, then two footfalls to make the U-turn on the landing, and four more stretches to the top. From the time we gained adequate leg-span, the three of us always took the sixteen steps two at a time. I think our six-foot-four dad did too, back when his body was an instrument of enthusiasm, but "trudging" would describe his footfalls for the greatest part of his years there.

The stairs were central in more ways than one. To manage the household, including everything from laundry and cleaning, to checking the furnace filters, to helping us get ready to go places as a family, Mother climbed up and down the stairs many times every day. In our teen years Carolyn and I began to compliment Mom on her beautiful calves and ankles. Her build was on the husky side, and although she stayed busy and active, she didn't purposely pursue physical exercise, which she would have seen as frivolous and unnecessary. But until the arthritic hip deterioration of her late sixties, her lower legs were strong and shapely.

The kitchen was the main reason for going upstairs. It saw more traffic and activity than any other room in the house. Entering the kitchen from the short hallway, the west wall was directly ahead, with a row of backless wooden stools at a long counter. Above the counter, wide windows displayed Puget Sound and the Olympic Mountains. This is where we kids ate breakfast.

* Lyric from "Me and My Shadow,, Dave Dreyer and Billy Rose, 1927

In the early days, Dad would bound up the stairs asking, "What's for breakfast?" If Mom was stirring a pot of oatmeal, cornmeal or Cream of Wheat, I loved to hear his exclamation, "Oh, good – mush!" His eagerness mystified me at the time, especially when to my ears, "mush" sounded like something for the hog pen. Knowing now how spare his childhood was, I think he may have felt especially nourished when someone bothered to cook for him in the morning. Once Mother returned to school and work, Dad sometimes lit briefly on a stool to inhale a bowl of bran flakes on his way to work, but often he just drank a glass of milk (the ulcer treatment of the day) before dashing out the door. Mother didn't eat the balanced breakfast that she pressed upon us (fruit, milk, cereal), or at least she didn't generally eat *with* us in the mornings. She always sipped coffee as she moved around taking care of our needs, but she rarely sat down until we cleared out.

The kitchen counter where we ate was a magnet for paper. In untidy piles were the ubiquitous flyers and mail pieces that get placed on any surface with, "I'm going to read that someday." There were also engineering sketches and notes made by Dad's professional "4H" pencils, along with some of our homework papers (only the ones that had been marked with A or B grades, of course), and the occasional magazine. When the stacks of paper reached critical mass, Mother would rail about the mess and glance roughly through it, throwing out a large percentage, leaving just enough, like a sourdough starter, to catalyze new growth.

Sitting on those stools eating our fruit and oatmeal had its perils. On many occasions Mother walked up behind my sister, hooked eight fingers over Carolyn's shoulders and jabbed both thumbs into her shoulder blades. "Sit up straight!" Now, if you've ever been six feet tall and sat on a high stool to eat at a counter, you know that sitting up straight is next to impossible. This scene was reenacted countless times. It was Carolyn's standing posture – slightly stooped – that really bothered Mom, but her 5'4" stature made it tough to attack her 6'1" daughter's shoulders if the two of them were standing! I thought the hunching was caused by Carolyn's shyness about being so much taller than her peers, with which I empathized. As with many physical issues (like my childhood exhaustion and menstrual cramps), Mother never considered that this might be a medical problem. To her it was a simple case of mind over matter. But as a young adult, Carolyn finally learned that she had a spinal curvature—scoliosis. Nonetheless, as she matured, my sister came to stand tall and lithe at her full height.

In the functional section of the kitchen, the appliances were arranged in the perfect "work triangle," with lots of floor and counter space. If the entire house was the realm where she reigned supreme, this room was Mother's most beloved principality. I remember how tickled she was when she painted the kitchen walls a daffodil yellow, and although other colors eventually superseded that one, I will always think of Mother in her sunshine-bright kitchen.

This room was like a light glowing in a window on a snowy night – visitors couldn't stay away. In the early stages of a party, guests gravitated to the kitchen. At some point Mother would wave a towel at the interlopers and say, with the full force of her personality eased by a chuckle, "Everybody get out of my kitchen! I need to get this food ready!" Despite this show of authority, people have told me that some of their

Barbie, Mom, and Kenneth in kitchen, 1952

warmest memories emanate from that kitchen.

First thing in the morning, on the back of the stove, the electric ring was turned to "High" under the percolator. Once it perked, and the grounds were removed, the coffee pot remained at a simmer all day, with Mother drawing off a cupful as often as possible. Outside of parties, she rarely had a visitor, but in case Grandma climbed the hill for a chat, the coffee was always ready. They both drank it black. Once as a little girl, when I was allowed to sit at the dining table while Mother and Grandma talked, I asked for a taste of coffee – it smelled so delicious, like waking up to a welcoming world. Mother let me drink the dregs in the bottom of her cup. I sipped and found it thick and bitter and grainy with grounds. I didn't touch coffee again until college!

At the top of the stairs was the telephone, primly perched on a special little shelf. Behind the shelf, a small door was cut through the wall, enabling us to pick up the receiver from the dining room as well as the hall. In those days, it was important always to answer the phone, even if you were at the dinner table. For one thing, it would keep ringing until the caller hung up, which could be several minutes (and phones couldn't be unplugged or turned off – to make the ringing stop, the cord would have had to be actually cut). There were no answering machines, voice mail, "call waiting," or caller identification, so if you missed the call, you might have missed a crucial connection.

Unlike today, telephone communication was uncertain. If you were away from home, or already on the phone with someone else, there was no way you could know that someone had called. A caller might have to spin that rotary dial several times over a few days before they could actually speak to you.

Mother eventually set a little stool in the hall in case we needed to sit, although she herself was so averse to lengthy telephone calls that she almost always stood, ready for a quick getaway. Later, when it became more practical to make changes to the instrument, a longer cord was attached. I took advantage of this enhancement in my teen years, when Mother and I were often the only people in the house and I wanted a little more distance for my hour-long conversations with my best friend. Of course I could have taken the call on the downstairs extension, but that opened the possibility that Mother would listen in on the line, instead of simply hanging up the upstairs phone for me. This was not a risk I would take.

The first room by the top of the stairs was the guest bathroom. Its large, obscured-glass window swung out over the ridiculous little concrete pond on the front lawn. That was the only window on the entire, long east side of the house, so if we heard a car pull in, we would sometimes furtively crack the window an inch and peek out at the parking area to see who had arrived, proud of our clever spy tactic.

The toilet, sink and counter lined one wall of the little bathroom, leaving a blank canvas on the opposite wall. At some point in my youth, Mother painted a colorful mural of a rainforest-like scene, with giant floor-to-ceiling tree trunks, spiky shrubs, huge flowers and life-sized forest animals.

Mom was an artist. Taking time to gaze out the west windows, she often commented on the changing appearance of the mountains, especially when they looked, as she termed it, like cardboard cutouts, arrayed behind each other in fading shades of blue. She loved that view.

There were a few summer days when the five of us drove to Deception Pass to picnic, play in the gentle surf, walk trails and climb boulders. Mother took along a sketch pad and I marveled as she rendered her beloved mountains in charcoal, beautifully capturing the shading of the water, rocky outcroppings, tree-covered hills, and peaks. I admired her eye, the accuracy and balance of her compositions. It seemed sad that she had so few chances to express this particular genius.

With that one exception, I felt she had entirely subsumed her powerful urge to create art into the tasks of housekeeping and raising children. She channeled her talents into home decor, craft projects with us, and practical, but sometimes also innovative, clothing design.

Just past the bathroom was a spacious area leading to the back door. This became Mother's sewing room, lined with shelves full of fabrics. (A few of those shelves were reserved for the canned fruits and jams that she and Grandma preserved year upon year.) This was a very convenient place for Mom to spend her copious stitching time, since we went in and out almost exclusively through the back door, and, as matriarch, she always wanted to know when we left the house.

The House: Part Four

Everybody eats when
they come to my house*

The kitchen was at the north end of the upper floor. Heading south, you passed through the dining room, which opened, unconstricted, into the living room. This long super-room was bordered on the west by huge picture windows extending from ankle height to the ceiling. The view of Puget Sound and the Olympic Peninsula was breathtaking. A couple of miles to the southwest, beyond the orchard and our grandparents' home, we could see a smooth stretch of beach and the Edmonds ferry dock.

There were drawbacks to the western exposure. The only thermostat in the house was

View of Edmonds docks beyond Grandma and Granddad's house, 1949.

in the dining room, directly opposite vast expanses of glass which amplified the heat of the afternoon sun. Mother never, ever allowed

* Lyric from "Everybody Eats When They Come to My House," Cab Calloway, 1942

the temperature to be set above 68 degrees. That's 68 degrees on the second floor, where warmth naturally collected. Even in winter, when the furnace heat was needed, if the sun shone, the thermostat clicked off. Looking back, I think of the upstairs as a hot, bright, expansive, public space, in strong contrast to the cold, dim, segmented, private downstairs.

The dining room was the site of family dinners every night. Mother sat nearest the kitchen, at what we called the foot of the table. Dad sat at the head, with his back to the living room. He had the chair with arms. Carolyn faced the mountains, and when we were small, Kenneth and I sat on the window side of the table. Like seating arrangements in the car, this lineup was based on length from hip to ankle. By his early teens Ken developed a penchant for tilting his chair back onto two legs, scaring us all with visions of his youthful body heaped on the lawn below, surrounded by splintered glass. But if he sat normally, his stretched-out legs could tangle with Carolyn's, instigating sibling conflicts. Soon Mother re-assigned him to sit next to Carolyn where elbows were the only likely point of contact.

Although we ate together, we were taught only a few basic table manners. Place settings had a fork, spoon and knife in correct array, with the glass at the tip of the knife. But we did talk with our mouths full. When the meal was served family-style, platters were handed around every which way, and after the first round, instead of asking for a dish to be passed, we often just leaned out to get it. We forgot to put the paper napkins on our laps before eating, and didn't pat our lips with them until we finished. "Boarding-house reach" and "no elbows on the table" were foreign expressions that embarrassed me at the homes of my friends in my teen years. Comically, when Carolyn, and later I, attended Whitman College, Wednesday night dormitory meals were called "gracious living dinners," where we were taught to use the correct pieces of flatware, take dainty bites, and pass dishes always in the same direction. Needless to say, our efforts to enlighten the folks back home with these rules were laughingly rejected.

Dinner conversation was stilted. At first, Dad would sometimes talk about his work. To me, this could be interesting, but he often spoke very slowly with long pauses to choose just the right word, which, over time, wore my curiosity down to a nub. Mother appeared to have the same reaction, because after a while she actively discouraged him from discussing his job. In the house, Mother's word was law, so Dad's work — the central material of his life — was set aside in a tightly lidded box, from which only the briefest of phrases escaped when they directly related to us: "Port of Everett meeting tonight," or "Got to work Saturday to get this report out." The silence was tense.

There were also periods when our parents made obviously forced efforts to engage each of us: "How was school?" or "What did you learn today?"

While the adults had prepared themselves by thinking up the questions, we youngsters were caught unaware and had no answers to give, other than "Okay" or "I don't know." Starting when I was about twelve, Mother became consumed with her own career, and we heard many stories from her work, often outlining difficult situations she had faced at school. While I found it ironic that her stories were just as conducive to stressful dining as Dad's had been, I had no thought of confronting her with the hypocrisy.

The Teufels visit at Christmas time in the late 1950s.
Far left: "Aunt" Helen Teufel. Far right: "Uncle" George.
At right, note the little door to the telephone.

Only when we had guests was dinner enjoyable for me. Out-of-town visitors brought new topics to the table, and at extended Burd family meals any tension was obliterated by chatter and activity.

My favorite evenings were when one or another of Ken's high school friends came to dinner. They were remarkably witty. In particular, he and Ralph effortlessly set up a rapid-fire repartee of one-liners that had the rest of us breathless with laughter. By this time Dad's hearing loss was affecting his ability to keep up – I think he heard sounds but needed a moment to process them into phrases – so I was sorry that although he was at the table, he was largely left out of the fun. With the callousness of youth, I forgot this fleeting concern in the sweeping waves of giggles that Mother, Carolyn and I shared as the boys' wisecracks ricocheted off our funny bones.

The record player was in the dining room. In my teen years, that spot became my after-school haven. Carolyn was away at college, Ken was at baseball, basketball or football practice, Mom and Dad were at work. Mom subscribed to the Columbia Record Club, and I sat daily on the floor playing records over and over. During the fall and winter seasons of short days, I watched scores of stunning sunsets while marinating in romantic, tuneful stories from the original cast albums of *Oklahoma, Carousel, South Pacific, My Fair Lady, The Music Man, The Sound of Music,* and *Camelot.* There's a theory that our brains have a limited number of cubby holes where information is stored, and I blame my inability to retain new information now on the fact that my memory cubicles are crammed with lyrics from mid-twentieth-century musicals. I can still sing nearly every song, word for word, and once I start, you may not be able to stop me.

The living room occupied almost the entire south half of the upper floor. The fireplace was on the east side, and the upright piano rested against the south wall. This piano had quite a history with us. It had belonged to my mother's sister until she replaced it with a baby grand at her home. Its surface had always been black lacquer, like most pianos of the day. When Carolyn was in high school, she decided that as an extra-credit project for her home economics class, she would refinish the piano. (Have I mentioned that she was always an A-plus student?) Her weeks of intensive work revealed lovely smooth-grained rosewood. This instrument never had the resonant tone of many other pianos I've heard, but it looked amazing, and faithfully served the family for all our lessons and songfests.

Nearly three decades later, Mother sold the house and we moved the piano to my house in Ballard. Before the annual Christmas carol sing, I hired the popular piano tuner in my neighborhood, who was known as "Blind Mike." After working for a few minutes, he said, "This is a beautiful piano."

Taking into account its rather thudding tone and the fact that he couldn't actually see the piano, I was taken aback by this comment. I couldn't help asking, "Beautiful? Do you mean as a musical instrument, or as a piece of furniture?"

For a beat or two he seemed to consider whether to hedge his answer, but then he said, "As a piece of furniture. I can feel the quality of the wood and the finish." From then on, every holiday when we needed a tuner, we always called Mike. I appreciated his honesty and diplomacy as much as his musical skill.

Although Mom had had difficulty starting her married life in the tropical heat of Hawaii, she loved the plants and flowers. Years later she was still telling us about the hibiscus, orchids and wonderfully fragrant pikake, and she always had an anthurium plant in the house. Her home decor in Edmonds was based on the tropical beauty she remembered. For the better part of our childhood, the living room was furnished with a wall-to-wall woven reed mat, and couch,

New Year's Eve party, late 1950s. Note wicker and rattan furniture, refinished piano, and silly game!

chairs and sectionals constructed of bamboo and rattan, for which she stitched bright Hawaiian-print cushions. Nobody seemed to take Ken seriously when he complained that he was embarrassed to let his friends see that his living room carpet was a grass rug.

Mother enjoyed having parties. Beyond occasions at her parents' or siblings' houses, she was uncomfortable at other people's events, but the hostess role suited her. She had lived at her parents' home through graduate school, and her letters from that time told of the great pleasure she took in gatherings of young friends there. Our large living room lent itself to this kind of entertaining, particularly the carefully choreographed carol sings and the family get-togethers for birthdays, Easter, and Christmas Eve.

Back in more innocent times, when Americans didn't feel the need to get drunk on December 31, she also arranged New Year's Eve parties where everyone played silly games. I was sometimes allowed to join in, and I recall one game that leveled the playing field for old and young alike – a team relay requiring each blindfolded player to carry a spoonful of dried kidney beans across the room, depositing them into a milk bottle. Teammates shouted directions, beans rolled on the floor or jingled into the glass containers, and winning and losing were equally fun. It's hard to picture in today's era of self-consciousness and sophistication, but the guests ended up laughing hysterically at their own antics. I remember my dad and mom sharing jokes, grinning at each other, and even doing a brief impromptu waltz one time.

Tired as I was after my bedtime, I was kept awake and happy by this unpretentious gathering. Most people went home before midnight, but my dad and his cousin "Bosie" Bosworth, and usually one or two other men, stuck around to set off firecrackers in the driveway as the new year began. I didn't like fireworks, and identified strongly with our poor dog, who couldn't quite tear himself away from the scene, but was unnerved by all the sudden explosions.

As far as I know, the flat roof on our house was a cost-saving measure of the day. I wished we had a pretty, pointed roof like the one on Grandma and Granddad's house, but once in a while there was an advantage for me. Periodically Dad would go up to examine the seams and the black tar coating, and on rare occasions Kenneth and I were allowed to climb the ladder and join him. The weather had to be just cloudy enough that the tar wouldn't be damaged by our treading. We were warned to be very careful about going near the edges. But there were broad rain puddles, slightly warm, for barefoot wading. I loved this rare adventure, and was thrilled with the expansive view from what surely seemed like the top of the world. There were some leaks over the years, but we didn't have severe water emergencies, as I would have expected from the pond-like puddles.

Dad took a tripod onto the roof sometimes to capture the overall scene. He later used these pictures, in sequence, to illustrate the year-by-year growth of the trees downhill from us. I thought these time-lapse sequences were marvelous historical documents. (However, they seem to be lost now.) To Dad there was a more urgent point. Those trees were a pet peeve of his, since they gradually narrowed the strip of Puget Sound we could see from our windows. Pat Hannah had bought Miss Ward's and Mrs. Bowden's house, and some of the oldest, tallest trees were rooted on Pat's property. He repeatedly asked her why she wouldn't clear them out or top them – not for his sake, he emphasized, but for her safety and her own view.

Pat Hannah and Dad, circa 1990.

His ruse was transparent. Pat, 15 years his senior, was a gardener, a plant person, and she believed the trees counted more heavily than the view. Knowing that there were certain topics he tiptoed around, such as aging and death, she decided to startle him and put a stop to his whining. In exasperation, she shouted, "Jim, you can cut all the trees you want when I'm *dead!*" He got the message. Her trees became a lighthearted joke between them after that. Pat and Dad ended up good friends for many years before she did, finally, pass on. Most of the trees were cut down by the new owners, but by then Dad had already moved away.

The House: Part Five

Country roads, take me home*

The name of our road was Dead End.

You turned off Snake Road at the Seaview Heights sign. The track up to the Heights was an unpaved, uphill, S-curved single lane, with a high bank on its south side and a deep gully along the north. It seemed to me that as soon as one crumpled car was pulled out of the gully, another went down, remaining for weeks until it, too, was eventually hauled out. This was not a route to navigate while under the influence.

At the top of the steepest stretch was a four-way intersection. Straight ahead, the lane leveled somewhat and led between a couple of old farmhouses and a field where a horse grazed. Turning right at the crossing led to a precipitous descent through a narrow elbow, with an upward slope beyond the dip. On both sides of this sweep were dense stands of twenty-foot-high lilac and rhododendron bushes. With zero visibility, one learned to drive slowly through "the Leightons' place." The spring floral display achieved by Mr. and Mrs. Leighton was absolutely incomparable, and the lilacs' perfume settled like a blessing in the hollow.

Instead of going that way, to find us, you turned left at the crossroads, where the "Dead End" sign was posted. In something under a half mile, this road made a gentle S-curve, then ended. In our garage. The bend must have slowed people down, because I don't recall anyone crashing into the garage. We did have occasional confused visitors who were looking for an address, but until

* Lyric from "Take Me Home, Country Roads," John Denver, 1971

Snohomish Couinty and the City of Edmonds made their way down every dead end road, attaching numbers, directions were given by landmark or by familiarity. "Well, do you know Dunc and Frances Thompson's house? No? How about the Bells? Well, just before their place, you turn up the hill. If you miss it, be sure you make a U-turn at the top of University Colony. Otherwise your next chance is down in Talbot Park and you'll never find your way out of there."

When I was in high school, more roads were cleared through the fields and forests above Seaview Heights. Normally I hated to see even one tree cut down, but these improvements enabled me to walk downhill both to and from school. In the mornings I would cross Pat Hannah's front yard and hurry down the long zigzag drive to catch the usual school bus, and then after classes a different yellow bus dropped me on 88th, above our place. I thought this was a great advance over tramping up Granddad's switchbacks every afternoon. The bonus was that my best friend lived along this upper route, so it was easy to stop there for long talks, when her parents didn't object. We always had so much to say to each other, things that couldn't be said to anyone else.

Dad had our driveway built with a handy L shape for backing up and turning around. I had a couple of mishaps in that spot. A low curb separated "the turnaround" from the lawn, and when I was eighteen, a late bloomer just learning to handle a vehicle, I once stepped on the accelerator to pull away from the curb. I had forgotten to shift out of reverse. The tires thunked backward over the concrete barrier. The divots in the grass were not hard to mend, and only my pride was hurt.

The other incident was more distressing. As every truck owner knows, you must be prepared to lend your vehicle to family members, even those who don't know quite how to drive it, but are eager to fake it. I was 21, and my roommate and I needed to move some furniture. I didn't understand the difference in magnitude between my compact Chevy II and a full-size pickup. One day when my mom's brother was visiting at the house, I went over to borrow my parents' truck.

As I backed and turned, somehow the momentum seemed to halt. I figured I hadn't given it enough gas, so I let out the clutch and gunned the engine. The truck stopped again. I checked the mirrors more carefully. Oh, no! I had crushed the front corner of my uncle's car.

I still feel bad about this! I ran through the front door shouting about what had happened, tears flowing. Uncle Sherman came out to look. Emanating calm assurance, he only said, "Oh, that's not a problem, Barbie, I'll take care of that."

"I'm so, so sorry! Of course I'll pay for the damage." I was working at my first job at the time, and knew nothing of the costs of car repairs, but I sincerely intended to pay. He wouldn't hear of it. I tried to bring up the subject later, but the car was fixed, and for Uncle Sherman, there was nothing to discuss. He was the epitome of kindness to me.

Our lawns were sites of great enjoyment, but also some strife. The front yard was large, but at least it was flat, as was the lower yard outside the bedrooms. But at both ends of the property, the ground was steep. Someone had to mow all of it. I remember Dad doing this a few times, before his job became all-encompassing. Then it became Carolyn's chore. She hated it. Wrestling the push mower up the grade was hard enough, but when she tried to cut downhill, the spiral blade fell off and performed a bouncing, rolling dance into the wild weeds that bordered the lawn. She retrieved it again and again. When Kenneth was about ten, he was deemed old enough to take over. Very soon after the job was transferred, Dad bought a power mower, which eased the task considerably for the boy of the family. Carolyn's indignation still echoes down the years: "It's *not fair!*"

Ken put a lot of effort into not mowing. With Mom, when his evasion tactics wore thin, he tried the direct approach, arguing with her about whether the grass *really* needed to be cut *now*. These conflicts with her son exasperated Mother — when we'd been younger, she'd been in complete control. But mowing was his job, and mow he did. Eventually.

Ken mowing front yard, 1959.
He also built the brick patio in background.

The final installment in the grass-cutting story is that, although I was sixteen when Ken moved out, I was never assigned that task. Literally nobody ever mentioned it. Certainly I wasn't going to volunteer, and with slight guilt feelings, I regularly heard Mother herself wrestling the power mower across those slopes – I heard, but never saw, because if I didn't look, it wasn't my problem! My siblings are right, I was spoiled.

There were all sorts of activities on the grass surrounding the house. Before the mowing battles, when we were small, we took delight in stretching out our little bodies at the top of the north lawn and rolling down the hill, often landing in a giggling pile at the bottom. And, naturally, doing it again and again. Serious matters were addressed here – should arms be stretched above the head, or elbows pressed in at the torso? Shoes or no shoes? We were generally free to play anywhere within hearing distance of Mother's powerful voice, but after the unpleasant drain field incident, she instructed us to check with her before rambling down the north lawn.

As teenagers, we played badminton on the west lawn all summer. Carolyn was so tall that she easily mastered the smash shot, and standard scoring became senseless. My favorite way to play was to see how many consecutive times the birdie crossed the net without touching the ground, with both players trying, in the next round, to increase the number of volleys. One could say I preferred a cooperative rather than competitive approach, but to be honest, if I had had a chance of winning by the regular rules, I probably wouldn't have been the one to propose an alternative!

For one day in 1960 the front yard became a track and field arena. It was an Olympic year, and Bror, our Norwegian foreign student, was with us. Mother went to great trouble to stage a series of "Summer Olympics" contests. Some cousins and some of Ken's friends joined in. Mom set up long jumps, "discus" throwing, an obstacle course, and several other goofy games with improvised props. For the winners she made cardboard medals in all the appropriate colors, and we laughed our way through a sunny day.

I don't recall any invented water sports that day, although the opportunity was there. Our pool was a circular, concrete-lined indentation in the yard between the front and back doors. Eight or ten feet in diameter and two feet deep, it had provided a spot for us to splash on hot summer days, predating, as it did, the collapsible plastic pools that are common now. As small children, Ken and I both were given small rubber dolls, and we took them "swimming." But my brother soon became convinced that dolls were not for boys – even if it was said to be a boy doll – and while he continued to join me in the water, at some point his doll spontaneously wandered away and got lost. He recently confided that he distinctly remembers throwing that doll into the woods as far as his young arm could hurl it.

Once we grew older, the pool became a lily pond, then koi were added. But the raccoons that lived just across the driveway

Kenneth and Barbie in pool, 1952.

81

welcomed this new delicatessen in the neighborhood, and my parents soon gave up on the fish. The pond could only be filled via garden hose. There was no regular provision for cleaning or even draining it, and nobody had time to pay attention. Whenever it began to smell, it was emptied, and eventually they stopped refilling it. From then on it was a great annoyance to Mother, spoiling the visual approach to her home. She wanted it removed, but to the best of my recollection, it stayed.

Woods bordered the driveway on the east. A couple of paths led into the shady ravine, where I sometimes went for secluded strolls. I've heard adults describe the forests of their childhoods as dark and scary places. That was never our experience. As soon as we began living there, Mother took us for nature walks. We learned to identify each species of evergreen tree – the spiky blue spruce, long-needled pine, hemlock with its drooping tips, cedar's branches draped with heavy fringe, and the upright Douglas fir. Mom taught us about alder (the caterpillars' favorite), holly (beautiful at Christmas), maple (but "we don't have sugar maples here") and vine maple (the most gorgeous fall display). We didn't know the term "nurse log," but she showed us that most often, the red huckleberry bush grew directly out of the splintering rusty remains of a cedar stump or log.

A stand of nettles indicated rich soil, and we all knew the risks of brushing against those serrated leaves. We were free to pick as many dandelions as we wanted, but we were never to pick trillium blossoms, as each plant produced only one bloom in a year. Mother made sure we knew it was always safe to eat composite berries we might find, like raspberries, salmonberries and thimbleberries, but with simple single berries, like huckleberries or deadly nightshade, you should never taste them unless you knew exactly what they were. We learned the difference in flavor among blackberry varieties – tiny native berries that grew on slender vines along the ground, large sugary Himalayan berries, which formed entire banks of thick, tangled vines, and the late-ripening evergreen berries with their deeply serrated leaves.

Cousin Nancy and I played house on the saddle of an enormous old maple tree at the edge of the conifers. It was an easy climb and we could watch the house and road, yet we had a sense of privacy because nobody looked up to notice us there. We squeezed white "milk" out of the stems of dandelions to feed to our dolls. The leaves of that tree were twelve inches across, providing generous blankets to wrap our babies.

The woods held a unique gift for me. I must have been about eight when I happened upon a little cabin that I had never seen or heard about. An elderly lady was outside the door filling a bird feeder. Hansel and Gretel never entered my mind, and I was not afraid. We exchanged greetings and introductions. At first I wondered if she was joking about her name, Mrs. Hutt, considering where she lived. She invited me into her two-room dwelling, and we talked. She told me she had lived there for some time with her husband who was now deceased. "Would you like to see my pet?"

"Sure!"

She held a bit of food in her fingers, lifting her arm toward the ceiling. Suddenly a creature leaped from a high shelf, swooped over us, snatched the food and landed on the other side of the room. Mrs. Hutt laughed at my alarm and reassured me, "That's Buddy. Know what he is?" Wide-eyed, I shook my head. "He's a flying squirrel!" I think she explained about the skin flaps that enable these mammals to fly, but I was barely listening. I could hardly wait to tell Mother about this funny lady and her funny pet. She invited me to come back any time.

Mother knew about this couple, although she hadn't known that Mr. Hutt was gone. She approved of my visiting our woodsy neighbor, and I continued. I saw Buddy and met a jay with an injured wing, a baby raccoon, and a few other nature pets Mrs. Hutt had adopted. She told me that she and her husband had donated their section of the woods to the City of Edmonds as a preserve in perpetuity. They retained the right to live out their days on the land. It's there today – Hutt Park – the only forested land that still stands in that vicinity.

We were about a half mile's walk from the water. At the far side
of the railroad bed, a wooden ladder led vertically down to sea
level. Sometimes we took our dog, Kandy, with us on an outing. He
couldn't master climbing down the ladder, so we carried him. But
after a romp, when we started up hand over hand, he outpaced us all.

It was a gravel beach, covered in small rounded rocks that shifted
underfoot, making a wonderful clashing noise. We splashed in the
shallow waves and rested on towels, searching through the rocks
for agates and shells. We found lots of limpet shells (which, in the
ignorance of the day, we called "Chinamen's hats"), plenty of small
thick-walled snail shells with the edges softened by the abrasion of
the sea, and an occasional fist-sized moon snail shell with part of the
crust broken off exposing the lustrous interior of the spiral chambers.
A sand dollar was a rare treasure, with its tiny birdlike teeth rattling
inside. We chased each other wielding smelly brown strands of kelp
like whips or snakes.

The trains were part of the beach experience. We stopped whatever
we were doing to wave to the engineer, and in case we didn't get a
wave back from him, there was sure to be someone on the back deck
of the caboose who would greet us. At home, whenever I heard a train
whistle, I thought of the friendly people who made the trains run.

When the tide was especially low, the extended family gathered
at Grandma and Granddad's house and trooped down the hill to go
clamming. We carried buckets, narrow short-handled clam shovels,
and a two-shovel contraption called a clam gun (it had no explosive
properties). On those occasions, at least one of us, with the dedication
of Ahab chasing the White Whale, would get caught up in the pursuit
of a fast-fleeing geoduck, sinking one or both arms to the shoulder in
a hole in the sand. Victory was mixed; geoducks are large and meaty,
but can be tough. Littleneck and horse clams, slower-moving, were
less muscular and easier to pull from their shallow subterranean
homes. Granddad always rolled up his trousers for this activity, but
I never understood why – by the time we had our quota of clams,
children and adults alike were drenched from top to toe in salt water

and sandy mud. Back at the grandparents' place, we rinsed off with the garden hose, and a chowder feast ensued.

As gatherings went, I liked this one nearly as much as I enjoyed the cider pressing party. A major factor was that my generation was segregated from the adults only for the time it took to cook the chowder. The sentence I always hoped *not* to hear was, "You kids go play, now." I was uncomfortable away from the grownups. I felt carefree and enjoyed the whole family when everyone was together, whether at the beach or on the porch.

Beyond the immediate environment, rich as it was, we regularly drove to Edmonds, back when the ferry dock was where you ended up when you coasted down Main Street right through the center of town. For years, Mother, Carolyn, Ken and I were summer foot passengers on the boat to Kingston, where we played on a beach that was almost deserted even on warm days. A huge picnic basket, which Mother lugged down the steep mud bank to the waterside, provided lunch and sweet snacks. I don't remember Dad joining us there generally, although he must have come along once, and snapped this photo of his wife and children on the boat deck.

Outings at Kingston are some of my earliest memories; I recall being so young that I didn't need a swimsuit, but was allowed to splash in the gentle surf wearing only my red

Mom, Barbie, Carolyn, and Kenneth on Kingston ferry, 1950.

cotton underpants. Many decades later, after Mother died, we three, her children now grown up, took a nostalgic ferry ride and scattered her ashes in the water at Kingston Beach, then celebrated her life by eating chocolate-chip bars baked according to her signature picnic recipe.

When Mom and Dad separated, they sold their north-end property. The buyer followed his plan to live there "as is" with his wife and children for a time, then build a new home. Periodically over the next eight years, I went to visit our former neighbor, Pat Hannah, always glancing up to see our old shoebox house. One day I got out of my car to knock on Pat's door, and my attention was drawn by an unnerving grinding roar from our old yard. There above me, a huge excavator was taking bites out of the house! I couldn't believe my luck to show up at just that moment. Most of the upper floor was already gone. I climbed the hill in time to see the fireplace room ripped open like a ragged dollhouse. Mother's familiar flowered wallpaper was still on the interior wall. I watched for some time, with very mixed feelings. Although I deeply loved the land and will always cherish memories of the activities, the woods, the hillside, and the beach, I had a certain antipathy for this building. It was a Pandora's box, crowded with complex interwoven memories. For the most part I was glad to see it splintered and crushed, opening its space to the sky and releasing all the old tensions, doubts, and anger that had seemed to dwell inside the walls. At the same time, it was a stunning end to the story.

I didn't even realize that as I stood just below the yard, Dad was in the driveway

Demolition viewed from south lawn, just before I arrived.

above, snapping pictures. I never saw his demolition photos until long after he died.

Out of curiosity, I recently drove out to the former site of our home. All the byways are paved. Snake Road has long since been renamed, and the others are numbered as streets and avenues. The warning sign has moved far from the junction, to the driveway entrance, and is worded with a little more gentility, "Road Ends." The current owners have lived in that location over thirty years, about the same timespan as our family. Their elegant house was built in 1991, and today, the entire half-acre is meticulously landscaped with thousands of shrubs artfully planted in manicured beds. Hutt's Park still adjoins the driveway, and even the rough, overgrown paths we followed into the woods are domesticated,

Current house on site, 2016.

their margins decorated with neat, seemingly randomly placed ferns and flowers. The whole property is *Sunset Magazine, House Beautiful, Better Homes and Gardens* in its perfection.

Without asking permission, I stepped to the edge of the slope. Several houses have sprouted in lieu of the orchard, and the massive evergreen trees below, whose growth Dad documented — and complained about — are gone, leaving a vast expansive view of Puget Sound above all the neighbors' rooftops. The whole scene is breathtaking, and for better or worse, bears little resemblance to the untamed environment where we grew up.

Bring in the dog
and put out the cat*

I don't remember Cuddles, but she's in the Christmas card photo from 1947 when I was nearly two. A cute little black and white pooch with a long nose and floppy ears. Cuddles was Carolyn's pet, and my sister was heartbroken when the dog disappeared. They took her away when Carolyn was at school one day, without telling her why. "She's gone to live with a nice family." Years later Mother and Dad joked that Cuddles should have been named Puddles, implying that she couldn't be housebroken. Later they told her the dog had been pregnant. Maybe both stories were true, maybe neither. Today there's research showing that children attach to pets and dolls and stuffed animals as if they were actual people, and the departure of what they recognize as an intimate friend is traumatic. But our parents – and probably most parents of that era – downplayed losses and endings.

Kandy joined us sometime after we returned from Florida. Due to his longevity, he really was a member of the family, although nobody treated a dog in those days the way people do now. He didn't wear a sweater, and we did not take him with us when we went to a friend's house for dinner. Mother named him Kandy because of his short, sleek, caramel-colored fur. He had an intelligent face with cocker-spaniel ears, a portly body and thin legs – we theorized that he was part spaniel and part Irish Setter. We thought he was pretty bright, because not only could he do the normal sitting up and shaking hands, but he would always go to the correct person on command: "Go see Kenneth," "Where's Grandma?"

* Lyric from "Yakety Yak," Jerry Lieber and Mike Stoller, 1958

We never hesitated to let him in and out the back door, although
once in a while Mother, exasperated, would quote, "In again, out
again, back again, Finnegan" (a 1918 saying that calls to my mind
a favorite definition from Ambrose Bierce's *Devil's Dictionary*: "Pet,
noun: An animal on the wrong side of a door"). Anyway, Kandy had
free run of the countryside, roaming the fields and woods. He could
have chased down onto Snake Road, but we must have figured he was
too smart to tangle with speeding cars. As far as I'm aware, we didn't
own a leash, nor did other dog owners we knew.

Another item missing in those days was the pooper-scooper.
Refined as he was, Kandy did not defecate on our property, which
for him included the orchard and our grandparents' house and yards.
If we ever found a dog pile, we knew that some other canine had
invaded. That was rare.

I was about nine or ten when, at Mom's Christmas party, one of
our rather distant neighbors saw Kandy and exclaimed, "Oh! Now I
can see why my neighbor's dog had red puppies!" I spent quite a bit of
energy alone in my room later trying to figure out how our dog could
be relevant to their puppies. This was the kind of question that always
drew oblique, useless answers from Mother, so I didn't ask.

But I did ask about something I saw around the same time. One
day Kandy was under the counter on his rug, as usual, but there was
something pink and shiny poking out of the fur between his legs.
That wasn't there the day before. Was he injured? Sick? I pointed
it out to Mother, thinking she, too, would be alarmed, but she just
looked away and said, "No, he's fine. Nothing's wrong." Another
puzzle to try to work out on my own.

None of our pets were neutered – it wasn't something people did.
When the feral calico showed up in the garage, there was nothing
to do but let her stay and have as many kittens as she would have.
Butterball and Dusty were the first.

Carolyn named Dusty for his lovely short grey fur. In some lights,
it looked as though there were a silver layer beneath, overlaid with a
faint golden veil. And he had personality. All the cats were standoffish

from time to time, but – except for the mother cat, who never entered the house – Dusty was the most aloof. He would curl up on our laps, purr when petted, lounge on our beds, but once past his first year or so, he periodically wouldn't come home. The first time he stayed away overnight, Carolyn and I wrung our hands with anxiety. What could have happened? Next day he came sauntering back. His absences grew longer and longer, until he was missing for two weeks. I was torn between resigning myself to losing him, and hoping that he was just having a vacation.

He came back, hale and hearty. Then one day we were at the curve in the road picking blackberries when a young woman walked toward us. She exclaimed excitedly, "Sammy! Where have you been? I've missed you!" She was talking to Dusty.

"What do you mean, you've missed him?"

"This is my cat! He just wandered off and I've been upset."

"No, this is our cat."

That faithless philanderer had been eating and sleeping with this innocent cat-rustler all the times he'd left us! We explained that he really was *our* pet because he was born in our garage. However, in the long run, we had nothing to say about it. One day Dusty went away and didn't ever come back. He had trained us, little by little, to let go, so let go we did.

Butterball had long golden fur with white markings. In contrast to his brother, he loved hanging around indoors and could often be found sagging into a soft chair or flopped rug-like on the floor under a sunny window. He did have one major adventure. One day he limped home from a field trip dragging one bloody leg behind him. He'd been shot with a BB gun. This was one of the very few veterinary occasions I recall with any of our pets. Mother and Carolyn wrapped him in a towel and drove to the vet, where a major financial decision was made. There was surgery, and Butterball wore a nine-inch splint on his left hind leg for many days, while we kept him indoors and watched him closely. He healed completely, and from then on, Mother wryly referred to him as "our $200 cat."

My parents didn't seem concerned about bringing cats into a house where the dog was king. Kandy was Mother's dog, slavishly devoted to her, and she was affectionate with him. Generally, I think he felt his place was secure. Although Mother didn't consider herself a cat person, eventually she was lured into the wordless comfort of Cat On Lap Syndrome. The only interaction between pet species that I recall occurred whenever Mother was holding a feline. Kandy would generate his most engaging unblinking, brown-eyed upward gaze that conveyed something between a plea and an accusation: "Could you have forgotten? You belong to me!" Her hand would trail down then and scratch his ears.

We didn't give a name to the mother cat. Human companionship didn't suit her – maybe like Huckleberry Finn she was afraid of getting "sivilized." She only sheltered at our place to have her kittens. There were three in the second litter, and Mom decided to assign one to each of the three of us. Carolyn's kitten wasn't strong, and died very soon. This death, like most others we experienced, was unaccompanied by any ceremony. The other two kittens were white – mine, a long-hair we called Snow White and Ken's, a short-hair dubbed Prince Charming. I bonded with Snow White as a sister "smallest girl in the family," until it was discovered that she was a he. The name was summarily changed to Snowball and my enthusiasm waned.

Me with Prince, 1956.

Living so near both woods and roads, the safety of small animals could not be guaranteed. Snowball vanished and the folks said he had probably been hit by a car. Prince, however, stayed with us, and he and Butterball lived long, indolent lives, generously demonstrating the art of deep relaxation.

We did have fleas. Our beds were especially problematic, but the straw carpets upstairs were also potential havens. Carolyn and I were quite miserable with itchy ankles. Flea collars and liquid treatments had not been invented. Pest-control products were limited to "flea bombs" or flea powder. Using the bomb was a big decision, because everyone (dog and cats included) must be kept out of the house for ten or twelve hours to reduce exposure to the poison. The powder, too, must have contained a weaker dilution of pesticide. Applying it to cats was useless, because of course they would lick it off as soon as they could (poisoning themselves in the process). When the infestation was greatest we would lock the cats out, take Kandy somewhere for the day – maybe to Grandma's house – and set off a couple of flea bombs. When we came back, we'd sprinkle flea powder thickly between the sheets at the bottom of the beds. Heaven knows how much toxic material we all took in through these measures. The fleas were generally reduced for a while, if not eliminated.

Butterball, 1963.

To us, Kandy's life was uneventful, but he had one close call. Mom had purchased a set of Compton's Encyclopedia from a door-to-door saleswoman. Every summer the woman (I'll call her Mrs. Carlson) returned to deliver the annual yearbook. In those days, the visit of a salesperson necessitated a coffee break and some socializing, so Mrs. Carlson had come to know a little about us. One day she showed up without an appointment. No one was at home except Kandy, who was on the porch guarding the front door. Suddenly he rushed at her and bit her leg!

Mrs. Carlson was shocked and appalled. When she reached my parents by phone, she threatened to report the incident to the authorities. This, of course, would mean the end of Kandy. Mother was worried. She talked at length, in private, with Dad. Then she gathered all her intellect, logic and debate skills and asked some pointed questions. It turned out that Kandy had started barking when Mrs. Carlson got out of her car. Unconcerned, she strode right up the walkway, greeting the dog by name.

"He should know me by now!"

"From one visit a year, he should know you? *You* should know that when a dog is at his own front door, barking, he is warning you away. You marched right into his territory. It was your mistake." ("Stupidity," not "mistake," was the word Mother used, to us, in describing the situation later.)

Carolyn, me and Kandy, 1952

The best news was that the bite had not broken the skin. The saleswoman's stocking, however, was beyond repair. Some sort of settlement was reached with Mrs. Carlson, probably involving new nylons, and the issue was put to rest, to our enormous relief.

Good old Kandy. I don't know whether he ever got a final diagnosis. With age, he grew more rotund, and we'd periodically hear him whine in his sleep. We started to worry that he was in pain. After a while he was eating less, and then began to have problems with incontinence. This went on for several weeks before Mother threw in the towel. She was more attached to him than I had realized, and clearly didn't want to see him go. But as with other deaths, this one was accomplished with no outward fuss. She took Kandy to the vet and didn't bring him back, and characteristically, Mom soldiered on.

He's gone away, for to stay*

I was five and Dad was 38 when he went away. I didn't know what the Army Reserves were, or, for that matter, anything about war (or "police action," the official designation of the Korean conflict). I don't recall anyone preparing us for Daddy's departure. Maybe that was the parental philosophy of the time, in the same way that they had avoided explaining to my sister why her dog had vanished.

Up until then, stability had been the theme of my life. Mother was a stay-at-home mom, if you didn't count organizing a cooperative preschool, being active in the PTA and community center, and serving as room mother for Carolyn, who had already completed fourth grade. Mother's parents lived steps from our door and I loved spending time with Grandma nearly every day. Dad went to work and came home, sometimes bringing friends to dinner, where we all talked and laughed together.

My parents doted on me from the start. I suspect they knew I was to be their last child, so they treated me like a cherished toy. This caused stresses among the siblings, but I was oblivious to that in my early years. When I was little, Daddy held me on his lap while he read the funny papers aloud. His favorite comic strips, "The Katzenjammer Kids" and "Li'l Abner," were written in dialects I couldn't comprehend. Laughing uproariously, Dad tried to explain the humor, which completely escaped me. What really mattered was being the special person who spent these moments so close to him.

All at once Dad was gone.

Some months after he left, Mother packed up the three kids for a

* Lyric from "He's Gone Away", traditional American folk song

train ride. A year-long journey began, transforming the predictability of our lives. We traveled from Edmonds to Fort Leonard Wood in Missouri, where Dad was stationed. After a long trip, eating cold food Mother had brought along and sitting for hours and hours in our train seats, we reached our destination and moved into a rental house.

Missouri was different than anything I'd seen before. The winter came early and suddenly. I was too young to start school there, but one day in his first few weeks of second grade, my brother wore a brand new pair of jeans to school. At the time, pre-washed clothing was not even imagined, and new jeans (or dungarees, as we sometimes called them) were dyed a very deep blue. A blizzard took the area by surprise, the school buses were cancelled, and Kenneth had to walk all the way home in knee-deep snow. He was chilled through, causing Mother some concern, but I laughed, because for several days, his legs looked like he had a rare, hilarious indigo skin condition.

Heavy snowfall continued. There was a lean-to shed at one side of the house, and my sister and brother took turns sliding off the shed roof to land in the snowbank below — until Mother discovered what they were doing. That was the end of that. On the other hand, nearby, through the woods, was a wonderful frozen pond where we and the neighbors went to skate or just slide on our smooth-soled shoes. Having lived only in the Seattle area up until then, I was amazed by this strange landscape of thick ice and deep snow.

I don't recall ever seeing Dad in Missouri. He later told us that he had been confined in an extremely rigorous military training program at the army base. At the time I knew only that he wasn't there.

In November, two months after our arrival, we were uprooted again. Not just a move, but to the climate antithesis of Missouri. Our father had completed both his boot camp and the training he was providing to his engineering brigade, and was assigned to an Air Force base in Orlando, Florida. Suddenly we were moving into the suburb of Winter Park, to live in a duplex, a new experience for all of us. We three children didn't enjoy the boy and girl on the other side of the common wall, although they were about the same ages as Kenneth and I. They were very different from us, and didn't seem to understand our sort of fun. From their Dutch heritage they had been christened Pieter and Mineer, names that made them perpetual targets of the bathroom humor of local children. Proximity required that we all get along, but for the most part, I steered clear of them, and Mother found little in common with their parents.

Mother was miserable in Florida. She hated the heat and she missed her parents and siblings who were back in the Northwest. Making new friends was hard for her. Dad was absent, for the Army sent him to Newfoundland and Greenland – yes, based in Florida to work in the Arctic – to survey and design airfields in support of the Korean War.

Florida law allowed five-year-olds to start first grade. Mother delivered me to a classroom where I couldn't decipher the deep Southern drawls of the teacher or students. Because of our time in Missouri, I started the school year late, and in addition, the students laughed at my northern accent. Back in Edmonds, I had attended only two weeks of kindergarten, which consisted of playing with blocks and doll houses, sitting in a circle on the rug, and taking naps. I was totally unprepared for the classroom with rows of desks and the requirements to study a chalkboard, write and read. For the first week or two, every time Mother left me at the school room door, I cried hopelessly.

The teacher was unlike anyone I had ever met. With her Southern accent, it was as if I'd stepped into "Li'l Abner," with no one to translate. Besides, she spoke so frankly! One day while my fellow students were working quietly, I went to the front of the room, hoping, no doubt, to be sent home.

"My stomach hurts."

"Whaya does it hurt?"

"What?"

"Whaya does it hurt? Show me." I put my hand just below my navel.

"Did you move your bayals this mahning?"

"Wha-a-t?"

"Did you have a bayal movement?"

Suspicious but unsure, I repeated, "What?"

"BM! Did you have a BM today?" Very matter-of-factly.

"No," in my softest voice. Right here in front of the whole class, she was asking me about my bathroom habits?! I'd never heard of anything like it! I was ready to be embarrassed, but the children didn't make fun of me. They seemed accepting of this kind of talk. Maybe she wasn't trying to humiliate me after all.

She closed the subject with characteristic straightforwardness. "Wayal, I think you'll be aw right. Go sit dahn in your chayah. I'll talk with your mothah laytah."

Something about this direct exchange settled my fears. After that, I began to trust Miss Campbell in a new way. Over time, she helped me very gently through the terrors of that first year of school, and I learned I could rely on her.

By contrast, the lunchroom was a nightmare, with crowds of noisy children of all ages and the sickeningly oppressive smells of the cafeteria food. In my entire life since then, I've never smelled a cafeteria like that one. When I complained about the terrible lunches served there, Mother pooh-poohed my whining, until one day she came to pick me up at school during the lunch hour and was immersed in the odors herself. Without comment, from then on, she made a peanut butter sandwich every day for my lunch. To this day peanut butter is my favorite comfort food – I felt it saved my life!

During recess I stood alone, as close to the wall of the building as I could, trying not to attract attention. In Edmonds, my only playmates had been children I'd known since birth, and I was an outsider here.

My outsider status was crystallized within a week of arrival when I was playing with my doll in the vacant lot by our house, and a friendly girl passing by said, "Hi, whatch'all doin'?"

After taking a moment to figure out her words, I said, "Who-all? It's just me." Recommended strategy for making a friend – criticize her way of talking! She just walked quietly away. My heart sank, seeing that I'd done something wrong, and at a loss as to how to undo it.

We went to the lake nearly every afternoon, and took swim lessons from a well-known instructor named Fleet Peeples. Mother admired this kindly, skilled teacher, and he was instrumental in getting Carolyn started on her path to being a champion swimmer throughout her early years. Ken not only learned to swim, but went on one of Fleet's regular camping trips with a group of other children. Peeples was so popular that later, in the 1980s, the city of Winter Park named both their high school pool and a city park after him.

I had a different opinion of this

Fleet Peeples with Kenneth, Barbie and Carolyn, 1952.

teacher. One of Fleet's talents was to walk into the water with a child on his shoulders until the water was well over his own head and up to the child's chin. I wasn't aware of this legend until he did it with me. As the water rose above my chest, I started screaming bloody murder. He couldn't hear me. I couldn't escape because he was holding my legs. I was terrified he would not stop before I went completely under. He continued up to my chin, then turned around and walked back to shallow water, as he did with all the children. He smiled. But the memory of impotent panic stuck with me.

He – or Mother – must have calmed me down, because after that, I recall a lesson when he tried to coax me to swim into deep water. When I said I was scared, he scoffed and said he had taught a two-year-old to swim all the way across the lake, and there was no reason I, at five, couldn't do the same. This tactic, rather than making me want to compete, increased my resistance. I never did quite trust Fleet.

Six decades later, my siblings and I were shocked to see an article in the Orlando newspaper reporting that Fleet Peeples' name was being removed from the Winter Park venues. His adult son had been arrested for pedophilia, and the deceased father – our teacher – was also revealed as a pedophile. Several women and a couple of men came forward describing their childhood molestation at his hands on the group camping trips, beginning in the early 1950s, exactly the time we were with him. We were lucky.

Dad came from the icy north down to Florida at least once for an R&R break. He was intent on having a good time in the sun, showing off what good shape he was in, swimming with us, telling jokes. He wasn't part of our daily drudgery and vexations, so his momentary presence seemed unreal. And then he was gone again. I think it was after this brief visit that I concluded he had personally abandoned me.

I recall this whole period as the first iteration of a recurring lifelong pattern – feeling utterly alone and unequipped in a new and mystifying situation. My aloneness was brought to a point by Dad's absence. I had always been with my parents or my beloved grandmother, and meeting their expectations had been simple, if somewhat stultifying: Be quiet, obedient and willing. I had never been asked, or taught, to meet challenges. Here, I was literally in a different world, separated from my loved ones daily for school and swim lessons, living in the confusing surroundings of the South without my indulgent daddy. Instead of summoning inner strength to turn challenges into opportunities, I believed I was powerless, and sought escape. Even while appreciating the novelty of picking oranges from trees in the back yard, or summer weather on Christmas, I always felt like I was somehow observing these experiences from outside myself, and playing the role of a happy child for Mother's sake.

At the end of the 1951-52 school year we returned to Edmonds while Dad wrapped up his Army assignment. No doubt Mother was overjoyed to be reunited with her parents, and when we first came back, we stayed with them – partly to allow time for cleanup of our own place. Through Granddad's contacts at the University of Washington, before we left, Mother had rented our house to the renowned poet Theodore Roethke, who was poet-in-residence at the University that year. (I like to think the house on the hillside contributed to his winning the Pulitzer Prize for Poetry only a couple of years later, in 1954.) It's now public knowledge that Roethke not only had a bipolar personality disorder, but was inclined to alcoholic binges. All I recall Mom saying, years later, with disgust verging on horror, was that she found the house in a filthy mess and littered with empty bottles. She was no appreciator of an artist's lifestyle!

When Dad returned home, he almost immediately started his own business. As a determined entrepreneur with a family to support, he no longer had time to read cartoons with his daughter. He worked days, evenings and weekends. For me, his absence from home was the capstone on his earlier abandonment. I felt that I was no longer interesting to him, and I believed that his desertion was permanent. In a way it was.

Throughout the remainder of his life, on the brief occasions when Dad was around home, he made an effort to lavish attention on me as he had when I was five. From my perspective, this erratic adoration seemed artificial. He didn't know who I was any more, and I didn't feel I could count on him to stick around and find out. To his credit, he was always a good provider – a central part of the husband and father role, at least in those days – but emotionally and physically he was missing in action. No more of his friends coming home for dinner, no more lighthearted laughter with him.

Now, more than sixty years later, I'm embarrassed to be dwelling on the perceived difficulties of my childhood. After all, my nuclear family was intact. Nobody hit me. Nobody died young. Dad's absence from me wasn't intentional and it wasn't personal. In reality, he didn't have the tools to invent a different way of being a dad. He did the best he could – given the era and his background – to demonstrate love to his family. I'm grateful for his persistent efforts to show his children more affection than his father showed him – which he did – even though those efforts often missed the target and went unrewarded.

Mama said*

I don't think of Mom as one of those people who was always spouting clichés. On the contrary, she was a real original. Yet when I reminisce with my siblings, one or another of us will often note, "Remember how Mother used to say..." Well, I've collected a few of the things "Mother used to say" that periodically replay in my head.

"Ye gods and little fishes"

"Ye gods and little fishes! How did the garbage get tipped over on the kitchen floor?" Because it referred to "gods" and not to "God," this was not considered cursing. I've discovered that it was already a commonplace expression in 1902, when my grandparents were little children. Although my friends chuckle every time I use it, I love the notion of carrying forward a saying that's probably crossed two centuries. If I had to characterize it, I'd say this was a much more entertaining version of the currently popular "OMG."

"Turnabout's fair play"

In early childhood my brother and I, being close in age and living far from other children, were each other's last-resort playmates. Our gender roles and game preferences presented challenges. Mom suggested that each of us play the other one's game for an hour, taking turns. For a certain period of our childhood, we accepted this compromise, and I learned to plow miniature roads in the dirt and move a toy car along until it crashed again and again, which apparently was entertaining for a boy child. But sometimes, when my turn came, "Mo-o-ther! He won't play dolls and he promised!" With

* Lyric from "Mama said," Luther Dixon and Willie Denson, 1961

a firm, penetrating look and the reminder, "Turnabout's fair play," Mother righted the balance – at least temporarily.

"Home, James, and don't spare the horses!"

This line dates from the 1880's, and formed the title of a popular song of 1934, when Mom was a college student. Our outings by car generally consisted of one holiday or another at Mother's brother's house in Bellevue or her sister's house in Seattle. After the festivities, we would take our assigned spots in the car. Dad always drove and one of the "tall kids" (after a certain age, both Carolyn and Ken were over six feet) sat in the front. Since the bench seat was adjusted for Dad's long legs, the front passenger was the only one who got real leg room. Mother and I, along with the other sibling, sat behind. Maybe Mom's position in the back seat inspired her to pretend she was being chauffeured. Since Dad's name was Jim, once we were all settled she would heartily call out, "Home, James, and don't spare the horses!" Looking back, this has a taste of irony, as nobody remembers Dad ever sparing the horsepower when he drove!

"Dog in the manger"

If I took one of my brother's toy cars just to keep it away from him, Mother's sermon was brief: "Don't be a dog in the manger. Give it back." Being compared to a dog made me cringe, as well as obey. I always thought it was some sort of reference to Baby Jesus, but that was a different manger. Apparently it springs from a second-century Greek fable: "There was a dog lying in a manger who did not eat the grain but who nevertheless prevented the horse from being able to eat anything either."

"Method to my madness"

Mother thrived on explaining things. When we were small, she taught us to make cookies. On the rolled-out dough, she carefully lined up the cookie cutter adjacent to the previous cutout. She would always both show and tell: "There's a method to my madness. We don't want to waste any dough, so we don't leave any space between." As the years went by, I was awed and intimidated by her unerring ability to outline her reasoning; it seemed she had already thought through every single thing she did. It's a skill I didn't inherit; to this day I often have the feeling there's no method to my own madness.

"A Boy in Bavaria"

Mother always seemed to know everything. I rarely ever had to search the encyclopedia for school assignments, because Mom would give me the answer. Once in a while, I – or one of her pupils at school – would ask, "How on earth do you know *that*?"

"Well, when I was a boy in Bavaria, I had to learn all about such things." People would, of course, do a double-take, since gender transition was unimaginable in those days, and it was apparent she had never been a boy. But this reply amused everyone and eliminated any need to really answer the question.

"A star in your crown"

Did Mother believe in an afterlife? I don't know. But when I told her I had helped a neighbor child find her way home, or worked with Grandma folding the laundry, she assured me that was another star in my crown (with the implication of a later reward in heaven). Because of the way this was expressed, I inferred that there was something improper about seeking accolades – you might be earning stars, but they were invisible and should remain so.

"Hide nor hair"

In my youth, by far the greatest proportion of extended-family meals were at Grandma and Granddad's house. Mother and we three kids would walk down the path from home, carrying Mom's potluck contributions. Dad was frequently late arriving, and someone was likely to ask Mother where he was. Setting down a bowl of Jell-O, she might shrug and reply, "Haven't seen hide nor hair of him!" After waiting some undefined amount of time, Grandma would say, "Well, if we sit down at the table, he's sure to show up." It rarely failed: Dad would breeze in, having driven straight from work, just in time to help himself to chicken and fresh applesauce – always with a polite apology to the hostess.

"Port and starboard"

In Mom's youth, her dad had a pleasure cruiser – the Ernum. Of course the professor used their family outings as educational, as well as fun, occasions. Mother once told me that she always remembered which seagoing terms corresponded to "right" and "left" by this sentence: "Port is wine, and wine is not right." Mother was, in fact, a teetotaler, but this was definitely a joke in her eyes.

"O ye of little faith"

"I don't see how you can get home from work and deliver me and the cookies to the Scout meeting on time!"

Mom's rejoinder: "O ye of little faith!" How could we doubt her omnipotence? This saying springs, of course, from the passage in the Bible where Jesus chides the fishermen and calms the storm. Like Jesus, Mother knew her own powers. And she generally had a calming effect on emotional storms, although I never saw her make an actual gale stop blowing.

"Wreck of the Hesperus"

On a Saturday morning, Mom might tell me, in terms I couldn't refuse, to clean up my room. "You have an hour." I had a knack for amplifying the disorder in my misguided attempts to make it neater. Mother would return to my threshold and in affectionate frustration exclaim, "This room looks like the wreck of the Hesperus!" I wasn't familiar with the reference until decades later, when I stumbled across *The Children's Own Longfellow*, published in 1908. In this little volume of pieces *selected for children*, the very first poem is "The Wreck of the Hesperus." I pity any unfortunate child who ever came unaware upon this horrifying tale about an ill-fated ship! In truth, with no broken spars or icy shrouds, and no innocent child's dead body lashed to a mast, my room looked nothing like the wreck of the Hesperus. But as we all know, disaster is in the eye of the beholder.

"Lazy man's load"

Our bedrooms were downstairs and the shared living spaces were above, on the main floor. In her youth, my sister did not like climbing the stairs over and over, so you might see her going up or down with books or laundry stacked up to her eyebrows. Like many long-legged young people, she also had a habit of taking two or three stairs in a single pace. Once she distinguished herself by being the only person we knew to emerge black and blue from falling *up* the stairs. At a time like that, she could count on two things from Mother: an expression of concern, quickly followed by the lesson, "You were carrying a lazy man's load!"

"It's all in how you hold your mouth"

Mom was the natural heir to this saying, as I also heard her parents tease each other with it. When I tried to translate black dots from the page to the piano keys, my front teeth gripped my lower lip in a certain way. Mother – or anyone watching – would seize the opportunity to say with a smile, "Reading music – it's all in how you hold your mouth."

"Come into my parlor, said the spider to the fly"

Based on the first line of the 1829 poem, "The Spider and the Fly," by Mary Howitt. There were many times when I had to be measured for a garment. Especially tiresome was standing on a chair for the pinning of the hem. When Mom invited me to her sewing room for a session, she often used these words to lighten the moment. I then entered with a smile in spite of myself.

"Who in this house"

When blame could not be fixed on any particular family member, we heard the free-floating accusation: "I don't know *who in this house* can't put a new roll of toilet paper on the holder!" Of course, we'd all avoid eye contact and scurry out of range. Even if I hadn't been the responsible party, this comment inspired in me a renewed vow to pay attention to details.

"Where is that dress *going* with that woman?"

After college, Mother nurtured a continuing fascination with clothing. She was familiar with costumes of every historic period, and with every current fashion. Her preferred styles were on the understated side, modestly complimenting the body's shape, rarely with frilly trimmings. When television first entered our lives, she found it possible to criticize performers with an unprecedented level of impunity – they couldn't hear her. Cinematography was in its infancy, and I remember once watching a singer step out on a vast, empty stage. I was open-mouthed at the courage of the woman to perform there, all alone without scenery or props, viewed for the first time by thousands via this new visual medium. She had a wonderful voice. But she wore a dress with puffy "leg o'mutton" sleeves and a wide ruffled skirt buoyed by crinolines, and Mother cut through my wonderment with the derisive question, "Where is that dress *going* with that woman?" It was one of the first times I realized how easy it is to forget compassion.

"Banty rooster"

Although Granddad had left his family's farm early for academia, once he was semi-retired, he and Grandma raised chickens and rabbits. Bantam chickens (informally called "Banties") are some of the smallest poultry animals, and the little roosters have an incomparably proud way of strutting around the farmyard, as if to compensate for their diminutive stature. At dinner one night, Mom described a new administrator at the school where she worked. He had recently been promoted from an ordinary teacher (my eighth-grade math teacher, in fact) to the elevated position of middle-school vice principal. He wasn't a tall man, but he walked erect with firm strides, chest puffed out, and defended himself vigorously when challenged, despite a limited mental arsenal. Throughout the day, he kept himself busy moving rapidly around the building. Mother theorized that he wore hard-soled shoes to make sure he was heard clickety-clacking up and down the halls, giving the impression that he actually accomplished something during the school day. "A real Banty rooster."

"Lo, these many years", and "Since Heck was a pup"

Naturally, as a parent, the daughter of a professor, and finally an educator herself, Mother firmly believed that quality public education should be available to everyone. But she was not naive as to the "quality" part of the concept, and often mentioned the failings of the school system. This was the arena where I heard two phrases that seemed to reach back into pre-history, as in this sardonic statement: "Sixth grade has been taught the same way for lo, these many years. Heaven forbid they should change anything now." Consistent leadership was one thing, but stale old policies were another: "Ring Goldspar has been Edmonds School Superintendent since Heck was a pup." The reference here is to Hector, the mythical Trojan War hero of the 13th Century B.C.E., and it had been even longer than "Lo, these many years" since Hector was a pup.

"Discretion is the better part of valor"

A variation on a line from Shakespeare. In vain Mother applied this phrase, and several other tactics, to dissuade me from arguing with Mr. Lyons, my eighth-grade history teacher. At the time, anyone teaching history was required to teach English as well. My knowledge of grammar exceeded the teacher's – I was the princess of gerunds, intransitives and prepositional phrases. Whenever Mr. Lyons countered my arguments by checking the teacher's manual for an answer, I was rewarded with the exhilarating experience of being proven right, something that rarely or never happened at home. My righteousness was insufferable. Needless to say, my fellow students did not admire me as a result. The great irony is that Mr. Lyons was a compendium of dates, battles, empires and presidents. His passion for, and knowledge of, history were miles beyond my capacity. I met my comeuppance. In balance to the "A" in English that couldn't be denied, I received very poor grades in history that year. Discretion would have been the better part of valor, and turnabout was fair play.

"They'll never see it from the balcony"

This maxim derived from Mother's intensive work in college theatre. While earning her Fine Arts master's degree, Mom had been the Wardrobe Mistress of the University of Washington Drama Department. Costumes needed to be produced quickly, and provide a convincing illusion of period authenticity, poverty or wealth, shine or raggedness. They got hard use, but they only needed to last for the length of the show. If a seam in a full skirt was not perfectly straight, or the inside of a jacket had dangling threads, it made no difference. During my semesters of sewing in school Home Economics classes, Mom was amused by all the rules I was taught. She scoffed at the standard 5/8-inch seam allowance and the many ways to finish the fabric edges along the seams – a waste of cloth, thread and time. "They'll never see it from the balcony" came to be applied to other unnecessary details, like dusting the books on the shelf. On the one hand, Mother wanted the important things done well; on the other, she retained the authority to define what was important and what wasn't.

"The back o' me hand to yeh!"

She was a hugger, and her hugs made me feel as if I were embraced by Mother Earth herself. Mom seemed solid and permanently planted in the earth. At five feet four inches, she was soon the shortest person in our nuclear family. One time, when Kenneth grew tall and strong enough, he shocked Mother in mid-hug by lifting her off the ground. Her squeak when her feet left the floor was uncharacteristic to say the least. But in a way she was, as she would say, tickled to death by this gesture. No sooner was she returned to terra firma than she laughingly pretended to slap him, and imitated an Irish accent to threaten this towering teenager. We all knew the back of her hand would never touch any of us. She wouldn't dream of it.

"One boy's as good as a boy, two boys are as good as half a boy, and three boys are as good as no boy at all."

Like many pre-teens and teenagers, my brother was just as helpful around the house as he was required to be. He sometimes brought a friend or two home in the afternoon and Mother would ask them to do a job around the place – stacking firewood, mowing and raking the yard, or sweeping the garage. I believe she offered to pay them some pittance. But being boys, while glancing around the garage for brooms, they might find a deflated football and go back for a pass.

Before you knew it, the job was forgotten in the jostling joy of contact sport. As far as my research has shown, Mother alone discovered the mathematical ratios outlined in this motto.

It's time we hung some tinsel
on that evergreen bough*

The tree was both broad and tall – the exact height that would cause the ornament on top to barely touch the ceiling. It was situated either in the windowed southwest corner, or just inside the front door, at the point where the dining room and living room joined. Setting it up was a big undertaking, with us children called upon as verticality inspectors.

"Is it straight?"

"No, it leans toward the wall."

"Tilt it toward the window."

"Pull it closer to you." The spicy scent of the freshly cut evergreen filled the rooms.

It was the day following Thanksgiving. Christmas had started, and Mom was in charge. Right after breakfast, she bought the tree and brought it home. Way back in history, I think Dad was involved in the preparations, but of course as time progressed he found himself unavailable. Mom's idea of Dad's natural role was to haul in the tree and wrap the lights around it. After all, he was a man (and thus suited to all matters muscular and electrical) and he was also tall (to reach the highest points with ease). But whereas we youngsters knew that, in holiday decorating as in life, our orders came from Mother, Dad couldn't get used to being directed in the minute procedures of arranging each bulb and wire. In my recollection he participated only a few times. Most of my life he was at the office.

*Lyric from "We Need a Little Christmas," Jerry Herman, 1966

But it was the holidays, and we adeptly turned away from the disappointment of a parent gone missing. Dad or no Dad, on tree-decorating days we had a party. Up and down the stepladder, circling the tree, Mom organized the lights. We lugged assorted dusty boxes upstairs from the furnace room, opening them like treasure chests to reveal glistening colors and mysterious packets wrapped in yellowing tissue paper. As we uncovered sequined hearts and feathered birds, each slip of tissue was saved for later re-packing. We linked a little black wire hook to each ornament, then we kids set to our task: making sure every single embellishment was attached to the tree. Mom was in a merry mood, trying to insist that we could leave off half the decorations this year. There were too many. But that concept didn't fly with us – in every aspect of life at Christmas time, our aim was super-saturation.

Woe betide the fool who chose a large glass ball for an upper branch – high branches were reserved for small objects. There were firm guidelines, and Mother had no problem correcting such major aesthetic faux pas. Elbowing or shouldering one another – but gently – we joked, reminisced and laughed as we decorated, and we bonded in a way that was challenging on other, more ordinary days.

Bing Crosby, the Ray Conniff Singers, Mitch Miller and the Gang caroled from the record player. The first record player was a component of a sturdy, waist-high radio console in the corner of the living room, and it played only 78 RPM discs. The second generation, with speed adjustments for 78, 45 and 33 RPMs, rested on a beautiful old cedar chest in the dining room. The third, and the one I recall best, was a wide black box perched on wobbly telescoping chrome legs, and boasted twin speakers. We had to be careful. On its spindly supports, if you bumped into the stereo while it was playing one of the LPs, the stylus would bounce, infecting Fred Waring and all his Pennsylvanians with hiccups, and possibly giving Frosty an extra "Thumpety-thump-thump" into eternity.

A relative had given an exquisite miniature blown-glass teapot to each of us, my brother, sister and me, when we were small. We always had a friendly dispute: "The blue one is mine!"

"No, yours is yellow, don't you remember?" (I didn't remember.)

After a couple of hours, bedecked like a dowager wearing all her collected jewels, the spangled tree shimmered and glowed. Brilliantly colored glass Santas, stars and bells reflected multi-hued lights. The radiance illumined our spirits, and the holiday feeling had been ignited.

The final special activity of the day was popcorn. Mother got out the popper, a blackened metal pan with a long extension made of heavy wire, finished off with a wooden handle. The pan had a hinged lid that could be opened with a lever on the handle. Once logs were crackling in the fireplace, Mom poured oil and corn kernels into the pan. We took turns shaking the popper over the flames, and as the corn exploded into fragrant white puffs, the lid gently opened. Usually a few kernels were sacrificed to the fire before we jerked the pan out of the heat and dumped the contents into a bowl. Mom judiciously added salt.

"You burned it!"

"Not all of it, eat this part."

"It smells burnt."

"Fine, then you try!"

Mom put a stop to our minor complaints and we devoted ourselves to enjoying the treat. It took more than one round of popping to make enough for four or five people, so we shared the first batch while agitating the second over the fire. There might be rich hot chocolate or warm, clove-scented cider to go with the crunchy snack.

The very next day the first packages appeared on the circular cloth "skirt" under the tree. Mother had already begun sewing our gifts, and now her stitching became almost constant. For us, the hum of the sewing machine was as central a sound of the season as holiday carols. Day by day she completed and wrapped more projects, placing them beneath the branches.

Mother loved to give presents. I sometimes suspected the point of selecting trees with wide-spreading limbs was to create a cavernous space below. One year, when my brother's daughters were small, there was such a crowd of presents that they spilled out in a wide circle beyond the branches, causing quite a navigational challenge when moving from one room to another. Of course, some of the gifts were from members of the family to one another, but Mom outdid us all in sheer quantity.

Reid kids with Christmas tree in southwest corner of living room, 1950.

Although Mother generally didn't use commercial sewing patterns, one Christmas she did buy a single pattern. She used it for two consecutive years to make plaid wool shirts in many sizes for eight or more of us, from Dad, a "big and tall" customer at 6'4", to me at 5'8".

Amazingly, every shirt fit the recipient. I loved both of my shirts and wore them for years until the elbows frayed.

My three nieces still chuckle as they remember the annual Christmas morning drive over to Grandma's house. "I wonder what kind of matching nightgowns she'll make for us this year!" One time the nightgown design was wide, roomy enough for a little girl to pull up her knees and stay warm on the couch. But that first night, as my brother's daughters turned and rolled in their sleep, the ample fabric twisted more and more tightly around their legs. In the morning, momentarily wrapped and trapped, they called to their mom, "Help, we're mummified!"

As she aged, Mother's playful nature came out mostly during the Christmas season. Maybe during the year she was so absorbed in her job roles (school counselor, teachers' union leader, professional woman) that a winter vacation was needed to let some of the rigidity drop away. In any case, one year she bought a brilliantly colored, silky, floor-length caftan in which she greeted holiday visitors, poking fun at herself in this bold and queenly garment. Another Christmastime, she acquired a knit pantsuit in solid scarlet. It became her informal holiday uniform for the next few years. We called her "Mrs. Santa" or "Christmas Elf," which always made her smile. Perhaps I should clarify that Mother was 5'4", allowing us to picture her as an elf compared to us. She was much shorter than any of her children; in fact when I finally topped her in height, I joined my siblings in occasionally slinging an affectionate arm around her shoulders and purring, "Poor little Mother!" Holidays or not, this always brought a laugh.

By the time Mother moved out of the four-bedroom house into her condo, most of her grandchildren were teenagers, and between limited floor space and arthritis, sewing became more challenging for her. Although she couldn't keep from buying and giving presents, her days as the excessively bountiful Mrs. Santa were largely past. But she gave me one final precious holiday gift.

It was early January 1986, the week of my 40th birthday. I had planned a low-key celebration for myself a few days later. Mom called and asked if I could come over that Saturday and help her take down her Christmas tree. As we lifted the ornaments off the tree, I recognized many of them as those I'd been hanging up all my life. And, as always, we wrapped them up in the antique scraps of tissue paper. It was a sweet and nostalgic afternoon. I felt close to her and thankful to have this time together. Afterward she asked me to drive her to my place, which was unusual, but I quickly agreed. "Sure, come to dinner, and we'll give you a ride home later."

As we pulled up in front of my house, I spotted my 4-year-old nephew in the open front door. "What's Reid doing here?" She answered innocently, "Hmm, maybe they came for a visit." No sooner did we step on the front porch than we heard, "Surprise!"

Now, I'm not a fan of surprise parties. But I absolutely love recalling Mother's impish grin throughout that evening, her glow of pride that she had successfully distracted me and carried off her role

*My fortieth birthday surprise party, 1986. Entering my own
front door, Mother following, nephew in foreground.*

in the secret plan. This memory is all the more precious because, sadly, within three weeks she unexpectedly died.

Thanks for all the Christmases, Mrs. Santa!

Don't you ever ask them why*

When I was seven, my friend Laurie and I visited each other now and then. We each had a life-sized baby doll. My Susie had short, dark hair painted on her rubber head. Laurie's Bobbie had no hair. We loved playing together with the dolls, dressing them, tucking them into cardboard-box beds, helping them have imaginary conversations.

That December, a couple of days after a visit from my friend, I was walking through Mom's sewing room on my way outdoors. What I saw of Mother, as usual during the holidays, was the back of her head and shoulders as she made her sewing machine rumble with new creations. Passing by, I glanced up at the shelves of folded fabrics, and noticed, perched on the very top, a life-sized, bald baby doll. It wasn't new – its face was smudged with dirt. It wasn't wearing any clothes. I said, "Oh! Did Laurie leave Bobbie here?"

Mom, still focused on her Singer, said, "What, dear?"

In those three seconds, I recognized that that wasn't Bobbie on the shelf. "Whose doll is that up there? I thought maybe it was Laurie's."

Mother swiveled to face me and said sharply, "Don't be looking around and asking questions. Don't you know Christmas is coming?"

Such a simple response, yet I was utterly floored. I had already learned to be careful what questions I asked in the family, lest my dad react by detonating angry words like a firecrackers, or my mom abruptly change the subject with a disapproving tone. I knew that my assigned role was to be quiet and compliant. But this was a new level

* Lyric from "Teach Your Children," Graham Nash, 1969

of constraint. Suddenly only absolute silence was safe. Where the doll was concerned, I was left to draw my own conclusions. Where Mother was concerned, I had to become more skilled at guessing what she wanted from me, without requesting first-hand data.

It may seem odd that I would take a single incident, a single comment, so seriously. But I was a literal child. For me, Mother's proclamations generally had the weight of universal law. People who are respectful, I heard her saying, do not notice what's going on in their surroundings. People who are acceptable to others do not ask questions. To be a good person, I needed to stop being curious.

Obviously this doll was to be a gift for me. I was further baffled. What did I need with another doll? One was plenty. What did Susie need with a sister, when she already had her friend Bobbie? Carolyn was thirteen, and I didn't find that having a sister was any great blessing at the time. I stewed on this long enough that, when I opened the package on Christmas, I was thoroughly unmoved. The doll had been nicely cleaned up and dressed in new clothes Mother made, but I didn't want her. Of course I knew enough not to show my true reaction. I smiled and said Thank you, as I'd been taught. I don't remember playing with that doll, or even giving her a name.

You can imagine the fallout over the years from my earnest adoption of the policy of not looking and not asking. I believe part of the reason I have trouble remembering people's names and faces – a personality flaw for which I was criticized from the age of 9 – is because at a deep level, I still feel I'm not supposed to look, observe, notice. As a school teacher, as a spouse, I ignored important aspects of my environment at great cost to everyone involved.

As we age and hopefully mature, we are able to change early beliefs that don't serve us. But we need to become *aware* of the dysfunctional beliefs before we can transform them. And this particular dictum, "Don't look, don't ask," created a self-fulfilling cycle that made it difficult for the belief itself to be discovered.

A tremendous gift was given to me decades later. A close friend and I were chatting about our daily lives. I had never told her about the doll debacle of my childhood. She related this story of an interaction she had just had with her young daughter. Martha had bought a doll as a Christmas gift for the little girl. She set the doll on a shelf in the back of a closet, thinking it was hidden, and the child found it. "Mama, what's this doll for?"

Martha's response came from a completely different place than my mother's. She said, "Oh! She's for you, honey. I meant to keep her as a surprise for Christmas. Guess I didn't hide her too well, did I? But now that you've seen her, would you like to help me pick out the fabric for the dress I'm going to make for her?"

They selected the material, and Martha made the doll dress for Christmas. She still created an unexpected treat — a matching dress for her daughter. Meantime, the girl started playing with the doll before the holiday, and using cloth scraps, expressed her own creativity by making simple skirts and capes for the doll.

My friend showed me a whole new approach to parent-child interactions, based on attentiveness and flexibility. Today, I probably resemble my mom more than Martha — I have trouble adjusting to the unexpected — but my long-term aim is to be *present* in meeting new developments. It's more rewarding for everybody.

Troll the ancient
yuletide carol*

It's still my favorite time of the year.

Mom noted all our appointments on the "Memo Calendars" that were sold as a fund-raiser for Children's Orthopedic Hospital (now Seattle Children's). We recently unearthed a few of these wonderful documents. They indicate that the first carol-singing party was on December 19, 1953. There has been a carol sing in our family every Christmas since then. In fact, starting by 1957 there were two per season – one for relatives and the other for Dad's employees and colleagues and their families. Once her own career was established, she often held *three* singing parties each December! This was one holiday celebration that Dad participated in, usually in a jovial mood.

Mother hosted the festivities for thirty-plus years. She hand-wrote the invitations inside the Christmas cards she mailed out, making sure to specify the hours, 7:00-8:30 p.m. She reasoned that since families were welcome, it was her job to assure parents that their children could be in bed at a decent hour.

The event involved a lot of upfront work. She liked being a hostess, but planning and control were key to her sense of success. So she returned to the same routines every year. She would decorate the living and dining rooms thoroughly, sometimes even wrapping the cupboard doors in Christmas paper and ribbon. The tree was decked in its finest, and holiday displays brightened shelves and piano. She made a profusion of cookies: at least ten kinds, many baked ahead

* Lyric from "Deck the Halls," Welsh melody, lyrics by Thomas Oliphant, 1862

and frozen. When we were teens, my best friend always came, and between ourselves, she and I referred to the party as "Cookie Day." Mother contracted with a musician acquaintance to accompany us at the keyboard. She never panicked – visibly – but she was busy and a little tense for some days beforehand.

Thirty to fifty people would fill the house. We sang traditional Christmas songs from a little blue book which, incomprehensibly, had been distributed by a local undertaker. The sequence of the evening was as strict as a church liturgy: a little socializing first, then music, then hot cider and cookies. Until time to serve, the cookie trays were covered with tea towels and set in the darkened kitchen – no noshing ahead of time! Children were expected to participate in the singing and to stay in the living room with their parents – no running or playing! If anyone objected to these rules, I guess they didn't come back. In fact, over the years some of those obediently repressed children grew up and actually brought their own children to the carol sing.

Small section of the back row, at my parents' house, 1979. That's me in white, singing the carol from memory.

As much labor as she poured into this event, I think that once it started, Mom thrived on seeing everyone singing the old sacred songs together. People were warmly welcomed, the house glowed with Christmas spirit, and an atmosphere was generated that allowed guests to share in creating the party, but at the same time, to relax and let the party happen. As for me, I loved the music even more than the cookies, and that's saying something!

When I was in my thirties, Mother downsized, gave me her piano and passed the torch. For nearly twenty years I was hostess of the carol sing. There was a shift in participants, as new and old friends, relatives and neighbors mingled. My house was much smaller than hers had been, but I stuck to the ritual form, and with the detailed planning, decorating, baking, and furniture-moving, before the event I was always just short of a nervous breakdown. The singing made it a delightful evening for me, but I collapsed for days afterward.

One year sixty people answered our invitation in the affirmative. Unlike my mother, I took this opportunity to panic. But fortunately, I talked with a wise friend, who assured me that if I made the decision to genuinely enjoy *myself*, the guests would have a good time. She was right. That night I learned that my passion for control was poison to the fun factor. Every time I felt myself tightening, I took a deep breath and let go instead. Sixty guests filled not only the living and dining rooms, but the kitchen and enclosed back porch/ laundry room, and even the stairway and landing. There was no place to hide the cookies, so people snacked as they wished. Rather than serving the spiced cider in my grandmother's cut-glass punch bowl in the dining room, we ladled it out of the kettle on the kitchen stove. It was sometimes hard to move around, but you could sure hear the voices of your fellow singers, and it was a joyful noise. A new, less ritualistic, jollier approach had forced itself on me, and I never reverted to the rigidly regulated format.

Guests began to request "Frosty the Snowman" and "Rudolf," so we printed song sheets, expanding the variety of music to include both sacred and secular. Every year I mildly regret that we ever printed "The Twelve Days of Christmas"! Next, we developed a collection of various bells and handed them out so everyone could accompany the pianist on lines like "Sleigh bells ring, are you list'nin'?"

Some years the number of children swelled, and with the march of time, youngsters were much less restrained in their behavior, making the proceedings more lively. We sometimes got to smile and laugh at two or three little dancers who couldn't help wiggling to "Jingle Bells."

Once I baked thumbprint cookies with a Hershey's Kiss pressed into the center of each. Later that night I found naked white cookies, missing their chocolate, abandoned on shelves and window sills. Another time I shaped chocolate cookie dough into little mice with a licorice tail. I just wish the children who liked chocolate had gotten together with the ones who liked licorice whips – cleanup would have been easier!

With the dawn of the 21st Century, my turn came to downsize, and my sister Carolyn stepped into the annual hostess role. At her house – and now in the central room at her co-op – the carol sings have continued, again with shifts in participants due to aging family members, new friends, and new generations joining in. The joy is rekindled every time we open our little blue books. Every year, as Mother always did, we close the party with a quiet rendition of "Silent Night," thanking her for this warm holiday tradition that she started over six decades ago.

After a long history with this celebration, both our parents said their final good-byes to life in close timing with the carol sing.

In January of 1986, Mother died only a month after helping me host the carol sing. Our sorrow was overwhelming. But thanks to my sister's insight and planning, at the end of Mom's memorial service, commemorating her warmth and the welcome of the annual celebration she invented, we sang "Silent Night." I'm pretty sure the last few dry eyes succumbed to tears at that point.

Years later, on an early December morning in 1993, my brother phoned to tell me our dad had died in Montana. The carol sing was already scheduled for that same evening. We knew everyone would understand if we cancelled. But even in our grief, after serious consideration, we decided to go ahead with the party, announce his passing, and sing with joy in his memory. It was the right choice. Nothing makes the loss of parents easy, but continuing a long family tradition helps them stay alive in our hearts.

Food, glorious food*

I'm staring glumly at a plate of once-piping-hot roast beef and vegetables. I won't raise my eyes even when Mother comes back to remind me that I can be excused from the table as soon as I finish my dinner. "Just eat three bites of each thing," she finally pronounces in a discouraged tone. The rest of the family left the room ages ago, it's been an hour — or maybe ten minutes, who knows? When you're only six or seven, each minute is such a large percentage of your whole life.

I choke down three bites of the meat. The soft, overcooked, cold broccoli is too much, and helpless tears start flowing. "I can't!" Mother sighs, takes away the plate, and frees me.

It happened more than once, but not enough times that I was persuaded to change my eating patterns.

Mom had rules about nutrition which I never thought to question, and in fact, they are still generally accepted as foundational. Protein at every meal. Carbohydrates in balance (with notable exceptions, at our house). Lots of fruits and vegetables.

Ah, but those vegetables. Frozen foods didn't make it into our lives until the 1950s. Even then, home freezer compartments, inside the top of the refrigerator, were tiny and did not hold their temperature well. So the answer to keeping vegetables on hand for quick access remained tin cans. Beans and peas were taken from the can and then cooked until just before they would have spontaneously pureed themselves. You haven't lived until you've been served canned asparagus which has been boiled on the stove for ten or fifteen minutes.

* Lyric from "Food, Glorious Food," Lionel Bart, 1960.

I say "been served" because to say "eaten" would be a lie. I was able to make such a revolting display of gagging and suffering that I don't believe I ever actually swallowed asparagus until I was 21 years old, far from home, and at the table of a really good cook. Fresh, tender-crisp asparagus was a whole new food.

We did have the gardens – Grandma and Granddad's huge garden, and usually one of our own as well. So we ate fresh produce, but it was nearly always cooked.

Reids' garden (in front of Miss Ward's and Mrs. Bowden's house), 1950.

About half of our grandparents' vegetable garden is seen in background, 1953. I'm in the center with dark hair and striped sweater.

Salads weren't a daily menu item, and when we had them, they were generally dense and substantial – coleslaws; chopped apples with celery; carrot-raisin mix. A salad I've never seen elsewhere is Mother's combination of iceberg lettuce with crushed pineapple. Every one of these dishes was dressed with Miracle Whip, a mock mayonnaise product which, manufactured without eggs, was considered safe for picnics and other unrefrigerated uses.

Although Mother and Grandma put up fruit in jars, the only vegetables they canned were tomatoes. As Mother explained to me, peas, beans and corn didn't have enough acid for home canning, and could develop botulism. Mom was nothing if not well-informed. They jarred applesauce, pears and peaches. Berries of all kinds were mostly eaten fresh or in baked goods, but there were also the jams and jellies, sealed with melted paraffin. In the winter, when we took a new jar from the pantry, if a bit of blue mold had grown under the edge of the wax, we just scooped it off and proceeded to use the rest of the jam. I never saw any deleterious effects from this. I'm a subscriber to the theory that a few germs are good for the immune system.

There were frequently big Sunday afternoon dinners at Grandma's house. Often these were celebrations of holidays or birthdays, grouped according to the month. My winter birthday was close enough to cousin Bruce's, and the family party was usually on Christmas Eve. In September a flock of small cakes commemorated at least five or six birthdays, including Mom's and Carolyn's. Ken's natal day was honored at our Easter gathering. Dad shared the October festivities with Aunt Frances, who, like him, had married into this tribe.

Each nuclear group brought contributions. Grandma and Granddad provided the meat, usually from the rabbits and chickens they raised. The four women gracefully performed an ever-shifting *pas de quatre* around one another in Grandma's tiny kitchen to prepare hot vegetables and mashed potatoes, and someone nearly always brought what was called, not just Jell-O, but a Jell-O salad – probably earning that terminology because there wasn't any other salad. Our parents seemed to think that Jell-O was a good way to disguise healthy foods so that children would eat them. I enjoyed Mother's version, laden with soft, sweet home-canned pears and peaches. What put me off were Aunt Peggy's continuing experiments with crunchy chopped celery, fresh apples or grated carrots suspended in the jiggly green medium.

Once oleomargarine became available, it was used in our homes almost exclusively. Until, that is, Uncle Van was hired by the Darigold

Company. By that time, the three families in my mother's generation had begun sharing the burden of entertaining the whole crowd. Whichever family hosted a big meal would buy a pound of real butter, Darigold brand, for the occasion. You might even feel free to accidentally leave the wrapper on the kitchen counter to demonstrate your loyalty to your relative's employer.

Springtime birthdays at Grandma and Granddad's house. I'm standing at left behind Mother. Kenneth is seated at far end and Carolyn stands behind him.

Food was complicated for me. I'd been a colicky baby, and looking back now, I wonder if my mother nursed me more often because it would quiet me down. In any case, to this day, whenever I'm uncomfortable in any way, food is first on my list of solutions. And the first food I choose is sugar. Mother was a well-educated woman who made it her business to know how to raise healthy children. But while she served wholesome, balanced meals, she also loved to bake. In some ways, she was the perfect example of the motto, "Do as I say, not as I do."

She expressed a belief that sweets in moderation were fine. In fact, we all indulged beyond moderation. Maybe it was more rewarding in some way for her to feed us desserts than meat and vegetables. Or maybe she herself craved the sweets and couldn't eat them without sharing with us. Apple and berry pies and crisps abounded throughout summer and fall, and if there were leftovers in the morning, she explained with a playful smile that it was "a perfect breakfast – you've got cereal in the crust, fruit in the middle, and a serving of milk in the ice cream on top."

Apples were ubiquitous. Because the Transparents ripened in August, Gravensteins in September, Russets, Winesaps, and other varieties through early December, there was a continuous supply. We were free to snatch one from a tree on our way by – which was how we learned the differences between an unripe fruit and one that was ready to eat. Once you bit into it, you were responsible for eating the whole thing or disposing of it correctly in the compost pile – no littering the orchard with experiments. There *was* the occasional stomachache! The Gravensteins were so abundant that one or two boxes of them rested on our back porch for weeks every fall. Their fruity fragrance accompanied all our comings and goings. They did not maintain their crispness, but I ate many a soft apple because they were so convenient. And they were perfect for baking.

Once when I was about eight, the troop leader, Mary Jane Thompson, hosted our Brownie meeting. Mother had said she'd pick me up next door to the Thompsons', at the home of my classmate, Bunny Lantz. On the Lantzes' dining table was a big bowl of grapes. My mouth watering, I asked Bunny's mother if I could try some. She laughed, "Sure! That's what they're there for!" My mouth exploded with these juicy little capsules of goodness. A new flavor sensation!

When Mother and I arrived back at our house, I waited for what I hoped would be just the right moment, then screwed up my courage and said, "Mommy, do you think we could have grapes sometime?"

She looked at me. "We have apples." Case closed.

Left to my own thoughts, I accepted this answer by reasoning that for us, apples were free, and grapes must be expensive. As it turned out, after a month or two, Mom did bring home grapes – very occasionally – proving she hadn't completely dismissed my request. I think now that she didn't want me to get the impression I could have everything I wanted. Even though, for the most part, I did.

There was no skimping on sweets. A defining characteristic of our house was the full cookie jar. Our cookies were always homemade, never "boughten." I ate as many every day as I could get my hands on. At first there were limits, but once I was tall enough to reach the cookie jar and master the art of stealth – lifting its lid cautiously, slowly, silently – no holds were barred. If she did happen to hear or see me, Mom might warn, "You'll spoil your dinner!" What did I care about dinner?

A daily supper where we sat down together was *de rigueur*. Even Dad, consumed with work, would generally show up for dinner, and he uniformly complimented the cook, although the way he shoveled it in never ceased to irritate her. He was always in a hurry, and his style of eating had likely been formed in a childhood when there was rarely quite enough to go around. Mother wanted her children to behave with more gentility, so she criticized him for scrambling the food together on his plate and downing his milk in breathless gulps.

I had the strong impression that fixing meals was no more interesting to Mother than eating them was to me. Food was spiceless and unimaginative. There was often red meat, because that was generally recognized as the best protein source available. For my part, I barely noticed the difference between meatloaf, pot roast, and sirloin steak – none of it had any appeal. Chicken and turkey tasted okay, but compared to chocolate-raisin clusters, poultry, too, lost its luster.

On a rare weekend morning, Mother made pancakes. For these events we sat at the dining table rather than the kitchen counter. When we were very young, she displayed her artistry by pouring the batter in the shapes of rabbits, cats, squirrels, turtles and teddy bears. They were fun to look at and fun to eat. These little masterpieces came out of the pan one at a time, and she spent inordinate energy delivering them from the kitchen, giving us each our share in turn. As we grew larger and more baby-bird-like, our beaks opening and closing with cries of "More, please!" the plan was simplified. She changed her recipe to include sliced apples or cooked rice – whether to make the meal more interesting, more filling, or more nutritious, I don't know – and fried round cakes, three at a time. And another set of three, and another, until she was able to gain on us and accumulate a platter full.

She would then circle the table with her spatula: "Just one more, they're all cooked now, let's finish them up."

"Oh gee... Okay, one more."

"Two? How about two?" She made it sound as if eating hot cakes was a duty to the family, like washing the dishes. Who could resist?

Once all of us were filled to bursting, she sometimes went so far as to sit down and join us with her ever-present cup of coffee, and do her part to "finish them up." Today, on those occasions when I overeat at a holiday meal, that leaden, overstuffed sensation calls up the specter of Mom hovering just behind my right shoulder: "Come on, just one more."

As a counterpoint to this peculiar pressure to load up on carbohydrates, Mother was always concerned that I was such an inactive child. There were a number of reasons for my listlessness. Like her, I was allergic to cats and pollens, so every morning and evening she gave me a pill from her own prescription bottle. I don't know if she ever checked with the doctor on this practice, because she could see that the tablets kept my allergy symptoms at manageable levels. I later learned that this medication was sometimes prescribed as a sedative to help patients sleep. The adult dosage I was receiving certainly must have depressed my daytime energy. Another cause of my lethargy was my dependent personality. I tended to stay close to my mom when I could, so that when she said, "Why don't you go outside and play?" my unspoken answer was, "Why would I do that, when you're inside?" On top of everything, I wasn't ingesting most of the nutrition that was offered at the dinner table. For some reason, I wasn't hungry!

It took a few years before I was diagnosed with iron-deficiency anemia. The doctor's prescription? Eat calf's liver once a week. A truly self-defeating treatment plan. I give Mother credit for trying that for several weeks, and Dad must have been on board the campaign too, as he would exclaim, "Liver, my favorite!" However, instead, in addition to the allergy tablets, I was soon taking iron supplements. And, of course, never stopped eating cookies.

Because we generally were raised on sturdy, home-cooked Scandinavian farm fare, I was unaware of fast food or even convenience products like Kraft macaroni-and-cheese-in-a-box. I never heard of Chinese take-out, never tasted Mexican food. There were no delis. The first several years I heard Dean Martin's 1953 recording of "That's Amore," I thought the lyrics were, "When the moon hits your eye like a big piece of pie." It made no sense, but I was used to living in a world that was often beyond my comprehension. Pizza was a concept I hadn't been exposed to.

We never ate out, and if a quick meal was needed, it had to be planned and prepared in advance. This often meant casseroles, which could be simply heated in the oven. Starting when I was a pre-teen, Mother left casseroles for us every week while she went to summer school in Bellingham, since neither Carolyn, Ken nor I had any talent or training in cooking. Our last-ditch, illicit pleasure during those weeks was an occasional night of Swanson TV dinners. My mild feelings of guilt only enhanced my enjoyment of those portion-controlled, over-processed entrees perfumed with the unique scent of hot aluminum foil.

For lunch at home, Mother gave us sandwiches with a piece of fruit. One of our favorites was Kraft American cheese with jam. Our friends looked askance at this combination, until they tried it. Delicious! Another specialty was simply cheese on a slice of bread, run under the broiler to soften the cheese. I loved melted cheese with bread, and until I was in my twenties, this open-face sandwich was the only way I knew to enjoy it. It was in New Jersey that a friend made grilled cheese sandwiches in a frypan with real butter and two slices of bread. Crispy bread drenched in warm butter! I've never gone back. On the other hand, peanut butter has been a staple of mine since early childhood, and a major comfort food. I'm only a little embarrassed to confess that today I sometimes eat two or three bites with a spoon, like pudding, calling up the transparent self-deception that it's really just protein!

Our drinks were milk, orange juice, fresh-pressed cider in season, or water. I still remember my jaw dropping when I went to a high school friend's house after school and saw in her family's refrigerator a case of Coke (for the kids) and a case of beer (for the parents).

We were proud when Ken was chosen for the high school football team. One day after school I was astonished to see him put a saucepan of water on the stove to heat. Cooking had never been of interest to him, to put it mildly. He opened a package of six wieners and dumped them all into the boiling water. When I recovered the power of speech and asked him why, I learned that the coach had told him to build his muscle mass by eating more protein. He perched on a stool and ate all six (while I raided the cookie jar). Somehow, throughout that season Mother stocked enough easy-fix protein in the house to keep him supplied.

Being the eldest child, Carolyn reached her full height ahead of Ken or me. Baking supplies were stored in the high cupboard over the stove, where we generally couldn't reach. One day after school, I saw my sister eating a handful of chocolate chips.

"Hey, where did you get those?"

She didn't want to tell, but when Kenneth got in on the question, she opened the upper door and showed us. "I only take them if the package is already opened. Mother will never see a few missing." To keep us quiet, she shared some with us. From then on, even if we had to climb on a stool, we would each take our turn at sneaking these bits of candy.

I was shocked, after months of this pattern, when Ken actually opened a new bag of chocolate chips to have a snack. "Mother's going to kill you!" The result was anticlimactic – she had become too busy to notice. Ken pointed out to me that there were also marshmallows and dates in the cupboard. Variety is key to an excellent diet.

Mother was seventy when we gathered to help her move out of the house, shortly after her divorce. I'll never forget discovering her *other* candy cupboard. The farthest corner cabinet beyond the sink had always been the storage spot for flower vases, fancy bowls and platters, and other rarely-used items. When I opened it to start packing the china, I found bags of Mars bars and candy corn, boxes of Frango mints, and every imaginable kind of chocolate-covered treat. The quantity alone was staggering, and I was swept with sadness. Knowing how I myself turn to sweets for consolation, I could only see this as Mom's security blanket. However difficult it was to live with her husband or to divorce him, to do her job or to let it go in forced retirement, to spend her days and nights alone, the candy would always be there.

My favorite family food event happened not long after she moved into her condominium in downtown Edmonds. She wanted to host Thanksgiving for the three of us and our partners – as she had in past years – but her new kitchen had very limited space and she had limited energy. "I'll roast the turkey, and you all let me know what side dishes you want to bring." An excellent plan.

Each of us called Mom and received her approval for our contributions. Little did we realize that Mother wasn't thinking clearly that week.

I brought my usual apple-raisin pie. Carolyn had found a new pumpkin pie recipe. Ken had picked up the specialty of the local bakery, a chocolate pie. When we all arrived, for a moment we were appalled. Then, hardly missing a beat, we designated the pumpkin pie "a vegetable," the apple-raisin pie "a salad," and ended up with only a single dessert: chocolate pie. At the table it was, "Please pass the sweet-potato casserole." Translation: the pumpkin pie. "May I have some more Waldorf salad?" The apple-raisin pie. That day provided some of the heartiest laughs we ever shared. Between the turkey trance and the sugar high, it's a wonder we were able to drive home.

The line is thinly drawn
'tween joy and sorrow*

One time, when I was perhaps eight or nine, I witnessed a collision of fire and ice that seemed to end in the final dowsing of the sputtering ember of affection between my parents. That night Daddy came home from work while Mother was standing at the stove cooking dinner. Smiling, he slipped his arm around her waist and gently kissed her neck. She stiffened, and aimed a sudden frown at the pot she was stirring as she stage-whispered, "Jim! The kids!" In the split second before he turned and left the room, I saw a heavy cloud of sadness well up to envelop them both like the dark smoke from a snuffed candle. After that I don't recall any other gestures of endearment between them.

It's impossible to write about Dad without writing about his marriage to my mother. In my lifetime, they operated for the most part in different realms, clashing when they overlapped. Mother's realm was the family, and increasingly over the years, there was no space for Dad to be active in that arena. Dad's realm was work, and increasingly over the years, he spent nearly all his waking hours working. Normally he came home to eat dinner with us, then immediately set out, either back to the office or to some meeting.

We three children barely knew him, and saw him largely through the dark lens of Mother's disapproval. Early on, the two of them stopped laughing together and spoke only about daily necessities. For her, his flaws loomed large: always late and rushing, never available to talk or help with homework or show up at ball games, irritable and

* Lyric from "Flowers Never Bend With the Rainfall," Paul Simon, 1966

impatient. At some later point we learned that Dad had the classic Type A personality, an explanation but not, in her eyes, an excuse. Mother remained convinced that if he cared for her, he would simply change these unacceptable behaviors.

When I was very small, I luxuriated in sitting on Daddy's lap while he read the comic strips. Before my birth, my sister Carolyn had enjoyed the same privilege. Now and then at Christmas time, he would get down on the floor and play with my brother Kenneth's electric trains. Beyond early childhood, these charming moments tapered off quickly, and what we saw of Dad was a preoccupied glance, or the back of his suit jacket as he left the house. Each of us youngsters had to grow up and gain some distance from our parents' home before we could believe what other people told us about our father.

Many people described Jim as "such a gentleman." In my pre-teen and teen years, I was sure this was a false front. He pulled the wool over *their* eyes, but *I* was not so easily fooled. He was frequently verbally abusive to my sister, distant with my brother and dismissive or scornful with Mom. But I had a special situation – in some ways my blessing, in other ways my problem. I was the apple of his eye. When you're little and someone adores you, I think you can thrive in that warm glow. But with the negative messages about Dad that I absorbed from Mother, the warm glow became a confusing strobe light: mostly off and then suddenly on, then off again for a while. Generally he wasn't around, and it was good not to have those strange flashes in my eyes. When he was there, he wanted me to appreciate his devotion. This became a burden.

The day I decided to start specifically avoiding him, I was 16. It was Christmas Eve, and everyone was dressed in their best. My mother, grandmother, an aunt, my sister and I were in our kitchen chatting and preparing food. Dad came home, walked into the kitchen and strode directly up to me, saying, "Barbie, you look so PRETTY tonight!" I was humiliated. Yet again, his tunnel vision focused only on me. I felt he had given the back of his hand to all the others in the room. Even at the time, I didn't think he meant to insult them, but he was oblivious to their presence, and in some mysterious way I was to blame for his rudeness.

As children, we had always kissed our parents hello, good-bye and good night with a peck on the lips. Recently Dad had started licking his lips before he kissed me. I believe this was unconscious, but it made me very uncomfortable. I began pointedly turning my cheek to Dad's kisses and answering his flattery with cold silence.

I want to make it clear there was never any inappropriate touching or direct sexual suggestion from my father. As I see it now, Dad was simply starved for affection at home and saw his youngest girl as a potential source of that affection. However, he didn't realize that in contrast to his fondness for the small child, the attraction he felt for the teenage girl was taboo. I could no longer be a central object of his love, and it was up to me to enforce this rule. Knowing only how uneasy I was in his presence, I replaced the soft and agreeable child he remembered with a closed and hardened teenager. He never stopped trying to convert me back into that compliant little girl, not even on his death bed, although by that time I had, to a large degree, come to accept him as he was. I traveled a long and wavering journey to create a more balanced way of relating to my father. I'm not yet done learning about his unique constellation of strengths and weaknesses.

At our house on the hill, we had only two near neighbors – my mother's parents, who saw Dad through Mom's frustrated eyes, and Pat and Dan Hannah, an older couple who were friends of Dad's through his civic activities. After Dan died, I used to stop by Pat's house sometimes after school, and as we chatted she would tell me again and again how much-loved Jim was in Edmonds. How many people he had helped with free advice and loans, how polite and mannerly he was. I simply couldn't see it. Pat was a straightforward, outspoken woman, so there was no doubt she was being honest about the way she saw him. But the notion that that kind, generous fellow was the same person as my father was inconceivable to me at the time.

In the summer after my junior year of high school, like my sister before me, I was hired to work at Dad's office. Suddenly I saw the other side of his life. The woman who served as office manager was totally devoted to my father and spoke of him with respect verging on worship. His overall crisis-management style caused some strife and grumbling, but generally staff and clients liked Jim and praised his skills as an engineer. Sometimes he displayed a dry wit, evoking chuckles all around. To me, all of this was brand new.

One morning I went into the Edmonds Bakery, a little storefront with a sales counter and two or three small tables. Warm yeast and sweet spices perfumed the air. Circled around a table, perched on wrought iron soda-fountain chairs, were four men in their business suits, drinking coffee and laughing. One of them was my dad. With a delighted smile he introduced me, and I noticed that his face looked different than it looked at home – his eyebrows rested at a higher point on his forehead. For the first time I saw him relaxing and enjoying the company of friends. The spirit of mutual encouragement was as apparent as the fragrance of freshly baked cinnamon rolls.

Another day Dad invited me to join him for lunch. We walked over to Brownie's café, and the waitress greeted him warmly. They exchanged pleasantries, and again he proudly introduced me, then she said, "You want your usual, Jim?" I don't know why I remember this short conversation, except that he seemed so lighthearted. These two had a daily connection that was vastly different from my daily connection with him. There was a simple friendliness in their exchange that I hadn't seen at home since I was very young.

Many years later, talking with my brother, I learned a little about the evening meetings that so often kept Dad from us. At one time he was simultaneously the city engineer for the cities of Edmonds, Lynnwood, Mountlake Terrace, and his childhood home town of Hermiston in eastern Oregon! In lengthy, overlapping time frames he was the contract engineer for the Edmonds School District and for three port authorities (Edmonds, Everett and Bremerton). He was a member and officer of two chambers of commerce and a Rotary Club, and chaired the Snohomish County United Way fund drive for years. In addition to these commitments, he attended hundreds of official

Meet Your City Officials:

City Engineer's Work Increases As Edmonds Continues to Expand

ENGINEER REID
with slide rule and map

It's a rare meeting of the City Council unless at some point in the proceedings the discussion comes to a halt, and someone says: "Let's ask the engineer!"

For the past 5½ years, that question has turned all eyes in the room to a big, slightly stooped man who proceeds then to start unfurling his maps and charts — City Engineer James H. Reid.

Sooner or later, about anything the city does goes through the engineer's office. If an annexation is petitioned, he maps out the area for the council, and estimates the population and property valuation. If it's a local improvement district for streets, sidewalks, or sewers, the engineer draws up the specifications and estimates the costs to the property owner. When a zoning change is being discussed, it's the engineer who draws up the maps.

And with Edmonds expanding and improving at the rate it is, the engineering work increases steadily — Mr. Reid estimates the volume of city work is six or seven times what it was when he first became the city engineer in the fall of 1953.

It was in March of that year that he opened an office in Edmonds, under the name James H. Reid & Associates. Despite the title, Mr. Reid worked by himself until Roy Middleton joined him in the spring of 1954. By now, however, the "associates" includes 23 persons besides Mr. Reid, and the operations cover the entire second floor of the former bank building at Fourth and Main.

NOT all this is due to the city of Edmonds, however — James H. Reid & Associates also is the engineering consultant for the city of Mountlake Terrace, Port of Everett, Port of Edmonds, Port of District 15, and Olympic View Water District!

A native of Oregon, Mr. Reid graduated from the University of Washington with a civil engineering degree in 1934, then went to work as a junior civil engineer in the U. S. Engineer's office in Portland. In 1937 he went to Hawaii, and after the outbreak of World

War II, was called to active duty from his reserve status, entering the Army Engineers as a second lieutenant and emerging in 1945 as a major, his service including a year on Okinawa.

Following the war, he joined the Seattle consulting engineering firm of James W. Carey & Associates, where he first became interested in municipal engineering work. He was called back to military service from 1951 to 1953, commanding a team of engineer specialists in Newfoundland, Labrador, Baffin Island and Greenland in constructing and designing air base facilities, and it was after that tour of duty ended that he started his own practice in Edmonds.

Engineer Reid has seen many a hot and heavy verbal battle swirl around his head during hearings on zoning, L.I.D.'s and all the other projects that come up for sometimes violent discussion, but his usual habit is to wait until the fireworks subside a bit, then resume his discussion or explanation in a low and unruffled voice.

Biggest job he's had for Edmonds so far is planning of the sewage disposal plant, and by the same token, the recent hookup between Mountlake Terrace and Edmonds to use the plant—all engineered by Reid & Associates.

This kind of work calls for lots of night meetings—"If I'm lucky, I get to be home about one night a week," he admits.

When he is home is at 18620 94th W., in North Edmonds. His wife, Jacqueline, is a sixth grade teacher at Lynndale Elementary School. A daughter, Carolyn, is a sophomore at Whitman College, and two children are in Edmonds Junior High School—Kenneth, a ninth grader; and Barbara, in the eighth grade.

meetings of commissions, city and county councils, and boards of directors.

I was aware at the time that he designed the Edmonds marina, the Edmonds sewage treatment plant, and a complex industrial loading dock in Everett. Through Ken, I've now learned that Dad was also responsible for the design of boat marinas in the Washington State ports of Everett, Port Orchard and Des Moines. He headed numerous projects for the City of Edmonds from 1953 on, and designed Lynnwood's first sewer system and treatment plant, plus many other projects for both public and private clients. In 1974, he was presented the South Snohomish County Chamber of Commerce's John Fluke Community Service Award (essentially "Man of the Year").

The company grew from "James H. Reid, Consulting Engineer" to "James H. Reid and Associates," and later, "Reid, Middleton and Associates," which still operates now, nearly twenty-five years after his death. He was an ethical, self-made businessman, driven to expand his business and provide ample, reliable income for his family. In the process he developed scores of mutually respectful relationships in the community. He had a deep commitment to civic improvement. But at home, I was never told that the evening meetings and projects for which he left us were part of a larger picture. Mother discouraged conversation about his job, so he rarely spoke at the dinner table about his work or service activities. We children were excluded from the positive circle that Pat Hannah had earnestly tried to describe. What I thought was a false front in the community was actually "the real Jim Reid" as he operated in an arena where he was at ease.

My brother got his professional start at Dad's company. Dad was not able to give full credence to his son's skills and talents. Contrary to receiving favoritism as the boss's son, Ken was largely treated the way Dad treated family members — that is, as someone to be ignored or criticized — rather than as a future colleague in the engineering field. My brother stuck it out for years and gleaned skills that later made him successful in related work. By dint of his own efforts, he himself eventually won the John Fluke Community Service Award.

In 1979, Ken organized a seventieth birthday party for Dad in a large Edmonds meeting space. Dad's friends, relatives and colleagues attended from throughout Washington and Oregon.

Oddly for a workaholic, Dad did have a hobby. During my teens, he took up photography. He loved the technical side of cameras, and periodically spent an hour at the Edmonds Camera Shop talking F-stops and apertures with his friend, the owner, and browsing and selecting new cameras or lenses. With all the energy he put into his job, he still had a desire to learn and hone a new skill.

I suspect the camera gave him a role both in our nuclear family and at larger gatherings of relatives. Not only was he somewhat isolated by his hearing impairment, but he had married into this wider company and I had the impression he never quite felt he fit in. The camera gave him a defined role in the group. In the long run, because he was behind the lens, we ended up with

Dad greets Uncle Sherm and Aunt Frances at 70th birthday celebration, 1979.

an extensive photographic record of events. There are many photos of the rest of us, but pictures of him are mostly limited to those for which he posed the family, set the timer, and rushed to "look natural" as he leaned into the edge of the grouping.

We still joke about some of his oft-repeated bumbling-cameraman moments. A common example was, "Did the flash go off?" We learned to preempt the question by calling out, "Flash didn't go off!" Because of his bad ears, and because it was more fun to shout than whisper, we usually employed our top vocal volume to convey this information.

If he felt he had missed a great candid shot, we'd hear the dreaded, "That was so cute, why don't you do it again?" This plea is recalled not only by my brother, sister and me, but also by my brother's daughters. I myself usually sullenly resisted the reenactments. But my sister-in-law genuinely liked my dad, and at her gentle urging, the three nieces would gamely troop back onto the lawn carrying their Easter baskets, or crouch again under the Christmas tree, and re-create whatever vignette he was looking for, but with a certain posed stiffness that hadn't been there the first time.

And the slide shows! They live to this day in the minds of first and second cousins. Not only was every presentation interminable because no snapshot was ever thrown away, but Dad's narration was uninspiring to say the least: "Do you think I overexposed this one? I thought F-stop XYZ would be right, but maybe not, hmmm," or, "Gee, that one's dark — guess the flash didn't go off," or, when the whole picture consisted of a wide black stripe with sprocket holes along the sides, "Oh, I guess that was the end of the roll."

I mentioned that Dad had a Type A personality. This pattern is characterized, among other things, by frequent hostility. I was thirteen when I wrote in my diary how unfair Dad was to my sister. On that day, we had started out on a car trip and Carolyn was reading a magazine in the back seat. Out of the blue, Dad began to rant at her for not looking around at the scenery, calling her selfish and uncaring. I remember exactly where it happened — at the Maplewood Club House, about a half mile from home.

That time, Mother defended my sister by saying his criticism was uncalled-for, since Carolyn was well aware of the scenery in the neighborhood and wasn't missing anything so far. But this was not an isolated incident and often there was no defender to take her part. As for me, I wouldn't have dreamed of stepping into a conflict so loaded with unsaid emotions. At different times I theorized that Carolyn might be some other man's daughter, for how could her own father dislike her so much? But once I was convinced that was impossible, I wondered if Dad resented her for being born and bringing an end to his carefree beach life in Hawaii back in 1940. In any case, by the time Dad was in his seventies, Carolyn, to my great admiration, had what I considered heroic success in reaching out to him and turning away from old wounds.

Dad's anger was expressed most often in silence – silence that seemed pre-volcanic. If he and Mother disagreed and he tried to speak, his words were jerky and explosive. Mother was able to unleash a river of rational support for her position, drowning his attempts to explain a different viewpoint. Where his feelings were concerned, his major strategy was to prevent himself from expressing them. His final resort was to leave the house, slamming the door behind him.

We looked for two signs of his silent fury. The first was the ever-present vertical crease between his eyebrows, which deepened when he frowned. But this could be misleading. On my sister's wedding day in Bogota, he said he was excited and proud, and I felt that he was. Yet as he walked her up the aisle, his scowl was more ferocious than I had ever seen. It was then that I realized his frown was a signal that he was feeling strong emotions – either positive or negative – and trying to hold them in. He had never been taught to manage deep feelings, and I believe that in that moment, despite his lifelong ambivalence toward her, he was overwhelmed with caring and concern for his first-born daughter.

The second, and rarer, sign of Dad's anger was the muscle in his cheek that contracted as he clenched his teeth in a massive effort to hold back his rage. That muscle was a sure sign that he wouldn't be in the room much longer – he had to escape. I can only imagine he was afraid of doing or saying something he would regret. Sadly, once he was on the other side of the slammed door, Mother sometimes made fun of his reactions – "Did you see how his cheek was twitching?" – as if this were just another in a long list of his failings, rather than a symptom of a problem to be solved between the two of them.

Dad also expressed his free-ranging frustration behind the wheel. The unspoken societal rule of the day was that if there was a father in the family, he drove – not the mother. Car trips were miserable, beginning with chronically late departures while we waited by the front door until Dad showed up. He habitually stomped on the accelerator with everything he had, and loved asserting his road dominance by passing other vehicles, even in dangerous settings. He didn't curse, but he frequently lectured other drivers behind closed windows. If anyone in the car commented on his driving, not only did he speed up, but the increased tension made the walls and doors press in, expelling all breathable air out of the compartment. I developed a trick of escaping by flinging my spirit outside of the car, through the fresh air, toward a friendly-looking house or woodsy cabin, like a spider anchoring her web to a distant blade of grass.

Sooner or later, most of Dad's professional acquaintances and friends refused to ride with him, even to a nearby meeting. "I've got this new car, Jim, why don't we take mine?" or, "I'll drive separately, I have to go somewhere afterward." But the family was stuck. He had tremendous confidence in his own lightning reflexes, and passengers had a harder time generating the same level of faith. Near misses are impossible to count, but through some kind of miracle, thankfully, he had very few collisions.

My parents' marriage ended after 40 years when they were in their 70's, and not surprisingly, both experienced a period of loneliness and depression. Before long Dad's many friends introduced him to Dibi, who was to become his next wife. Their romance was exciting and passionate at first, and they remained married until his death. But despite his promise that "I'm not going to let this one go bad," the two were no longer friends when he died some years later. He married strong-minded women, then resented the fact that he couldn't control them. Intimate relationship was not his strong suit.

Did he have an affair, or affairs, earlier? Of course it's possible, but he had a phenomenally strong conscience and old-fashioned values. In my thirties, I was living with my husband-to-be. At the time we planned to stay together long-term, but not necessarily to marry. Dad told me this arrangement was not okay with him, and later took Charles aside for a serious talk. "Do you realize you're ruining

her reputation? If you don't marry her, no other man will want her!"
Privately, the two of us laughed at Dad's naïveté, but we respected his
courage in making the speech, and the firm uprightness of his beliefs.
I didn't think this was the behavior of a fellow who had, at any time,
turned his back on his own vows of faithfulness.

Every human is an unfathomable mash-up of conflicting qualities.
Dad's days seemed to swing pendulum-like from a narrow world,
where he was isolated from his loved ones, to a wide community full
of connections. But he had a strong core that linked the two extremes.
He cared very much about people and had no desire to hurt or hate
anyone. I'm thankful to have been part of his life. I loved him, and
even though he didn't have the power to create the relationships he
would have wanted, he tried to learn, and loved us in the best way he
could.

On the bonnie, bonnie banks*

I don't swim there now, although that's more out of inertia than by conscious decision. I don't swim anywhere.

After Mother died, I asked Aunt Peggy for some family stories. Green Lake surfaced right away. When Peggy was a child, she and her brother and sister (my mom) had walked with their mother from their house in the University District to the lake every day for summer swim lessons. This was a round trip of at least four miles, which was considered reasonable in those days. Grandma never learned to drive, but even if she had, she wouldn't have had a car at that time in history, as every young mother requires today. The Red Cross taught swimming classes on the wide concrete steps at the west side of the lake. Not until the siblings were eight, eleven and fourteen was a bathhouse built there to provide toilets and a private area for changing out of wet swimsuits.

As Aunt Peggy told this story, my mind flashed on my own childhood years. Although we lived fifteen miles away, sometimes Mother and I drove to Green Lake to meet Peggy and her son Bruce, a favorite cousin. Bruce and I loved splashing on the concrete steps that led down into the water – the very same steps where, unknown to us, both of our mothers had taken their first lessons. After our water play, I sometimes got to spend the night at my cousin's house in the Ravenna neighborhood.

On special occasions we met grandparents, aunts, uncles and cousins for picnics in Woodland Park just across the street from the water, frolicking up and down the grassy hills and looking over the

* Lyric from "The Bonnie Banks o' Lock Lomond," traditional Scottish song

fence at the deer in a spacious, forested enclosure that formed the back edge of the city zoo. The lively afternoon was followed by a show at the Aqua Theater, located in the lake a few hundred yards south of the bathhouse. This unusual entertainment venue consisted of a stage – and an orchestra pit – floating in the water, flanked by two high diving platforms. We would rush from our picnic to clamber up to the best seats in the grandstand for the show. Musical flourishes and dramatic spotlights highlighted the daring divers, and sometimes songs or skits were performed onstage. But what thrilled me was the synchronized swimming. The water was always clear there. In front of the stage, up to twenty swimmers would arrange themselves into pulsating flowers and stars, ending with breathtaking underwater acrobatics. While we watched, the summer sun set behind us, and in the dusk the theatrical lighting took on added brilliance.

Some thirty years later, having become a busy but non-athletic adult, I made the startling discovery that physical exercise benefitted me personally. Living in a house just beyond a mile from Green Lake, I started walking that mile and rediscovered my childhood play place as a perfect spot to take a refreshing dip on hot August mornings. I liked to swim laps from one raft to the other early in the day, before the lifeguard and the crowds of children showed up. The feeling of my bare feet on the cool, rough concrete steps took me back to my early youth.

Green Lake is not a natural lake. It started out as a marsh and has been through several major transformations. The shoreline was privately owned until 1911 when, as part of a plan by the famous designers the Olmsted brothers, the water level was lowered by seven feet to create public parkland. Dikes were built – edged with the now-familiar concrete steps on both the west and east shores – and the bottom was dredged. As a result, we now have beautiful lawns and groves, and the most-visited park in the state of Washington. The tradeoff was that the creek that had provided outflow from the marsh dried up. Later, when city officials recognized the high level of pollution in street runoff, the storm water inflow to the lake was redirected to sewers. The lake is now fed only by rainwater and the rare transfusing of a city reservoir, and with neither inlet nor outlet, it sometimes stagnates. This condition has worsened over the decades, but the city manages the lake's condition as well as possible.

There are seasons when the algae bloom is actually considered hazardous, and warning signs are posted for swimmers. But most of the time the water is completely safe (although it is recommended that people towel off vigorously to defeat the annoying but short-lived parasite known as "swimmer's itch"). The historical view helps me remain unperturbed about the recurring issue of algae, as it has been part of Green Lake since the beginning. Hence the name.

Today, lying just below my windows, the lake is at the center of my thoughts for at least a few moments every day. I gaze at it – a jewel set in the middle of the city. Canada geese and swallows who make their homes at the lake fly over my apartment frequently. I live only a half mile away, often stroll through the neighborhood to the water, and sometimes circle the lake on the circumference path.

To my mind, there are two ways to walk the lake: alone or with friends. I treasure both ways. Alone, I notice the many variations in the surface of the water, from placid and mirrored to choppy with white-capped waves and slashing rain. I may stride along purposefully, or I may stop to notice red-winged blackbirds whistling among the cattails, carp jostling the lily pads in mating season, turtles waggling their pleated necks as they sun together on a log, a bald eagle resting on the pinnacle of the tallest tree. Arborists originally planted a wide variety of trees throughout the park, which form an ever-changing canopy. I'm always amazed at the number of birds supported by the specific ecology of this place, including herons, cormorants, mallards, widgeons, mergansers, wood ducks and coots, all managing to hold their own alongside the ubiquitous gulls and crows. Multitudes of squirrels provide entertainment for the leashed dogs accompanying their masters on the circular path. Thankfully, the path is not lighted at night, allowing nocturnal creatures to live in their natural rhythm, and if you're there just after dusk in winter, you can feel wind gusts from a posse of small bats rocketing past your head.

Walking with friends offers a different perspective. The environment provides a public yet private setting for conversation, since people you pass may overhear a phrase or two, but rarely more. Because of the beauty of the setting, discussions may go in unexpected directions, deeper and sweeter than the ordinary. There's a casual timelessness to this space. People take babies out in prams, briskly exercise their dogs, zip along on rollerblades, or stroll slowly together sipping from bright paper Starbucks cups. Now and then a drummer or guitarist perched on a bench sends sonic waves out over the water.

Even time itself seems to differ between the two ways of walking the lake:

Green Lake Relativity
Yesterday
I circled the lake alone
It was a long path
2.7 miles, they say
Only 42 minutes
I made good time

Today
I circled the lake with a friend
We arrived back at the start
before I ever expected
A short path, 2.7 miles
Something over an hour
We made such a good time

Another thirty years have passed since my first pedestrian forays to Green Lake. There have been a lot of changes to the lake and park. The bathhouse has been converted to the Bathhouse Theatre, where I have served as usher for just about every play for fifteen seasons. The former changing rooms are now the backstage area. I think the old fixtures were still in use for a long time; until the plumbing was upgraded recently, there was a sign in each rest room stall: "Please do not flush during the performance. It can be heard in the theatre."

The hillside where our family picnicked was long ago cut back to create a flat parking lot by the street. The Aqua Theater has been dismantled and a crew house stands in its place, with a couple of preserved sections of the grandstand used for stair-climbing exercise. Regardless of changes, regardless of algae, I can honestly say I love Green Lake. My connections with this little gem go back before my birth. In my eccentric way, I consider it my own.

The sweetest days I've found, I've found with you*

Mother and Grandma were best friends. Before I turned ten and Mom went back to school and to work, I was often privileged to sit at Grandma's big plank table with the two of them, listening to their conversation while they sipped coffee and I watched the birds outside the windows. The quieter I was, the more I was able to understand about my two dearest people in the world, and I wanted to hear it all.

They talked easily and openly about the events and people in their lives. They planned the necessary daily activities that they shared – laundry, gardening, food preservation. Some of their discussions amounted to gossip, as they came together from their different arenas. Mom would talk about other Cub Scout mothers or the latest PTA meeting. Grandma would share stories about her sewing group members or her faraway relatives. I didn't hear much about their husbands, and I suspect they censored themselves, saving those discussions for times when I was in school.

Grandma and Mother, circa 1955.

* Lyric from "Through the Years," Kenny Rogers, 1981

Once, though, Grandma did mention Granddad in a negative light. The day before, she had received a letter from her sister, who still lived in the small Midwestern town where they had all grown up. Before she even opened the letter, Granddad had remarked, with cutting wit, "Another 'organ recital' from Esther, no doubt."

"He says," Grandma continued, "that Esther 'enjoys poor health.' It's true she has a lot of problems, but why does he have to say those things? She's my *sister*!" My grandmother actually had tears in her eyes, an extreme rarity. Self-appointed judge and jury, Granddad had decided Esther was nothing but a complainer, and he had no qualms about insulting her. Always the dutiful wife, Grandma didn't feel she had the right to reveal her hurt feelings to him. Her solace was confiding in her daughter.

Another narrative I overheard at that table involved a luncheon planned by the spouses of Granddad's University of Washington colleagues. For the sake of her husband, Grandma felt she must attend. Despite her iron will which forbade open displays of emotion, anxiety showed in her pursed lips and fidgety fingers. For the first time, I came to understand that she was acutely aware of being much less educated than most of her counterparts in University society.

Both my grandparents had been raised in the farming settlement of Armstrong, Illinois. After high school, he went away and completed his master's degree. She stayed with her parents and helped raise her siblings and work the farm. They married on Christmas Day, 1912, in their early twenties. Obviously she was pregnant immediately, as my mother was born thirty-six weeks later on September 6. Henry earned his Ph.D. and his professorship, working what jobs he could find along the way, while she raised three children on a tight budget through the First World War and the Depression. She may or may not have wished for a college education, but she didn't get one.

Many of the other professors' wives had met their mates during their own college careers. She was terrified that neither her appearance nor her conversation would be up to par.

I knew nothing of this as we sat at the table, and the concept that my grandmother felt inferior to anyone was beyond my comprehension. My mother, however, was familiar with the issue, and was ready to bolster her mother. "Mom, conversation won't be a problem. You're the best listener I've ever met – just ask a question and start listening. Don't ever think you're not a *lady* with the best of 'em. You'll do just fine." Then they adjourned to the bedroom to comb through the closet and choose the most suitable clothes and jewelry for the luncheon.

She survived it. The post-event debrief involved several detailed descriptions of the various women's personalities and attire. Grandma's best dress was, indeed, more simple and matronly than those of the other participants. Her hair style was basic, and lipstick was her only makeup. Mother's comments were unfailingly supportive: "Some of these women have to dress to the teeth because they don't have any substance under their furs and rubies." "Oh, that one, I remember her. She *looks* so attractive, but butter wouldn't melt in her mouth."

"It sounds like you did really well, Mom." Grandma received positive remarks with a downward-glancing, almost imperceptible nod, or a slight relaxation in the pressure of her mouth, although she would never actually smile at a compliment. In the end, she seemed relieved that she had done her civic duty. I didn't hear about any more luncheons after that. But she continued to rise to her husband's social requirements, arranging and hosting a number of large but less formal gatherings of faculty at her home.

Sight and sound were mingled in the tapestry of my grandmother's life. She had an almost mystical affinity for birds. Seated at the table three abreast, we gazed beyond the porch to the front lawn, dominated by two gigantic evergreen trees. A couple of birdhouses were attached high up on the tree trunks, almost hidden in the branches. Three different types of feeders were suspended alongside the bench swing. Grandma interrupted the conversation to name the birds that performed in our little floor show, a great gift rounding out my early education.

"Oh! There's the goldfinch! Isn't he pretty? We don't see him too often." Another time, "You can hear that red-headed woodpecker all the way in here, rat-tat-tatting on the tree. Let's go see if we can spot him. Look up high, now." "Seagulls are greedy. But they'll just keep circling until they give up, because they can't get under the trees to where the bird feeders are, you see?" "There's that squirrel again, he thinks he's going to get away with all the food," she'd say, and go to the door and clap her hands. At this sound the offender scampered up the tree to a high perch and began to broadcast his scolding chatter.

Mother, too, generally enjoyed explaining things, like the names of plants and animals, but on these occasions she was uncharacteristically close-mouthed. I think she respectfully left the space for her mother to be the educator for once.

Our grandparents' house was surrounded on two sides by a covered porch that measured perhaps a dozen feet in width. The big windows over the kitchen table, recessed under the broad eaves, were in deep shadow and nearly invisible to birds. A couple of times a year, one of these winged missiles would slam into the pane. Grandma tried to rescue these wayward beings. She held the stunned little character in a warm, still space between her palms, feeling its panicky heartbeat, and the scratching of its tiny claws if it was strong enough to struggle. As long as the heart was beating, she had me put crumpled tissue paper in a shoebox, then gently tucked in the bird, covered the box with a ventilated lid, and put it in a warm place. We kept our voices soft and soothing. About half the incidents happened with baby birds, and to these she fed sugar water from a medicine dropper. The verdict on the success or failure of these efforts was never delivered until the next day. When I returned in the morning, it was either a sad, "The little fellow didn't make it," or, "He's alive. Let's put him out on the edge of the planter and see what he does." The survivors were always able to fly away into the wild. It sounds heartless, but I quickly forgot about those that died, since they just disappeared in the night.

I spent large parts of every weekend and summer with Grandma. She was, as she said, up with the birds, so I could run down the trail at seven in the morning and count on finding her in her beloved flower garden. This garden was on the low hill across the path from the rear kitchen window. Thanks to Granddad and his Rototiller, year by year the flowers claimed more territory from the wild. He built trails and steps of dirt or stones up and around the incline. One spring morning I was baffled not to see Grandma in the flower beds that sloped down toward the house, until her disembodied voice answered my call from the far side of the knoll and I realized the garden had expanded again.

She was in charge of maintaining the planting areas surrounding the house on all sides, filled with shrubs and perennials. And she asked Granddad, or maybe Uncle Van, to build long planter boxes bordering the front porch. After that, all spring and summer, while we watched birds from the kitchen, our view was edged with red geraniums and blue lobelia.

Her gardening outfit was a slight variation on her daily costume. I remember her always – at least into the late 1950s – wearing button-front, short-sleeved dresses with flared skirts. Short sleeves left her arms free for all the chores, and the skirts were wide enough to give freedom to climb, bend and kneel. All day every day, she wore stockings and sturdy black leather shoes with one-inch heels. For outdoor work, they were the oldest, most worn-out shoes, and the nylons that already had runs in them.

Grandma, more than anyone, taught me to work. I was beside her, helping or observing closely, among the flowers morning after morning for years. The first regular job I ever held was picking the pansies. They were all around the yard, and she wanted them all picked a couple of times a week, explaining that this would encourage the plants to keep blooming all season. I was probably six when I started skipping everywhere, seeking out the rainbow-hued blooms, and bringing them indoors where she arranged them to show off each one to perfection. What a sweet, ruffled fragrance! Not until five years later, still picking Grandma's flowers, did I tire of the nickname the family had given me, "Pansy girl."

She taught me about planting seeds and seedlings, and especially about weeding. Her teaching was mostly by demonstration, in contrast to Mother's didactic explanations. Words came in short phrases, always illustrated with actions. "You want to pull up the entire root, or it will sprout again." Long pause while we labored side by side. "Here's why that one's so hard to pull. Dandelions have a tap root, you may need to use your trowel." More peaceful concentration. "Chickweed has thin runners, see how hard it is to follow them? Now, do your best to get them all." "This kind of grass is easy to pull. But once it goes to seed, you'll have it everywhere. You want to pull it early in the spring." "People talk about 'picking weeds,' but that's just silly. You *pick* flowers. That means you leave the plant in the ground. You *pull* weeds."

One day, at home, I heard Mother trying to persuade Kenneth to do some chore around our place. He shouted angrily, "I *hate* work!" I idolized my brother and wanted to be just like him. So the next morning, while Grandma and I were on our knees in the St John's Wort, and I was struggling to extract weeds from the dense stubborn roots of the ground cover, I asked, "Grandma, is this work?"

Her answer was oblique. "Mmm, I guess you could call it work. Why do you ask?"

"I *hate* work!" I imitated the passion in Ken's voice.

This triggered the only lecture I remember from her, and it was a short one. "Why would you *say* such a thing? Work means doing something useful, something that helps. You can't hate work if you're in the world. You just do it. You don't have to *call* it work, and it doesn't have to be hard, but you'll *always* want to be doing something useful."

She was right, of course, and in addition, there was work that was also fun. I was delighted the first morning she tied an apron around my waist and showed me how to locate the eggs in the hen house and carry them, oh, so gently, by holding up the edges of the apron to "make a basket." Of course she transported most of the eggs in her own apron, but I was bursting with pride when I made it to the kitchen with all five of mine unbroken.

She had only one enemy in nature. She loved just about all of God's creatures – including people. But before stepping outside to head for the chicken house, she always grabbed a special pair of kitchen shears used for just one purpose. When we entered the patch of thick grass beyond the driveway, she bent down over and over. Snicker-snack! Another slug sliced in two. The first few times I witnessed this unflinching operation, she muttered, by way of explanation, "That one's not going to get our spinach," or simply, "Nasty thing." But soon words weren't needed, and after a while I even asked to use the scissors myself. Since those times I've always had a disaffection for gastropods, and today in my gardening, as I callously bisect a slug or crush the shell of a ground snail, I often think of Grandma – the tenderest, toughest woman I've known.

Let's see that dust fly
with that broom!*

At the time I didn't suspect, as I do now, that Mother may
have taken advantage of my devotion to my grandmother by
sending me down the hill often to "help Grandma." Grandma did
her best with a pampered little girl. Although she tried to teach me
housekeeping tasks, I think we were both happier outdoors with our
hands in the soil. She gave me a soft dry cloth to dust the side tables
and knickknacks in the living room, and demonstrated how carefully
to proceed. A weekly requirement, she said. I did the job a few times,
and was sorely disappointed that I couldn't see any difference between
before and after. In my quiet voice but with manipulation in my heart,
I complained until eventually she took the job back from me.

Sweeping the painted concrete floor of the porch was another
assignment that fizzled. Declaring that every tool has its specific
uses, Grandma gave me the push-broom and had me practice short,
springy strokes with it. At the time I fancied myself a singer, and once
alone, I kept pausing, leaning on the handle and singing at the top of
my lungs with visions of someone discovering my incredible talent
and taking me away from all this. The porch was, indeed, large, but
after I was there for nearly an hour one day and hadn't finished the
sweeping, Grandma saw she couldn't delegate that job to me.

When Granddad had built the house, he included a sizable
room with two deep iron sinks, a large electric stove, and miles of
counter space. Its title on the design drawings was "Utility Room,"
but, I suppose in imitation of one or another of the family's children,

* Lyric from "Yakety Yak," Jerry Leiber and Mike Stoller, 1958

ninety-five percent of the time we called it the tiddly room. On laundry days it was in those iron sinks that Mother and Grandma hand-scrubbed any stains before starting the wash.

From my earliest memory there was an electric agitator (with a detachable wringer) for the actual washing. Mom often took our family's clean clothes home and hung them on a folding rack in our north yard. For whatever reasons, I didn't hang clothes at home. It's likely that Mom found it more efficient to do such daily tasks herself than to teach me. I may have also been more resistive to taking instruction from her than from her mother!

When I was at Grandma's, she and I hung the clean laundry on two long wires stretched between sturdy posts, a pair near the north brick wall of the house and the other two almost all the way to the yellow plum tree with the twisted trunk. I would hold up the far end of a sheet or tablecloth while she pinned its length to the wire. Clothespins were stowed in a handmade gingham pocket stitched to a coat hanger so that she could slide it along the line. Later in the day, Grandma and I held opposite ends of the linens and walked toward one another like dancers on a stage. This choreography was repeated at least three times for each bed sheet, and once I caught the rhythm, I felt as proud as if I'd mastered a ballet step.

I imagine that my siblings and cousins think of Grandma mostly in connection with food. Given the opportunity, she taught us all how to harvest the crops. Cousin Bruce and I occasionally spent whole days at Grandma and Granddad's house together, and we had some silly moments, repeated over the years until we were teens, as we proceeded in parallel down opposite sides of the raspberry row. We devised, of course, a competition regarding both quantity and quality. The canes grew so thickly that even on the sunniest days it was hard to discern colors in the center of the row. One of us would reach into the middle to take hold of a berry, and the other would warn, "Don't pick that one, it's not ripe enough and Grandma won't like it." (She was insistent that no fruit be picked before its time.) If the berry was the desired deep red color, we'd discourage each other with, "That's on my side, you better not take it!"

"Nuh-uh, it's mine!" Small fingers met in the middle, but we were careful not to squash the berry in contention. These squabbles were always settled quickly – we were picking, not for ourselves, but for Grandma.

There was a high bank between the vegetable garden and the driveway above, and blackberry vines gradually took over the long slope. On family dinner days, we kids sometimes paraded down past the rabbit hutches to gather blackberries. Meanwhile, Grandma finished roasting the meat, worked with our mothers to set up the rest of the meal, and made the pie crust. Naturally, we snacked as we picked, but in general we were pretty earnest about filling our coffee cans with berries, because a wonderful dessert depended on us. Were we proud when the steaming pie was brought forth!

One of my great delights was harvesting peas and sitting with Grandma on her shady porch shelling them, just the two of us side by side. Back then we shelled all our peas, and there was something very satisfying about the fresh fragrance and the "pop" when the pod opened, followed by the pattering sound like gentle rain as the little globes cascaded into a bowl. This was one of those old-fashioned activities that provided time for the peaceful silences and spare conversation that I enjoyed so much with my grandmother.

On the other hand, one Saturday, at Grandma's request, I stood at one of the deep sinks in the tiddly room, engulfed in an unfamiliar odor – the hot, raw flesh of two scalded, headless chicken carcasses. Grandma, bent over a chicken in the sink on my right, was ready to show me how to pluck a chicken. She laid the other bird in the left-hand sink and told me to do as she was doing. I could hardly bring myself to touch the poor dead creature, but obediently tugged on a few feathers. They clung stubbornly, strongly anchored under the skin. I felt brutish and primitive, never having wrested my food from a dead body, and leaning over the reeking sink gagged me. Without warning, having removed not a single feather, I turned and ran for the kitchen, leaving Grandma to finish the work. Her only comment was to call after me with a sigh, "Wash your hands, now."

Interestingly, my disgust did not cause me, even temporarily, to become a vegetarian. The following day, I sat down with all the relatives and savored my share of those birds. The only lasting effect of this experience was that, as an adult, I have never bought a whole chicken at the market, because the very form reminds me of that smell, that rubbery skin, and those tight feathers.

The most dramatic activity in the tiddly room occurred in July and August, when Mother and Grandma canned. During what always seemed to be the hottest week of summer, Granddad would arrange for a friend to bring peaches or pears from Eastern Washington. In their twenty-pound wooden orchard boxes, they filled the room with the rich perfume of ripe fruit. There was a sense of urgency – the produce had to be dealt with quickly before it began to spoil. Paring knives, clean jars, and washed fruit stood on a table in the center of the room. Against the south wall, counters flanked a six-burner electric range on which massive pans of water were heated. The room started out hot and grew hotter.

Mother and Grandma would devote two or three long, steamy days to sterilizing the jars, parboiling, peeling and cutting the fruit, dropping the halves into each jar, and filling them up with simmering sugar syrup. Then the rubber rings, boiled by themselves, the lids tightened just enough, and the jars in their wire rack lowered into the huge canning kettle full of bubbling water. From early childhood I watched these processes, amazed at the apparently heat-proof hands of my forebears. The two of them worked together with an ease built over a lifetime. There were times when they conversed briefly, but comments for the most part were short and focused: "This one's not worth the effort," as a half-rotted pear plopped into the compost bucket; "Coming through!" as Mom swept across from sink to stove carrying a full kettle as if it were a leaden beach ball. Sweat poured down their faces. When, rarely, a muffled "pop" emanated from within the rumble of the boiling water bath, they recognized the sound of a broken jar. The two women's only reaction was annoyance at the wasted labor and fruit – and the mess to be cleaned up.

When I reached the age of nine, Mother invited me to help cut the fruit. Pears and peaches, once peeled, were awfully eager to slide out of small hands! At first, between dropping perfectly good food on the floor and struggling to cut perfect halves and slices, I was pretty near useless. Even with improvement, I was never as skilled as the two of them. Nevertheless, canning became part of my life, and once grown and living in my own place, I was pleased with the conservation and frugality of putting up fruit from local back yards.

She served innumerable meals to big groups, both family and others. I have an indelible image of Grandma reaching both hands to the small of her back to tie or untie her apron. It was a gesture repeated many times a day. For family meals she wore an apron through all the hustle and scurry of kitchen preparation with the three other women, then removed it just as she sent one of us through the house to call everyone to the table. If "company" (non-family visitors) were expected, the apron came off before she answered the door. The apron reappeared for washing the dishes. These seemed to be her rules for proper attire.

She was especially well-known for a couple of desserts. Mother told me that as a young homemaker, Jennie had built a reputation among her

Grandma saying good night to Aunt Frances and two granddaughters, 1962. The apron is on, following kitchen clean-up.

diverse social groups for excellent angel food cakes. They were tall and lighter than air without being dry. The recipe was demanding, calling for twelve egg whites beaten to a high froth. When cake mixes first came on the scene, she tried a blind test on her husband and children, and they couldn't tell the difference! After that, she continued using the mix, sparing time, effort and expense, and her reputation did not falter. As Mom and Grandma saw it, the moral of the story was to let go of traditional ways if a less labor-intensive approach became available. Don't be a purist. Be practical.

By the time I came along, Grandma's specialty was apple pie. She was so adept at this, family legend held that if Granddad gave her short notice to expect people for dinner, the first thing she did was make a pie. Once this crowning glory was in the oven, then she thought about the meal. Thanks to the orchard and the cool room by the walk-in freezer, apples were available nearly year-round, and a peel rolled off her knife in a single long red or green coil. She had a simple recipe, and mixed up the dough by using an ordinary dinner fork with the strength of her arm. As an adult, I used her recipe and method many, many times. I will admit that after a few years, feeling like a pathetic weakling, I gave up the fork for a labor-saving hand tool called a pastry blender.

The seasons are passing
one by one*

Like many brilliant people, he could be gruff and highly critical. He expected everyone to live up to the standards he held for himself, and could snap at someone who disappointed him. Interestingly, none of us today can recall exactly what he said, but a critical glance and a few short words made it obvious when he was irritated. You just didn't want to irritate him. My brother remembers Granddad, in his well-ordered shop across the porch from his kitchen, teaching Ken about various tools and tasks. Ken spent these sessions feeling intimidated, knowing that the smallest mistake would bring brusque correction.

Early in their marriage, when the food was cooling on the table, Grandma had learned about her young husband's sharpness when she repeated, "Supper's ready, Henry!"

His forceful reprimand stayed with her for a lifetime: "*Never* call me twice for dinner!" It seemed she had interrupted his concentration as a then-Ph.D. student.

Yet he could be playful and even tender, and only rarely did I feel put off by his formidable personality. With few words or gestures, but the occasional smile or gentle comment, he welcomed me into his home. This was important, since I spent so much time with Grandma and shared the lunch table with both of them on innumerable ordinary days.

He was a professor at the University of Washington for thirty years, finishing with nine years as chairman of the Department

*Lyric from "Times of Your Life," Paul Anka, 1971

of Marketing, Transportation and Foreign Trade in the School of Business Administration. Earlier he had specialized in business communication and in fact, a 500-page book he authored in the early 1920s, titled *Commercial Correspondence*, was re-published in 2015 by Palala Press "as being culturally important, and... part of the knowledge base of civilization as we know it."

U.W.'s 'Mr. Chips' Will Retire Again

HENRY A. BURD

Henry A. Burd, the University of Washington's version of "Mr. Chips," is getting ready to say good-bye to the university once again in June.

Burd, acting dean of the Graduate School, began a "semiretirement" in 1945 and a permanent retirement in 1954, only to be called back into year-around service each time.

Retirement is no idle word to Burd, however. His plans include work on the three-acre grounds of his Edmonds home, independent business-consultant work and a bit of fishing.

"I never have thought of retirement as vegetation," Burd said. "There's no need to undertake an entirely different mode of life. My plans are to work right along—at my own pace."

At U. W. Since 1924

Burd joined the University of Washington faculty in 1924 and moved up to head the Department of Marketing, Transportation and Foreign Trade in 1927. He also became director of summer quarter in 1927.

The summer-quarter directorship lasted until the summer of 1945, when Burd resigned that post to begin building his home in Edmonds — a task which took him two years and four months. That summer quarter, however, was Burd's first summer vacation in 21 years of administrative work.

Teaching, administrative duties and one year as acting dean of the College of Business Administration in 1948-49 kept Burd busy until June, 1954, when he retired.

That retirement lasted only until September, when Dr. Henry Schmitz, then university president, interrupted Burd's fishing trip on the Columbia River with an urgent plea to accept a "temporary" post as acting dean of the Graduate School.

". . . A Little Longer"

"Each year I was asked to act as dean a little longer," Burd said. "So, for four years that's what I did."

Burd was graduated from Illinois Wesleyan University in 1910, received his master's and doctor-of-philosophy degrees from the University of Illinois and received a doctor-of-laws degree from Illinois Wesleyan in 1957.

Burd says that his wife, Jennie, two daughters, Mrs. James H. Reid of Edmonds and Mrs. C. V. Donaldson of Seattle, and a son, Sherman K. Burd of Bellevue, plus his eight grandchildren, will provide plenty of extra activity for this retirement.

"If I had it to do over again, I wouldn't want to change a thing," Burd said. "I've been fortunate enough to be the right man in the right spot at just the right time. What more could I want?"

Unlike my dad, Granddad was at home quite a lot. During the day, I would often see him in his book-lined study, smoking a pipe and poring over materials or writing a presentation. He had already retired, although he was called out of retirement at least twice to fill interim positions.

In our family, "the book store" was never a generic term – it referred only to the University Book Store. We never patronized other book shops. As a child, I reaped one concrete benefit from my grandfather's vocation. From 1954 until 1959, his call-back job was as acting dean of the Graduate School, and this, with his pre-retirement Business Administration connections, gave him VIP access to the Book Store. One August evening every year, when Seattle's Seafair Parade marched and drummed along University Avenue, we had balcony seats, looking down from the upstairs windows of the store. We felt like royalty.

Granddad always maintained his connection with the university through return invitations to the ivied halls, as well as through clubs and associations and numerous friendships. Periodically he threw a party for

Granddad hosting a faculty barbecue, 1956.

current and former colleagues – often a summertime barbecue, flipping burgers himself on the solid brick grill he had built by hand. I enjoyed the novelty of seeing him in his big striped apron, so relaxed, informal and friendly in the midst of the intelligentsia.

I was ten or eleven when Mother told me Granddad was planning to host a faculty cocktail party. Grandma had asked if I would like to help out. I was generally eager to do what she requested, because she made tasks interesting enough but not overwhelming, and she accepted me warmly just the way I was. At home I usually felt inferior, but not with Grandma.

I walked down the hill in my best bib and tucker, and she said she wanted me to serve drinks. I didn't know what that meant – to serve drinks. Grandma explained that I would carry a tray of mixed beverages around the living room and offer them to the guests. (As an aside, on long car rides Mother had always lullabied me with the song "Jacob's Ladder," but I had never understood the phrase, "If you love him, why not serve him." The next time I heard the song after learning to "serve," I was more confused than ever, picturing the "Soldier of the Cross" carrying a tray of cocktails to Jesus.)

Bunny hop, cousins watching, 1951. Mom and Dad are standing. I'm on Granddad's lap, Kenneth is to the right of Kandy, Carolyn (in motion) is at far right.

Even as shy as I was, circulating with the full glasses was easy. At some point in the afternoon, when I didn't have a tray in my hands, Granddad called me over to the rocking chair where he was momentarily perched. "Try this, Barbie." Standing nearby were a few professors and their wives (yes, all the professors were male!), wearing indulgent smiles. I tasted his drink – the first alcohol of my young life. It was sweet, and I liked it. He offered me another sip, to the sound of gentle chuckles all around. Then Grandma, somewhat abruptly, called me to the kitchen to help with cleanup.

Granddad's humor was revealed in small ways. He laughed easily. Generally he wasn't demonstrative with his affection, but he enjoyed his grandchildren, on his own terms.

His bread trick never failed to distract us. For group meals at their house, there was usually a plate of Wonder Bread on the table, and nearly all of us helped ourselves to a slice. During the meal, someone seated near Granddad would look the other way and, turning back to her plate, discover her bread was no longer there. "Didn't I have a piece of --?" Everyone had a first time as the butt of this joke, and my younger cousin Nancy was a frequent target, because she responded to teasing with such a jolly spirit. Whenever someone brought a friend to Sunday dinner, we were in suspense until Granddad got his chance. He would maintain a poker face just long enough for the victim to feel confused and foolish, then he'd wink and give back the bread, while everyone chortled. Personally, I had a mixed reaction to this little game, because I hated being made to feel stupid. I felt sorry for myself and anyone else who might not "know how to take a joke."

Swearing was strictly forbidden in our family, but at least once a year Granddad got his chance. At Labor Day, about 25 of us would spend a week or ten days in Long Beach, Washington. Arranging to rent the four cabins took some serious planning, and several months prior to summer, it came time to make the reservations. Granddad would get up from the dinner table, cross to where the Children's Orthopedic calendar hung on the wall over the telephone, and project his voice with a dramatic flair. "Well, who wants to go to Long Bitch?" Aunt Peggy tittered nervously, Mother harrumphed, and Grandma's lips pressed into a tight line as she rose to clear the dishes. Then Granddad took the calendar in hand and the scheduling discussion began. Of course, in the intervening decades, the word that appalled our mothers has now become completely acceptable in many settings.

The other time I heard him curse was at "the adults' table" one holiday, when I walked into the room to hear, "That's just *one* thing that's wrong with the God-damn Catholics." I never found out what had led up to that, because my mother saw me and stage-whispered to her father, "Dad!" Conversation stopped until I fetched my second serving of Jell-o and returned to the children's table, out of hearing distance. Mom was determined not to let us grow up with any prejudices – or profanity – if she could help it. I think her planning worked pretty well on the prejudices, but oh my, I hope she doesn't hear me now when I drop a dish.

At the four or five faculty parties where I helped out, I learned that Granddad enjoyed telling off-color jokes. He was generally known as a quiet, dignified man who spoke only if he had something important to say, so the effect of these "naughty stories" was enhanced by the element of surprise. Owlish expressions overtook Grandma's face and she kept busy in the kitchen alcove. Looking back, it's apparent that his inhibitions were loosened by alcohol and the admiration of a crowd he wanted to impress. To his credit, he created an atmosphere where academia let its hair down but didn't go wild.

There was a whole other side to Granddad, and this was where my daily life overlapped most with his. He had been raised on a farm and thoroughly imbued with farm-boy values. Like his wife, he epitomized these commandments from start to finish: you took care of your land as independently as possible; you reused everything you could; you spent just enough money to provide a good life and a bountiful harvest; and you never shirked hard work.

He tirelessly did the physical tasks around the place. All summer – and often throughout the year – he was outdoors. His summer work clothes were incomparable – a once-white string undershirt beneath suspenders that held up a loose pair of chinos above old canvas shoes or, for mowing, beat-up leather boots. The crowning glory was his hat. He would cut off about eight inches from the top of one of Grandma's nylon stockings, creating a tube. Turning it upside down so the reinforced section would rest just above his eyebrows, he tied a string around the other end, and pulled it over his bald head – a unique take on the "stocking" cap.

The most amazing feat I saw him perform – repeatedly – was dragging the road. Our grandparents lived at the top of an unpaved driveway shared with a neighbor. It was much longer than an ordinary driveway, and we called it "the road." Because the hill between the arterial and their house was so steep, not only did the road have two switchback curves, but in the early days, people regularly stalled out their car engines on the way up. Granddad erected a large hand-painted sign at the bottom: "USE LOW GEAR." The sign grew old, and when the lettering faded to grey, he repainted it. Not until automatic transmissions came on the scene did the sign outlive its usefulness.

Granddad maintained the road through a system I've never heard of, before or since. It involved an old watering can filled with used motor oil, and a rusty bedspring with a rope attached. He looped the rope around his chest, as if he were a mule, and walked the length of the road. As he trudged, he sprinkled the oil evenly over the surface and dragged the bedspring behind to mix the oil into the upper layer of dirt and gravel. He performed this feat twice in succession, warming up by dragging the contraption down the hill, and then at the lower end, reversing direction and pulling the heavy spring slowly back up the intensive incline, scattering oil as he went. Of course the job had to be done in dry weather, which meant warm temperatures. Seeing him out there in his nylon skullcap on a blazing summer day, I was in awe.

The surface thus created was remarkably durable, and substantially reduced erosion. A frugal man, he also found it satisfying to recycle his used oil. Sadly, at the time, we didn't realize the oil was poisoning the ground. Granddad's rules for living were being honored in the most tangible way. Sometime after the Low Gear sign came down, after protesting for years that his way was the best way, he finally gave in to family pressure and had the driveway paved.

With a lot of help from Grandma, he took care of the property. She planted, weeded and tended her extensive flower and shrub beds, fed the rabbits, managed the chickens and eggs, and worked full days in the huge vegetable and fruit garden. She gathered the family and prepared the food. He maintained the three acres, plowed the vegetable garden, pruned the berries and the fruit and nut trees, and slaughtered the livestock. He turned the compost and chopped the wood for their two fireplaces. Water to the house was provided through community channels, but for irrigation, there was a well, located between the house and the rabbit hutches, and getting the pump into working order sometimes required days of troubleshooting and repair.

The bane of the orchard was Scotch broom, a strong, fibrous, invasive weed that infested the orchard. It formed dense stands that could grow up to five feet tall, and was impossible to eradicate, since strong herbicides couldn't be used around the fruit trees. He tried to keep it down with a sickle and mower, but cutting off the above-ground part of such a stubborn plant barely discourages the roots from reaching ever farther. The Roto-Tiller, a great help in the vegetable garden, plunged wildly down the hill when he tried to use it in the

Granddad painting sealant on a pruning cut, 1942. (Orchardists no longer use sealant.)

orchard. It was an unending struggle. I never admitted to Granddad that I secretly loved inhaling the honeyed summer fragrance of the broom's golden blossoms.

There was a wide variety of apple types, ripening from summer through winter. In October, when the bulk of the apples were ready, Granddad hired one or two teenage boys to help pick them. He stored a huge stack of wooden boxes throughout the year. Attaching a trailer to his small tractor, he hauled the full boxes to his wide covered porch, where the annual cider pressing took place.

Every member of the family, and many of our friends, have joyful memories of this event. The chilly weather didn't discourage the crowd of people of all ages from actively participating. Granddad was the overlord. We dumped the fruit into a washtub full of cold water, and one by one the apples were fished out of this bath and quickly perused. Standing with one or two other women, wielding sharp paring knives in our freezing hands, I cut out major bruises or cast aside rotten apples for the compost pile. I took pride in this task, but at times I was somewhat resentful that the males got to do the more exciting jobs farther down the line. Yet I wouldn't risk trying to wedge myself between the eager, impatient youngsters at any other part of the cycle.

The clean apples were passed on to the grinder, where men and boys took turns at the crank and the chopped apples splatted into a container at the bottom. Next, the press, also operated by energetic young fellows. Then the cider was poured through a filter into sterilized gallon bottles. And the tasting began! This was the only time of year I remember Grandma making doughnuts – in fact, she may have only done it once. In any case, on that day I learned there is no better treat in the world than a hot doughnut and a cup of fresh-pressed apple juice.

There was so much cider! Afterward, each family took home a few gallons, and Granddad decided what to do with the rest. Much of it was stored in the walk-in freezer in his basement. This was a six-by-six-foot room which he had built in the days before free-standing kitchen freezers were available. It was a little tricky to make sure the glass bottles weren't too full, and sometimes one of them split open in the freezing process, a mess to clean up. Nevertheless, we always had hot spiced cider at Christmas and cold glasses of juice for other gatherings during the year.

Next to the freezer was the cold pantry lined with shelves of home-canned goods – including applesauce, apple butter and other produce that Grandma had "put up" earlier in the season – and some of the cider would be kept there for use in the coming weeks. A few times Granddad and my uncle tried to make hard cider. The right balance of conditions was difficult to achieve, and when the efforts failed, nobody could find enough ways to make use of four or five gallons of cider vinegar! This practice, labeled as wasteful, was soon discontinued.

Below the house, in the bent elbow of the road, was a small filbert (hazelnut) orchard. It sometimes seemed more trouble than it was worth. Filberts will not mature if picked unripe, but must stay on the tree until the husks surrounding the shell are brown. At that point they instantly fall from the branches. For a three or four-week period every year, Granddad gathered nuts from the ground every day or two. He rubbed off the dry leaf-like husks, then spread the filberts in shallow wooden boxes to develop their characteristic crispness.

The orchard had been neglected for some time before Granddad bought the property, and as he nurtured the soil and the trees, more nuts were produced. However, with the increase in available food, non-human scavengers also became more numerous. Granddad developed a vendetta against Steller's Jays, the obvious raiders in that patch of land. One day he declared war, went out with his shotgun and managed to kill a jay. He strung the dead body on a wire above the nut orchard with the intent of discouraging other birds.

I had always thought the jays were the most beautiful birds I'd ever seen, with their unlikely brilliant blue feathers. On the day when, returning home from the school bus, I saw the carcass swinging over the filbert trees, I was sickened. Who could have done such a thing? Mother found out the truth and explained it to me as gently as possible, but I couldn't accept killing a bird as an answer to any problem.

We didn't get noticeably more nuts than the year before. The jays may have been repelled or not, nobody was sure. But because we kids walked by the trees every morning and afternoon in the fall, we became eyes for the family.

And what did we see? Dozens of fat, busy squirrels. Squirrels, not birds.

Soon we could no longer give the nuts-in-shell as gifts, because a large proportion of the ones we gathered were empty. The squirrels had a knack for gauging by weight whether there was a nutmeat inside, and they left the hollow shells intact for the foolish humans. We cousins were then drafted for nut-cracking parties after the drying period, a rather tiresome task when so many shells opened to nothingness. The filberts we did find, Grandma glazed in a sugar syrup. She gave jars of this confection to friends and family.

I was never allowed to see my grandmother's response to the jay incident, but her silence on the topic was thick and expressive. After all, it was primarily from her that I had absorbed an abiding love of birds. I imagined that, like me, she felt jays were only seeking food and couldn't help their marauding habits. Teaching them a lesson was as likely as persuading them to change the color of their feathers.

The final episode of the nut story gave me a perverse satisfaction. A neighbor had heard the gunshots that brought down the jay. Although the police could hardly believe her claim that the esteemed Dr. Burd was the culprit, they had to act on the complaint, and came to the house. Granddad confessed to the crime and received an official warning for discharging a firearm in a populated area. I had never heard of him shooting anything prior to that, and I never heard of it again.

As my grandparents aged, they seemed to become even more companionable. In a play on their last name of Burd, they called each other Twit and Twitter. They maintained traditional gender roles until the end, but they increasingly seemed like helpmeets as their work was more often done side by side. In the evenings they watched TV, both falling asleep in their chairs, then rousing themselves just enough to cross the hall and climb into the bed they always shared.

Grandma died first. To my knowledge, Granddad had not set foot in a church since their wedding some seven decades earlier, and I suspect that whatever evil he attributed to "the God-damn Catholics" had tainted all religions in his mind. When Grandma died, to the dismay of her children and grandchildren, Granddad adamantly refused to allow a memorial service of any kind. She had attended the local Methodist church whenever she could get a ride there, and the pastor sided with her children in this controversy. In the end, forbidden an actual funeral, this minister devoted an entire Sunday morning worship service to Grandma – sermon, hymns and readings. Many family members, notified in advance, were

Granddad and Grandma on their fiftieth wedding anniversary, December, 1962. Grandma blinked!

present for this touching tribute. Granddad stayed home.

Once she was gone, he came completely unmoored. Family and friends helped as much as they could, but he was dazed by the loss. Months later, as an undergraduate at the UW, I was shocked to see Granddad's name listed as a guest speaker for a course I was taking. Something prevented me from telling my fellow students, "My grandfather is coming!" I ended up relieved that I had not bragged. His lecture, read woodenly from the podium, was one of the dullest presentations I had ever seen. There were about seventy-five students in the class, and I never told him I'd been in the auditorium when he spoke. Today, I realize that not only was he nearly eighty years old, but Grandma had died no more than a year earlier. The worst of bad timing.

After a mourning period, with some intensive match-making by Aunt Peggy, Granddad married Ruby, a dear old friend whose husband had died earlier. She lived in California and the newlyweds moved there. Sadly, before long he was diagnosed with dementia and lived in a Seattle area nursing home for a time before passing on. I'm ashamed to say that I never made an effort to visit him there. My parents discouraged it. Granddad had been an almost revered patriarch and intellectual, and Mother wanted everyone to remember him that way, not as an incoherent and unruly patient who needed to be confined in a secure facility. I accepted her guidance. Paralleling her desire to protect me from all unpleasantness, I guess that's what I wanted for myself too.

He died in 1972. True to form, Granddad had made one thing clear. The newspaper obituary read, "At his request there will be no funeral services." It went on to state, "A memorial service will be announced." In the end, there was no memorial, which probably would have suited him fine.

I've loved you since
heaven knows when*

Since Grandma never learned to drive, it was fortunate that some aspects of the world came to her. Every few days, the milkman delivered glass bottles of milk with the cream floating on top. She poured off some of the cream, then shook the bottle well – home-style homogenization. The full bottles were stored in the stubby, round-cornered Crosley refrigerator that had recently replaced her icebox.

Wednesday was bread day. The bakery truck forged its way up from Snake Road to stop between her tulip bed and the porch steps. When she heard the truck climbing the incline in a growling low gear, she hustled out in her shirtwaist dress and apron to make her selections. Frugal as they were, she and Granddad rarely bought anything beyond plain bread or rolls, but I welcomed the chance to peek into the truck and inhale the mouth-watering fragrance of cinnamon buns and doughnuts.

For major grocery shopping and necessary chores, Granddad seemed very willing to chauffeur his wife when he wasn't at the University. She was healthy and active, and for smaller shopping trips, she often walked and took the bus. The nearest bus stop was at the end of the line where the bus's northeasterly direction swiveled to return southwest to downtown Edmonds. From her house, this turning point was nearly a mile's trek on the narrow shoulder of Snake Road. I thought nothing of this fact until one day when I accompanied her to catch the bus and fetch a few groceries. Getting

* Lyric from "There! I've Said It Again," Redd Evans and David Mann, 1945

there was a hike. Coming back up the driveway carrying the parcels was a real climb.

Her top-priority weekly commitment was to what she called her "Orthopedic group." This was one of many local women's guilds dedicated to stitching hospital gowns, robes and blankets for the medical center that started its life as Children's Orthopedic Hospital (now called Seattle Children's). I accompanied her to the meeting place once or twice. We met in a one-room cabin in Mrs. Watts' back yard. There were several sewing machines, only a few of which were electric. After initial greetings, the ladies went right to their tasks, and in minutes treadles were clacking, needles thrumming and garments rolling off the machines. Grandma must have taken me there as a favor to Mother, because there were no activities for a child. I was allowed to watch quietly, look at magazines, or work the treadle on an out-of-service machine whose needle had been removed. I was also free to walk around the yard, a grassy area surrounded by colorful hydrangeas and rhododendrons.

Their conversation as they stitched, and during their lunch break in the main house, was much less interesting than the talks between Mother and Grandma, and I wondered how they could bear to come together every week for such dull entertainment. Looking back, I'm sure that having a seven-year-old in their midst, listening intently, had a dampening effect on their expressive freedom.

I had met a few of the women on different occasions when they visited Grandma. I especially remember the ladies who are in the right-hand side of the picture. Mrs. Bell, to the right of my grandmother in the photo, lived with her husband not far from us. Their green-roofed white house beside Snake Road was hidden behind a hedge as thick as a city wall. I visited her home a few times with my grandmother, and she was as sweet as anyone I've ever met. Lotchie Woodruff, next to Mrs. Bell, was a rather outspoken friend whose name was often mentioned in Grandma's *tête-à-têtes* with my mother.

At far right is Mrs. Hollowell. Her home was on our own dead-end street. I believe she was a relatively young widow – she lived alone, which tinged her with a certain outsider status in our hyper-traditional world. Her place was always completely darkened on Halloween, leading the neighborhood children to declare that a witch must live there, and dare each other to dash down the curving driveway and

North Edmonds Ladies Have Enjoyable Time Sewing For Red Cross & Hospitals

Edmonds Tribune-Review, 1953. Grandma is fourth from right.

knock on the door. Then we – pirates and hobos, princesses and pumpkins – ran like hell, not knowing whether we were excited or scared. We never saw her. Meantime, Mrs. Hollowell was probably happily spending the night elsewhere. Being introduced to her at the sewing circle, I was abashed to find that she, like the other women there, was very kind to me. I made a mental note: No witch.

Being opposed to religion of any kind, Granddad didn't give Grandma rides to church as often as she would have liked. As a child, I didn't realize how important this must have been to her. She had a small pump organ between the kitchen and hallway, and on its music rack rested a hymnal, but I didn't hear her play or sing the sacred songs, and never knew Grandma was devout. In fact, we kids often fooled around with the organ, pulling and pushing the stops and pumping our feet madly, and more than once we broke one or the other of the pedals, rendering the instrument silent yet again. This would bring a droop to

Grandma's shoulders, which made me sad, but I didn't connect the loss of the organ with a more important loss for her, the opportunity to connect with her spiritual source in her home.

When *my* mother died, more than two decades after *her* mother's death, I found a small two-ring binder Grandma had kept. On the cover she had pasted what must have had an earlier incarnation as a greeting card, bearing a hand-colored illustration and the familiar poem "God's Garden" by Dorothy F. Gurney:

> The kiss of the sun for pardon,
> The song of the birds for mirth,
> One is nearer God's heart in a garden
> Than anywhere else on earth.

To make pages for the little notebook, she had cut up unused stationery from some of the colleges where Granddad worked, and punched ragged holes for the rings. She hand-copied poems onto some of the pages. On most, she pasted one or two quotations clipped from magazines. The first fifty pages or so contain odes to nature, gardens and the seasons. This is consistent with how I knew my grandmother.

Past the halfway point, however, there are increasing mentions of God, and increasing sadness in the poems. Here is the first stanza of "Faith" by Edgar Guest:

> When sorrow comes, as come it must,
> In God a man must place his trust;
> There is no power in mortal speech
> The anguish of his soul to reach.
> No voice, however sweet and low,
> Can comfort him or ease the blow.

The air around me grew heavy as I read one of the few unrhymed poems, "Loneliness" by Dorothy Arnette:

> Loneliness is a fog
> Covering my soul;
> Through its wrap

My heart reaches out
Desperately
In vain
Trying to free itself.

Here is one in Grandma's handwriting, that got me thinking: "Unity" by Leona Bacon:

Can two walk together
Except they agree?
This ponderable question
Was presented to me;
So in quest of an answer
I have searched near and far,
I have queried with sages
And men of the bar,
Who shake their heads sadly
And boldly declare,
Though many have tried it
Exceptions are rare.
In the Book of the Ages
This answer I find:
Be ye equally yoked
And of the same mind;
For the yoke, they will find,
On the steep up-hill road,
Must be equally borne
To balance life's load.

She took the trouble to copy this out. It makes me wonder about the sacrifices – physical, emotional and spiritual – that she made to maintain her marriage as an effective partnership. How many times did she find she must agree with her husband, when if her deepest truth were told, she was not "of the same mind"?

Mother and I took Grandma to church with us sometimes. She seemed to find special meaning in the Methodist hymn "Are Ye Able:"

Are ye able, said the Master, to be crucified with me?
Yea, the sturdy dreamers answered, to the death we follow Thee!
Lord, we are able, our spirits are Thine.
Remold them, make us like Thee, divine.

Along with several favorites of my own, through repetition I
memorized the first verses of this song. I wish I'd explored why it
meant so much to my grandmother. It's apparent that she had a much
harder life than I imagined, and relied on her spiritual beliefs to lift her
from hardship and heartbreak.

For my twelfth birthday, Grandma gave me a new Bible, and signed
the flyleaf with both their names. I had an inkling of Granddad's scorn
for religion, and found it curious to receive such a religious gift in his
name. As far as I knew, no one in the family read the Bible, and even with
my very own book, I've never read it either, except for a few selections.
But I do use it as a resource, and I'm deeply thankful to have this gift that
meant so much to her, with her own handwriting inside the cover.

Outside the circle of family and close friends, Grandma was often
shy and uncertain, so she wasn't generally interested in travel. She made
an exception when her first grandchild entered the world thousands
of miles away. She found her way to San Francisco and boarded the
Matson steamer
Lurline. It was
1941 and Carolyn
had been born the
previous autumn.
My parents,
with their new
daughter, were
living at Hickam
Field, adjacent
to Pearl Harbor.
Grandma
enjoyed the
baby, and made it

Jac, Carolyn, and Grandma in Hawaii, 1941.

back to the mainland a few months before the devastating December 7 bombing of the harbor and the commissioning of the *Lurline* as a troop transport. (The day following the terrifying attack, Carolyn toddled across the back yard and found a solid hunk of iron shrapnel nearly as big as her head. It had been fired from a US anti-aircraft gun, and had half-buried itself in their lawn.)

At five, I learned to tie my own shoe laces. It was Mother whose steady attention brought me to this grand achievement, but it was Grandma who, to my way of thinking, had to be told – immediately! I can still feel my little-girl heart swell with pride, still feel the packed-earth path pounding joyfully against the soles of my feet and the wind breathing against my face, as I charged down the hill to her house. I found her busily tending to some chore in the tiddly room. She stopped everything and listened to my proud announcement. Then she made me untie and re-tie the shoes as proof of mastery, and gave me a big hug of congratulations. Her response was ample and sufficient.

Other than the Bible, I don't recall many gifts Grandma gave me, except for the one that was a mistake. I celebrated my sixth birthday in Florida, missing my grandma. To make matters worse, a few weeks passed before a package arrived from Edmonds – it had been delayed in the mail. I was amazed that Grandma could give me a present from so far away, and I could hardly wait to see what it was. She had always known me so well.

But inside the box was a truly perplexing item: a dress made of paper. I'm sure my face fell, because Mother immediately came forth in a lilting tone with, "Oh! This is the latest thing! I've heard about these new dresses, they're very pretty – and fun to wear. Blue, your favorite color. You're going to look so cute in it!" The dress crumpled and crackled as I lifted it out of the box, and when I obediently put it on, it was wrinkled, scratchy and stiff. Impossible. Mother directed the scene and I posed, with a smile, under the orange trees. I'm sure Grandma enjoyed the photos and Mom's letter of thanks, and I never saw the dress after that day. In my childish mind, I created the convenient fiction that there had been some mix-up and it wasn't really Grandma who sent this present!

As a farmer's daughter, she had learned home crafts early. In her living room and the sitting room off the kitchen, the floor coverings were braided rugs. At age eight, I asked her to show me how to make them. I had no concept of the lengthy process involved. After several requests, she outlined the steps: collecting old woolen clothing, tearing or cutting it into strips, stitching those strips into long tubes ("Some people don't do that, but then the edges ravel, and you have a rag rug. My rugs don't look like rags."). These long sections were joined end to end to form a tube the length of several boa constrictors. You needed three of them, and the braiding was heavy labor. You had to make sure the braids lay flat as you hand-sewed them into a coil. "It's a lot of work," she smiled. "I might not be making a braided rug for a while." She probably already knew that "a while" would last the rest of her life.

On the other hand, she taught me to crochet when I was seven, and we often

Barbie, just turned six, in the paper dress, 1952

sat together doing our needlework. I mastered the "granny square" at her knee, which seems singularly appropriate. She herself, meantime, was crocheting her own plentiful granny afghans or other items for gifts. She fashioned thin cotton thread into intricate doilies and antimacassars. A couple of the doilies rested on tables in her living room, but in general she didn't like fussy decor, and gave these items to friends. The largest of her thread projects that I recall was a double-bed cover that made me think of lace snowflakes. Every summer morning, she arranged it atop a yellow sheet that she and Granddad used as an under-spread, and every night they removed it together, folding it on the cedar chest at the foot of the bed.

My most cherished memories of Grandma are our beach breakfasts. Once in a while when I arrived at her place early on a warm morning, she put a pint bottle of milk, two tiny boxes of dry cereal, and spoons into a basket and led me to the lower garden. We picked raspberries into a little square box, then we set out for the beach. We strode down her steep, zigzag driveway, across Snake Road, and down the University Colony road until we crossed the makeshift bridge and the train tracks. Re-juggling our burdens, we descended the ladder and made our way southward, finding our footing on the gravelly surface.

Among the tumbled boulders supporting the railroad bed, there were one or two large granite slabs with flat horizontal surfaces. We designated one of these as our table, and settled ourselves on driftwood logs next to it. The waves made rhythmic shushing sounds as they slipped up the beach, then a sort of hissing rattle as they receded, drawing clattering pebbles back toward the deep water. Our wax-lined cereal boxes were cleverly designed to be opened along the side, so we could add the berries, pour in the milk, and eat our breakfast together in this phenomenal dining room. My senses reeled with the taste of berries, the salt smell of parched seaweed, and the piercing remarks of gulls. I'll always treasure these moments of pure connection – connection with this dear, loving person, and also with the earth that provided our fruit and the unique setting on the shore of Puget Sound.

There's a photo showing the moment of return from one of Grandma's rare trips, this one with Granddad. During the 1950s he was a marketing consultant and faculty member of the Advanced Management Seminar of Western Canada, and made a number of visits to Banff, Alberta. When he was gone, I often stayed overnight at Grandma's, sleeping on the day bed in the study or, at her request, sharing their bed with her. But one time he persuaded her to see the northern Rockies with him, and afterward, when we met them at the Edmonds train depot, she looked very happy – whether she had enjoyed the adventure or was just glad to be home, I don't know.

Although in my own way, I continued to love and admire my grandmother, in the teen years I was challenged to hold myself together. At sixteen, I was just beginning to emerge from the despair of an undiagnosed three-year depression. Oblivious to my mental state and baffled by my ongoing surly behavior, Mother directed her concern at my hay fever. She and I both had difficult symptoms including long-lasting nosebleeds. She heard about an injection treatment for young people with respiratory allergies, and the nearest available clinic was in Portland, Oregon. Since Mom was working, she drafted Grandma as my traveling companion.

Mother, Grandma, me, Granddad and Ken at Edmonds train depot upon grandparents' return from Banff, 1958. Granddad wears the enigmatic expression of a professor who just told a well-timed joke.

The two of us arrived at Seattle's King Street Station a little late. I hardly ever went anywhere either, and was already nervous and excited, and then we had to run for the train. Something happened to Grandma on the way. By the time we reached the steep steps into the train car, she was gasping for breath to the point of nearly sobbing. She wouldn't tell me what the problem was, and throughout the next three days she was tense and preoccupied. I thought that her responsibility for handling arrangements and finding her way in a strange city was weighing on her and making her edgy. A semi-stable, self-absorbed teenager, I couldn't (or didn't) find a way to reach out to her – her clamped lips and furrowed brow were forbidding.

It was a year or so before Mother explained the mystery. Grandma confided in her that dashing through the station had triggered a bladder emergency. She had wet herself. Even though I was right next to her for hours and I never guessed, nonetheless she was humiliated and ashamed. How she managed to deal with the immediate problem, I haven't figured out, but she spent the rest of our trip rigid with fear that it would happen again.

Grandma had always been hale and hearty, a steady source of acceptance and assurance in my life. For the 1964 Christmas holidays, instead of returning to Edmonds from college in Walla Walla, I accepted a classmate's invitation to visit her family in Montana. This novel trip meant I was away from my own family throughout the winter. Long-distance phone calls were unusual in my world, but in January Mother called me at school to say that Grandma was very ill. Shocked, I asked if I should come home, and when Mom said Grandma didn't want me to, I accepted her recommendation.

That decision is one of my few serious regrets in life. I wish I had looked her in the eye once more and given back a scintilla of all the love she had poured into me. A tenet of our family culture was to avoid things that were defined as unpleasant. Dying was certainly in that category. Grandma died February 9, 1965.

The disease was multiple myeloma, a rare diagnosis at the time. It had taken the doctors far too long to identify the problem. In those early days, the only treatment was total blood transfusion, and she was transfused twice. These procedures were painful, difficult, and only briefly effective, since the bone marrow continued to produce blood teeming with cancer cells. Bone marrow transplants hadn't been invented.

I missed her last days on earth, and a light had gone out in my world. A Sunday morning church service was dedicated to her in lieu of a funeral. I'm so glad this bit of ceremony was concocted in spite of Granddad's objections to memorials of all kinds. The pastor had interviewed family members, and supplemented his sermon that morning with appreciative words about Jennie Burd. Congregational voices lifted, like a toast to her, in her favorite hymn, "Are Ye Able":

Thy guiding radiance above us shall be
A beacon to God, to love and loyalty.

I didn't know her as well as I wish I had. But I always loved her, and I always knew that she loved me without reservation, a gift beyond measure.

Every summer we can rent a cottage in the Isle of Wight*

Bruce and I jumped out from the back seat and ran across the sharp rocks as fast as our bare feet would take us.

"Ow, ow, ow!"

"I won!"

He almost always beat me. "You practiced at home!" Innocently rolling his eyes to the heavens, he gave me a one-sided smile of victory with a hint of apology. He had figured out that the annual race required preparation, and he'd been toughening up his feet on rough surfaces for a week.

This major track event consisted of a sprint from car to cabin, a distance of four or five yards. But it was the ceremonial starting flag, for the two of us, of a week of carefree fun.

Long Beach, Washington, was a one-street town where our extended family spent every Labor Day. We always stayed at the City Center Motel, composed of about twenty cabins arranged in a horseshoe around a crushed-rock courtyard.

The centerpiece of the court was the boat – or, more accurately, the statue of a boat – a simple fishing vessel made of concrete. The stern was concave, about the size of two bathtubs. If you were small, with some effort you could pull yourself up from that sunken hold onto the narrow side deck or the bow, and climb into the cabin through a window. The tiny cabin was one of the rare play places where the littler kids had an advantage over the bigger ones, and as we crouched in that cramped space, we did gloat a bit. Two of us could squeeze

* Lyric from "When I'm Sixty-Four," Paul McCartney, 1967

inside – no more – and year by year, we all sadly outgrew the arched openings. Nancy, youngest and most petite of the seven of us, was the last to leave it behind, until her little sister Stephanie was born a long while later and we all gathered around to indoctrinate the baby into the joys of the boat. We were, by turns, pirates, captains and mates, and wrestlers in the hold. Once I stood on the prow for some minutes, envisioning myself as a graceful carved figurehead angled bravely into the oncoming swells. (In fact, absorbed in my mental imagery, I leaned so far forward that I nearly toppled into the foaming brine–I mean onto the gravel.) It's amazing how much entertainment we invented on that boat, since to the untrained eye it was nothing

City Center Motel and the boat, 1966.

but a hunk of cement surrounded by gravel.

The real fun, though, was in the town and on the beach. The little settlement was the only populated place in my young life where I was allowed to wander around without an adult. Nancy, Bruce and I, the youngest of our respective families, were a troupe who went from store to store on our own as soon as we were old enough to understand a dime and a quarter. With my deep-rooted sweet tooth, naturally I was most drawn to The Candy Man, whose name was George. He had a square, open face, dark hair, glasses, and a white apron. His shop was clean and white and redolent of vanilla and butterscotch. George was friendly to us kids, but not too friendly, and his businesslike

198

manner made us feel quite grown-up. After the first couple of visits, he recognized us, but didn't use our names, just a simple, "Well! Here you are again! What are you thinking you'd like today?" We gravitated to his candied popcorn loaded with caramel and peanuts. The rich chocolate fudge was his most expensive item, so it was a fudge day only if we were carrying a little extra change. At least once per summer we asked for cotton candy, partly for the joy of watching George twirl the long paper cone in the glass-sided machine until it was thickly wrapped with airy pink spun sugar.

Across the street from George's was the Milton York Candy Company. For the longest time we didn't patronize that store. They didn't sell individual servings, and their products were on the costly side. I had the impression that slightly grubby, barefoot children weren't really welcome. But eventually we discovered salt water taffy, those soft, chewy morsels individually wrapped in waxed-paper squares. Amazingly, George didn't carry this confection. I think it was Nancy who came up with the idea of getting money from the grown-ups to buy a taffy assortment for the whole family. Then with a little effort, on the way home we managed to unseal the white cardboard box imprinted with the Milton York logo and skim off one piece for each of us.

The other establishment where I remember shopping bore the word "Notions" on the front window. (I think spools of thread were among the items for sale.) When you unlatched the door, an indescribable odor came out to meet you – the heavy, musty scent of damp old books, combined with a tired, salty smell like seaweed at low tide. We bought an occasional comic book or magazine there, but I suspected that if you went in looking for a newspaper in 1956, you might accidentally go home with the 1939 edition. We were fascinated not with the products, but with the proprietress. Our name for her was "the bun lady," because she wore her hair in two thin braids, coiled into tight spirals which covered her ears. This style amused us greatly. I had nothing against braids – my mother had them, but Mom's were full-bodied, and bountifully wound around the top of her head like a crown. This narrow lady with the human-hair ear muffs watched us with squinted eyes and barely spoke except to snap, "Don't touch those comics unless you're buying them!" The suffocating atmosphere confirmed that customers rarely opened the front door to the fresh breezes outside, and you got the feeling the shopkeeper preferred it that way. She was so exceptional that in our private conversations we invented a number of alternate back stories for her, favoring the Russian-princess-in-reduced-circumstances version.

We went with some of the older kids to Marsh's Free Museum, near the far end of town. Its outdoor display boasted such curiosities as The Largest Frying Pan in the World (14.6 feet), which dangled from a beam laid across a pair of sturdy posts; an authentic totem pole stolen, no doubt, from a native tribe near or far; and Jake the Alligator Man, a crude carved human head stuck on a very realistic stuffed alligator's body, the whole thing coated in glossy black paint. Marsh's, to us, was the world center of oddities, a large, warehouse-like space with glass cases displaying other supposed wonders of nature, along with table arrangements of cheap souvenirs, racks of postcards, and genuine sea shells which were probably imported along with the trinkets. We came to look and marvel, rarely to spend, although I did once hand over twenty-five cents for an irresistible South Seas shell.

When we were small, two or three of us were allowed to play without adult supervision on the first sand hill that rose behind the court, as long as we stayed within sight of the back of the cabins. Although no one watched us out the back, if anything happened, one of us could find help within seconds. This freedom would be unheard-of today, but we were able to trust the world in those days. And we stayed in sight, knowing we needed to earn the faith that our parents were placing in us. I remember making roads in the dry sand, burying each other's feet and legs, and studying the tiny flowers on the spidery plants that survived in that desert environment.

The front of our motel court was on the road to the beach, but we preferred to avoid the road and wend our way over the dunes. The dunes weren't massive like those on the Oregon coast, but at low points you could still lose all directional clues. It was fun to master a simple "orienteering" skill: ascend to the top of the closest hill, listen for the steady roar of the ocean, and look back at the cabins to get your bearings. I loved ploughing through the soft sand, up into the wind and down into the protected valleys. Outings to the beach comprised different assortments of children with one or two adults, until we were teens and allowed to go in our own group. Nobody went alone.

The beach itself was always windy, and the wind had a sweep of several long, flat miles. It was no place to relax or sunbathe, although our dutiful parents cheerfully took their turns watching the big kids in the surf and the little ones on the sand.

Barbie, Bruce and Ken, Long Beach, WA, 1947.

The grownups memorized the tides to keep us safe. If the tide was coming in, we could float, and I remember the buoyant delight of letting the waves carry me to the beach – always at an angle, as the prevailing current landed us a dozen yards north of our entry point. At changing or ebb tides, we were permitted to go into the water only up to our knees. On such a flat surface, the water was shallow for at least a football field's length from the edge. This gave us nothing to do but jump miniature breakers, chase each other, and splash. We'd walk out to see how close to the actual ocean we could get and still be in the shallows. The parents kept a close eye and hollered, almost loud enough to be heard over the waves: "That's far enouuuugh!" We'd turn and look, heads tilted to the side, as if we didn't know what they were saying. "Come baaack!" was accompanied by full-body beckoning gestures. We never quite believed the ocean was as dangerous as they said, but their concern made us nervous enough to obey.

These annual respites started before I can clearly remember. Probably I was four or five. Altogether, there were our two grandparents, Peggy and Van with two boys, Sherm and Frances with two girls (later three), and the five of us. This assemblage was "the whole fam-damily," an exceptional term which was *not* considered profanity.

The patriarch and matriarch rented what we called "the main cabin," where the living room and kitchen were (barely) large enough to feed the crowd. Each of the other nuclear families had a smaller cabin, used mostly for sleeping. Perhaps because the smaller cabins had space for only four, I often stayed in the extra bedroom in Grandma and Granddad's place. Nancy was invited to join me overnight once in a while. I really loved "belonging to" the main house. If you lived there, you didn't miss much of the action. And I was away from any nighttime friction between my siblings or Mom and Dad – when Dad's work commitments allowed him to join us there.

Sometimes the aunts and uncles and cousins had breakfast or lunch in their own little kitchens, but most meals – except the picnics – were in the main cabin. Throughout the dozens of Labor Days, the dinner planning consisted of variations on a single theme: each household of my parents' generation planned and provided one supper for all of us, supervising its preparation in the main kitchen. That took care of Friday, Saturday, and Sunday, the evenings when most everyone was there. Grandma and Granddad arrived in Long Beach early, and there were years when they stayed until Tuesday to miss the weekend traffic, since they didn't need to get children back to their neighborhoods for the first day of school. There were occasions when Cousin Bruce and I rode all the way to the coast in our grandparents' car – a huge privilege – but we were stuck with our own families for the drive home.

Aunt Peggy was by far the most extraverted and fun-loving of the adults. She established a tradition that created a crazy sort of clan bonding – the flotsam and jetsam parade. One morning she would announce that today was the day, along with the cheerful yet firm proclamation, "If you do not march in the parade, you don't get dinner tonight."

Costumes had to involve some object found at Long Beach. You can do a lot with cast-off clam and oyster shells, but beyond those, there weren't many ornamental nautical materials in the area. We might stoop so low as to bejewel ourselves with little plastic toys that forgetful children had abandoned in the sand. Lucky the person who found a round glass float that had washed in from a Japanese fishing net across the sea! A prize as special as that didn't have to be worn – you'd just carry it like a king's orb. Once in a while someone planned ahead and made a coconut shell bra or a cowrie necklace, but this was considered cheating, since coconuts do not wash up at Long Beach. For color, we were encouraged to wear our brightest, most mismatched clothing.

No parade is complete without a band, so we clamored out a marching rhythm with spoons on cooking pots like nursery school children, nearly hysterical with the absurdity of it all. Aunt Peg led the parade around the inside of the motel court, circling the boat twice, to ensure that all other guests had the chance to see and hear us before we went in to supper. There really was very little public exposure, but we all whooped in sympathy in the middle of one procession when Peggy's embarrassed son Bruce, a dried-kelp hula skirt tied over his cut-off jeans, cried out, "Sometimes I wish I was a motherless child!"

Picnics and campfires were high points for me. At least one evening every summer – unless the fog came in too thick and early – we packed up blankets, firewood, hot dogs, marshmallows, and all the accoutrements and trooped across the dunes to find some lovely secluded spot, protected from the wind and still warm from the sun, where we ate and sang and laughed. We all chimed in while Uncle Van plunked out "Peg O' My Heart" on his ukelele and Aunt Peg

blushed and shook her head. Cousin Janice learned to play guitar as
a teenager, and she led us in songs of the day, starting with "Michael,
Row the Boat Ashore." And no campfire went by without "Swing
Low, Sweet Chariot." Before it was fully dark out, we made our way
back to the cabins, warm of heart and sandy of trouser.

One morning each year, I was awakened well before dawn by
men's voices on the other side of my bedroom wall. It was fishing day!
Grandma made breakfast at four or five in the morning, sending off
thermos bottles of hot coffee with Granddad, Van, Sherm, and Dad
(if he was there) as they drove to Ilwaco to go salmon fishing on the
charter boat owned and operated by Art Randall, a friend of Granddad.
When they grew old enough, Dale and Kenneth joined the other
fellows on this expedition. I neither knew nor cared anything about
fishing itself, but we were all included in portions of the annual ritual.

When the fishers returned, they showed off their prey, and proud
photos were taken of each one holding up his catch. I learned that
a big fish was a badge of high achievement and seemed to have
something to do with graduating from boy to man. Once in a while,
one of the fellows got "skunked" – that is, caught nothing while
everyone else pulled in fish. Congratulations and mild insults were
exchanged as the men gutted their fish at the outdoor cleaning stations
at the edge of the motel court. Granddad's rule was, "You catch it,
you clean it." I avoided watching this smelly, gory procedure, even if
someone exclaimed, "Wow, look here! This one's full of eggs!" To my
knowledge, caviar was never a delicacy enjoyed by the Burd family.

That night we had plentiful, fresh-caught, baked salmon for
dinner. And when the catch was especially bountiful, we canned what
we couldn't eat right away. Yes, we canned it then and there! The
commercial cannery at Ilwaco offered hand-canning machines for
rent. I never understood how this process could be safely done in a
motel kitchen with people constantly walking through – chances of
contamination must have been very high. But as I recall, various people,
led by Granddad, took turns cutting the fish in chunks and packing it
in the wide cans. Then the youngsters had their chance to rotate the

crank, sealing the lid. By some means the cans were heated, cooking the salmon within. In that way, we were all able to take home portions of the catch, in the era before freezers were commonly available.

One year my mother made a bold and unheard-of decision. She requested to go out with the men on Art's boat. Somewhat baffled but agreeable, they opened their ranks and included her. They all departed in the dark that morning, as always.

In mid-afternoon the motel office received a rather alarming phone call. Art had radioed the harbormaster, who called the motel to ask someone to meet the boat when it landed – one of the party wasn't well. With the women talking among themselves in hushed tones, we rode down to Ilwaco. "There it is, that's Art's boat coming in!" The vessel tied up to the dock and Mother staggered off, gray and weak, rain-drenched, scarf triangled tightly over her head, feet wobbling in borrowed rubber boots, arms supported by a pair of the fishermen. My mom, normally the Rock of Gibraltar to all of us, had been defeated by the elements. To use a common expression of her own, she looked like she'd been pulled through a knothole.

The one outing she chose to join happened to be the stormiest fishing trip Art ever remembered, and Mother was seasick as soon as they pulled out of the harbor. He had offered to bring her back in. She absolutely refused. She reasoned that once they crossed the bar at the notorious mouth of the Columbia River, the waves would settle down. But out at sea a tempest raged, and Art wrestled the pitching, rolling boat through massive waves. There were a few non-family charter customers on board, and the majority voted to keep fishing, since this was everyone's last day of vacation. Most likely Mom didn't vote to throw in the towel either, not willing to be the weak female ruining everyone's day. She was sick for hours.

Although I asked, I never learned what had motivated her to undertake this outing in the first place. I wonder if she just wanted to know what it was like, or perhaps wanted to show her daughters (and son) that no activity is the property of one gender. It was many decades before the term "women's liberation" was coined, but she was an exceptional person. Characteristically, once her normal heartiness was restored, she minimized the experience. "I was fine, no need for anyone to worry." On the other hand, she did admit, "Well, no, I don't think I'll want to go out again next year."

Beard's Hollow is an ocean inlet near the south end of the Long Beach Peninsula. In a short convoy, we drove through the settlement of Seaview on a series of two-lane roads and parked on the shoulder to hike down into the hollow. Hills and rocky outcroppings surrounded the fjord, and storm-tossed driftwood was jumbled on the shore. The topography of the hollow created a zone of bright, fickle sea breezes, in contrast to the strong steady wind on the Long Beach waterfront. Fascinating beachcombing finds could be snagged among the rocks. We kids played in the low surf and balanced along the helter-skelter weathered logs.

Our supervisors found a shaded indentation in the base of a bluff to set down the picnic basket, then puttered among the driftwood and stones to find treasures. I believe it was here that Mother found the J-shaped log that became her living-room table lamp. Here also, Mom started her collection of small sea-polished rocks and bits of driftwood, from which she crafted unique natural pendants for gifts one Christmas.

My cousins and siblings had some lively adventures climbing around on the tall rocks. For complicated reasons, I refused to join them. At first the crumbling cliff faces frightened me a bit, but I was more scared of making a fool of myself than I was of anything else – slipping, falling, not finding a handhold, and especially being made fun of for my clumsiness. I was a year older than Nan, and I was in safe territory as long as we both stayed at beach level. But when she began climbing, the others taunted me. "Baby Barbie!" I was the only one left on the ground. The more they teased, the more adamant I became. In all our years there, right through high-school age, I never joined them in mounting the heights.

Despite that particular drama, I remember Beard's Hollow as a singularly lovely place combining steep hills topped with twisted pines, a crescent beach with lapping waves, sunshine and cool shadows, and fogs that draped the cliffs so that they stood out in receding layers, each paler than the one before it.

As I approached my teens, life became confusing and Long Beach changed for me, in both obvious and subtle ways. We never foresaw traffic becoming an issue, as it did when the road between the shore and the town grew crowded with cars and RVs parked along the narrow asphalt lane. Vehicles were also allowed on the damp sand parallel to the coast, and the flat 28-mile stretch had a tendency to turn

Beard's Hollow, 1951. Guess who's at the base of the cliff?

into a speedway, so it was risky to cross from the dunes to the water, and once you got there, the roar of engines competed with the rush and shush of the ocean.

And of course, we cousins changed.

Dale bought a Jeep. Outside of a buckboard, I can't imagine a more jarring ride – hard tires, hard suspension, and hard seats. It was a basic, or sub-basic, model. He told us that a police officer had tried to cite him for insufficient equipment because his vehicle had no windshield wipers. "But officer, it has no windshield. Why would it need wipers?" According to Dale, that got him off the hook.

In spite of everything it lacked, the Jeep was a cool venue for adolescent posturing, so we all rode in it from time to time for a few years. And it didn't take Dale long to find a profitable use for it. He noticed that a lot of inexperienced drivers veered off the firm surface and got stuck in the soft sand. He equipped the Jeep with towing cables, and when he spotted one of these flustered tourists, he called out, "Can I help?"

He approached them like a good Samaritan, then once they were extricated and began thanking him, he charmingly explained, "Glad I was here, you might have had a long wait for a tow truck. Pulling a car, though, is hard on my transmission, and I'd appreciate it if you could give me something to defray the damage." I don't know what he normally netted, but I was with him once in the 1960s when a man was persuaded to hand over $50 – a lot of money in those days. I was uncomfortable with the deception, but, always one to avoid conflict, the only action I took was to stop riding along as window-dressing. Soon enough, Dale was taking either his brother or my brother out with him to help with the jobs, and before driving down to the oceanside, they'd have a little ceremony, asking fate to provide plenty of stuck cars. Eventually the local gendarmes had a pointed chat with Dale, explaining that, as he wasn't running a licensed tow company, he'd better cut it out.

Janice met a boy one Labor Day and spent quite a bit of time away from the family, which worried her parents. They had a sit-down meeting, and afterward – probably in order to keep her privileges – she brought LaMar to join some of our activities. Then he invited the cousins to go out with him and his friends, an excursion that was indescribably exciting to me. It was the first (and last) time I participated in that curious custom called "cruising the strip." We crowded into the open bed of a pickup truck and rolled along at a crawl, exchanging smiles and smart remarks with other young people on foot or in convertibles.

That was as close as I wanted to get to boys. I found them an intriguing species, at a distance, but I was completely out of step with the boy-crazy girls my age. I lived inside my head and was reluctant to reach out. At ages thirteen and fourteen I had schoolgirl crushes on boys who had been in my class the prior spring – first Tom, and the next summer, Dennis. They were both marginally "bad boys," not the kind who greased their hair and rode motorcycles, but the ones who disobeyed teachers and acted up in class to distract from their lack of academic gifts. Of course it was nearly autumn, and I hadn't seen the boy *du jour* for many weeks, but that was irrelevant since neither of them ever had an inkling of my adoration. When I was mooning over Dennis, my enraptured mind found it deeply meaningful that my City Center Motel bedroom window looked out at a lighted sign that simply read, "Dennis." By chance, our cabin that year was directly across the street from the hardware store – the Dennis Company.

More changes. Ken married, and Carole came to Long Beach – and went fishing with the men, with little or no fanfare! Dale married, and Bid joined us. Babies were born. Grandma died, and we kept going to Long Beach, with my mom (the eldest Burd daughter) stepping into the matriarch role. Granddad remarried, and at least once or twice Ruby came to the ocean with us, before Granddad died and Ruby returned to her life in California. My recollection is that we only stopped our annual visits to Long Beach because the City Center Motel was sold in the late 1960s.

Labor Day continued as a reunion weekend. With the new families sprouting up, we needed more cabins. After a hunt for another affordable spot, we discovered the Cama Beach Resort on Camano Island. Muriel Stradley Risk had been managing the place since her father died in 1938, and she had a unique approach. The flyer advertised "Modern Cabins," which had been built when Muriel was a child, and had never been updated. When it rained, if you made a request, Muriel would provide buckets to catch the roof leaks. There were electric lights but no refrigeration. Unbelievably, ice blocks were delivered every two or three days to keep food cool in the forty-year-old, metal-lined wooden iceboxes!

Dale and his family brought canoes to Cama, and we all learned to paddle. Deprived of a suitable venue for a parade, Peggy instituted the water-balloon-toss and other inventive outdoor games for all ages. The waterfront boasted a stony strand with driftwood logs scattered about, and a fire pit for evening sing-alongs – although Muriel had strict limitations on the size of the fire. If she looked out her bungalow window and saw flames higher than two feet, she marched out and gave us a scolding then and there. We learned that you didn't want to make Muriel mad, so we nodded gravely and promised to be good, and saved our chuckles until she had gone to bed.

Most of the next generation of grandchildren had entered the world by the time we shifted our festivities to Alderbrook Resort on Hood Canal. The place was more upscale than our previous accommodations, but each living unit accommodated six or eight people, so in a way families were reunited under each roof. There wasn't any beach to speak of – there was a small marina and fishing pier instead. Uncle Sherman tied up his boat to the dock and taught his grandsons and great-nephews and -nieces to fish. Someone brought a sailboat. We hiked wooded trails up the steep slope to the golf course and back, then indulged in a dip in the hot tub. In various groupings, we played canasta and put together jigsaw puzzles. Dale acquired a hot-air balloonist's license. After attracting the attention of the whole resort by laying out the colorful fabric and cords on the front lawn and lighting the whooshing flame to inflate the balloon, he took little clusters of us – and other tourists – up in the basket on

The whole fam-damily at Alderbrook, 1986.

a long tether. Our last Labor Day reunion was at Fort Worden in Port Townsend. The physical layout wasn't conducive to the various nuclear units spending unstructured hours together over meals or cards, and I recall that weekend as generally unsatisfying.

By the late 1980s, when Mom died, the family had begun to seem so extended that it lost a lot of its cohesiveness. When my mother and her siblings had married, the spouses were grafted onto the Burd family tree – Burds weren't absorbed into the Stickles, Donaldson or Reid clans in the same way. Sunday dinners, holidays and Labor Day weekends carried a tinge of "command performance" – based in love and appreciation of Grandma and Granddad, to be sure, but with an undercurrent of non-negotiable expectation. The sense of duty dissipated as my generation became the designers of our own lives.

My nieces and their age-group cousins hadn't grown up together in the way that we had – they were, in fact, second cousins, and they had nearer relatives who weren't part of the Burd tribe. And unlike the marriages of my aunts, uncles and grandparents, several spouses in my generation divorced, shifting the nuclear constellations. Also unlike our forebears, siblings and cousins moved hundreds or even thousands of miles away and weren't free to gravitate to an annual vacation weekend. New family trees sprouted from the seeds scattered by our parents and grandparents, and even today, as the seasons pass, every fresh seed and sapling contains both the history and the future of the entire orchard.

My brother Ken is to be congratulated for reviving summer get-togethers. These are attended by families of several of the cousins who were our best friends in childhood. Choosing dates and locations to maximize participation is always a challenge, and it's an admirable effort that has succeeded for numerous years. Old traditions perish, and new ones spring up!

Take me riding
in your car, car*

"James H. Reid & Associates/ Consulting Engineers" was
emblazoned on both sides and the tailgate. Dad was a solo
entrepreneur at the time, so we concluded that we must be the
Associates. One or two summers, we drove all over the West in that
car. It's amazing to think we packed three teens, two parents, and
all the food and camping gear for the lengthy drive to Yellowstone
National Park into that 1955 Ford Ranch Wagon.

I don't think any of us were crazy about camping. I'm sure it was
a cheap way to travel and spend time in beautiful woodsy places
with dramatic mountains and geysers. Perhaps because I didn't
enjoy family outings, I've forgotten more than I remember about the
Yellowstone vacation, but we did see bears at close quarters. Living
near a boat dock, at home we had already coined a phrase explaining
heavy traffic heading toward us on Main Street in Edmonds – "The
ferry just came in." Yellowstone added a variation on that – a solid
row of oncoming cars meant, "There's a bear in the road up ahead."
Those were the days when many people considered the wildlife in the
park to be tame. While signs advised everyone to stay in their closed
vehicles if animals were near, some tourists were not cowed by such
overly protective guidelines. At least once, Dad and Carolyn jumped
out and strode confidently to within easy reach of a black bear, while
Mother hung back at the car, with her hand on her heart as if to still
its pounding. I approached more uncertainly.

* Lyric from "Riding in my Car," Woodie Guthrie, 1954

I've always wondered what suddenly possessed our parents to undertake these camping expeditions, which had not been a part of our early childhood. Maybe it was the imminent departure of their eldest child for college. I was very fond of the comforts of home, and while I didn't strongly object to sleeping on the ground or keeping warm by a smoky fire, it seemed to me an unnecessarily difficult lifestyle. Just unpacking and setting up the camp and creating meals took such a lot of energy, and after all that, what did you have? Dirt, bugs and a faraway toilet, with only an occasional toasted marshmallow to take the edge off the inconveniences.

Carolyn with Yellowstone bear, 1956. Dad and Ken are behind the camera, I'm in the center, and Mother is standing by the car, hand on her heart.

Riding in the car, too, was challenging. No matter where we sat, we were three fractious siblings cooped up for long spells. Dad preferred to drive absolutely as far as possible without stopping. There were no official highway rest areas – you generally had to get off the main track into a small town, which interfered with the forward momentum that Dad always seemed to crave. So on many legs of the trip, bathroom breaks were few and lunch was held off until we were all whining.

Here Mother, accustomed to being the sole decision-maker in family matters – while Dad was always at the office – was like a tigress on a short leash. Speaking up on behalf of her offspring, and trying to hold back on the authoritative tone of her voice, she did her best to persuade Dad to pull off. Without a word of response, he kept the car hurtling through space. They both ended up silently fuming.

These interactions were emblematic of their ongoing unresolved power struggle. In the car, we were all trapped – Dad couldn't walk out and slam the door as he would at home, and we kids couldn't retreat to our rooms and avoid being witnesses. Here in the cabin of our spaceship, Mom, the only one who could rescue us all, would turn her attention to us kids, and pasting a thin veneer over her anger, lead us in "I spy" games. We spotted license plates from different states, or pointed out objects whose names started with different letters, but rather than actually being fun, these were makeshift distractions from an unpleasant circumstance.

We drove until it was almost night. I recall pulling into one campground very late in the day, where just one site remained available. We felt lucky to get it. In only minutes we realized why this spot was empty. It was raining caterpillars. Every nonessential item was quickly tossed back into the station wagon while Dad and Kenneth set up the tent. We pulled up our hoods or put on hats. Mother cooked supper on the blackened grill of a small wood fire, as the wiggly creatures added an extra sizzle to the burning logs.

As she had done while cooking, we held tin pie plates over our individual meals, and you could get your fork to your mouth without extra passengers once you mastered the precise angles coordinating the aluminum cover with the brim of your hat and the bend of your back. Dinner music replicated the cymbals

Yellowstone photo opportunity, 1956.

of a percussion ensemble – Ping! Ding! Ting! sounded as flocks of caterpillars were deflected by the pie plates. Immediately after stowing the dirty pan and dishes (no cleanup that night), we zipped ourselves inside the tent and dozed off to a "Tap-t-t-tap-t-tap" lullaby on the canvas. Needless to say, breakfast was a picnic – several miles farther down the road!

Once we were inside the park, Dad turned over a new leaf, temporarily – he eased up and became willing to give us time to enjoy the scenery, read plaques, and peer through telescopes. Before long we had sharpened our eagle eyes and were chorusing from the back seat, "Viewpoint!" If the previous stop had been more than a few short miles earlier, he would cheerfully pull into the turnout. Now that he had delivered us to our destination, some of the pressure was off. Perhaps just as importantly, he had a new camera, and was excited about learning to use it. Regardless of the reason, with the more relaxed pace I felt a unique light-hearted freedom, and I'd swear we *all* became more cooperative during that period.

In addition to the Yellowstone trip, there was a journey the three of us joked about for years – The Great American Sewage Treatment Plant Tour. The city of Edmonds had, at long last,

Snack break by a river, 1956. Barbie, Carolyn, Ken, and "poor little" Mother.

decided that it was time to end the practice of dumping raw sewage into Puget Sound. As City Engineer, Dad had been commissioned to identify costs and timeframes for building a new treatment plant. I have no sense of geography, and so no notion of where we traveled, but what was billed as a vacation turned out to be rife with hours of boredom at a picnic site or streamside, while Dad conferred with one town's civil engineer after another. My net gain from that trip? On the afternoon we spent waiting by a tranquil lake, Kenneth taught me to skip stones on water, a pastime I've enjoyed ever since.

In 1956 we delivered Carolyn to Whitman College in Walla Walla, the station wagon crammed to its rafters with everything she would need for nine months. There were later, more direct repeats of this excursion, but the first time, it was a two-day family adventure. We paused to view the capitol building in Olympia, the Columbia River, Grand Coulee Dam. In her usual fashion, Mother brought along an overflowing basket for picnic lunches.

Unpacking the car in Whitman College's circular drive 1956. Left to right: a student greeter, Mother, Carolyn.

To me, the most important stop was a visit to our second cousin, Shirley, her husband Les, and Laura, their toddler, in Pasco. I'm still impressed that they welcomed five extra people into their home. They fed us well, and even escorted us to a local swimming pool to cool off in the southeastern Washington heat. As far as I was concerned, those two were — and have remained — paragons of generosity.

Closer to home, periodically we drove from Edmonds to Bellevue to celebrate Thanksgiving, and sometimes other events, at Aunt Frances and Uncle Sherman's house. With no freeways, the route roughly followed the shore of Lake Washington through Bothell and Kirkland on two-lane asphalt roads. It was a long drive. Dad was always late getting home, often skidding to a halt outside our garage half an hour after it was time to leave. This guaranteed Mother's tight-lipped fury, and the whole family was set up for yet another tense journey. It seems to me that often, the November darkness fell en route. When we got behind another car moving at only the speed limit, Dad would accelerate right to their bumper, impatiently wait for a straight stretch of road, then punch the gas pedal and pull out to pass. It was especially scary in the dark. His favorite term for other drivers was "Idiot!" I'm sorry to say his angry shouts entered my DNA, and that word still bursts from my mouth now and then when I'm behind the wheel.

The entire East Side along those roads was forested, with a few houses and small farms. Many, many times I spent long intervals staring out into the shadowy surroundings. Many times I saw a light in the window of a cottage or farmhouse and imagined the happy, peaceful family that lived inside. One Thanksgiving I actually saw a group of people entering a dining room and seating themselves around the table, and Norman Rockwell had nothing on the pictures that my mind painted. I fervently wished I was in that bright room rather than in this dark chamber with its dark undercurrents. It didn't occur to me that our own family would look the same from outside a window, and that the tightly held emotions that pressed me into the car seat could just as easily exist within that seemingly idyllic cottage.

What else can I be but what I am?*

O nce her youngest was a pre-teen, innate ambition led Mother to extend her horizons, but she was bound by her parental code to continue fulfilling all her established functions at home.

She had already won the uncontested title of Super-Mom, long before the press invented the term, by establishing the first of every local service for children (first cooperative preschool, first Cub Scout troop, first Brownie Scout troop, etc.), and leading the PTA and the community club, and cooking all our meals from scratch including the always-full cookie jar, and sewing all our clothes, curtains and pillows, and painting and wallpapering every room in the house, and managing the family finances, and inventing craft projects for her kids, and chauffeuring us around to see our friends, and setting us up in swim lessons, art lessons, piano lessons.

When I was ten, Mother decided to pursue another degree. After a year of evening classes in Seattle, earning the final credits she needed for a teaching certificate, she had begun teaching the elementary grades. It wasn't enough – she wanted to continue her professional growth by becoming a school counselor. The University of Washington didn't offer this major, so she traveled to the state college in Bellingham for classes. In those days, colleges made few, if any, allowances for older students. Although Western Washington State College (now WWU) offered selected night classes in Seattle, one of their degree requirements was residency on campus for a minimum of two quarters.

* Lyric from "I've Gotta Be Me," Walter Marks, 1967

In those days, Bellingham was nearly a three-hour drive from Edmonds. For two summers, in order to meet the residency rule, she lived in a dorm five days a week, then drove home for the weekend. She must have planned our week's menus as she drove southward. Nearing home, she stopped to cram the car with groceries, then arrived Friday night to begin cooking, washing our clothes, and catching up on bills. Sunday evening was thick with good-byes, then she was gone for another week.

During these summers, Dad was our nominal leader, but as always, he was only at home to sleep, so the job of corralling the younger siblings fell to my sister, at 16. Our brother was 12, and for a year or two he had already been spending most summer days either hanging out with friends in the area or playing pick-up baseball at the field a mile away. The field was the only large, flat, grassy space around. We knew that when Kenneth took off for the Church of God campground, he'd be home around dark. (I never learned anything about the Church of God itself, and only once in thirty years did I see a camp meeting there. Generally, no one interfered with the baseball boys.)

I didn't have friends close by, and had never been an adventurous child. Yet, though I may have been bored, I definitely didn't want to do anything my sister told me, especially the necessary household chores. Mother had been my sounding board, as well as my social secretary, making plans and transporting my friends and me. I don't remember pining for her, but I recall a frequent feeling of annoyance and unfairness. With my willing participation, she had made me totally dependent on her. My childish mind protested that somebody's sole support shouldn't just go away! When she came home for a weekend, of course, she was so relentlessly busy setting up the mechanisms for our survival that she was unreachable. I had no comprehension of the strain she was under — only my own.

I consider now how that life may have been for her, and wish she were here to talk about it. The long drives every single week, laboring to exhaustion Saturdays and Sundays, missing out on her children's summers. By contrast at college, the lightness of staying in a room she didn't have to clean, eating what someone else prepared, and focusing exclusively on intellectual pursuits and discussions for days at a time. I know the trade-off was worthwhile long-term, because she loved her career, but I hope the process itself had its little joys as well.

During those two years, she taught school from fall to spring. After a couple of years with first graders, Mom "graduated" to sixth grade. She was especially drawn to this age group, and in her evening counseling courses she focused on information that could help her work with pre-teens and teenagers.

I was in seventh grade. Junior high school was painful and difficult for me, and I was depressed most of the time. I hated the changes that puberty was imposing. I had few social skills. My mom was not around to talk things out. In hindsight, I'm guessing Mother was worried about me, but she didn't say so, and in fact, seemed always preoccupied. I began adding this line at the end of my diary entries: "I will be alone," meaning *always*.

On the other hand, one of Mom's sixth-grade students delighted her almost daily, and she would bring home stories about Mike Trenton. How alert he was in class, how sociable, how eager to learn, and the things he said – oh, he was impressive. I never met Mike, but I hated him with every cell of my being. Clearly he was superior to me in every way, and a year younger to boot. Unable to compete, I tried to dismiss him from my mind, but next night at dinner, there was his specter.

One day Mother told me that she and a fellow trainee were taking a course for which they were required to administer a psychological test. They each needed a guinea pig. "Would you mind letting Mr. Astor test you, as a favor? To pass the course, he has to do a practice run."

Sullenly, I yielded. "OK, fine."

In the part of the test that's stuck in my memory, Mr. Astor said he was going to say a word, and I should respond with whatever came to mind. So he read a list of words, and in response to each, I gave him a word.

Guess who Mother chose for her guinea pig? A couple of days later, apparently unaware of rules of confidentiality as well as completely blind to the feelings of her daughter, she entertained us at supper by sharing Mike Trenton's answers on some of the test questions. "Oh, you should have heard him – the stimulus word was 'sword.' He told me about broadswords, bayonets, épées and all kinds of fencing swords, and outlined the history of weaponry and the place of the sword in it. Amazing."

Here's my exchange on that prompt.

Mr. Astor: "Sword."

My complete response: "Sharp."

Not only was I intellectually and socially inferior, now I had proven myself psychologically inferior as well. After that, although I wasn't conscious of it, I wonder if I took a perverse pleasure in being the counselor's slow and obstinate kid whom the counselor couldn't help.

I don't recall any family announcement or celebration when Mother achieved her counseling credential. Did she think that her vocation had to be downplayed for fear of outshining the man of the family? Did she believe a person shouldn't celebrate her own milestones, only those of others? Or was she always "on to the next task" without pause for ceremony?

Mom seemed to find deep satisfaction in her role as a counselor. She always fought for the underdog. The continual

Mrs. Jacqueline Reid's school picture, 1960.

expansion of her career seemed to be a natural expression of who she was, not a ladder-climbing project. She was a leader in the district's teachers' union and the counselors' association. During her last few years at Meadowdale Middle School, she was given the honor of being selected by the Washington State Superintendent of Schools as a member of a three-person consortium. The other two team members were professors, one from Western Washington University and the other from the University of Washington. The mission of the consortium was to design the first statewide

Jacqui Reid honored by school counselors

Jacqui Reid, counselor at Meadowdale Junior High School in Lynnwood, has been honored by the Washington School Counselors' Association.

WSCA at their annual

JACQUI REID

meeting in Spokane, awarded Mrs. Reid a certificate of merit "for outstanding service as a professional member of the Washington School Counselors Association, for efforts above

and beyond assigned tasks in the field of guidance and counseling and for exceptional ability which furthers the status of our profession."

The award was one of six in the state to be presented by WSCA president Marilyn Budd. This was the first year of the awards. Mrs. Reid was nominated for the honor by the Snohomish County School Guidance Association.

Mrs. Reid has many years experience counseling. She has served in the development of the program for certification of counselors already in practice and is now working on a proposal for training future counselors under the regulations and requirements of the state superintendent of public instruction, working with The Edmonds Education Association, and the Edmonds School District 15.

Mrs. Reid is active in the local counselors association, the Edmonds Education Association and has received letters of commendation from district superintendent Harold Silvernail and director of secondary education Al Christensen for this award.

criteria and college curriculum for school counselor certification. They succeeded by studying, researching, consulting with the few known experts, and becoming experts in their own right. The standards they created became the model for other states nationwide.

Despite her elevated accomplishments, one of the most cherished honors she received was the proclamation by a formerly troublesome middle-school student, summing up her impact on his behavior with "Mrs. Reid, you're a far-out lady!" More than once she reported this significant compliment to us, always with a self-deprecating grin.

When Mother was 64, the district required all faculty members to retire by age 65. That very year, the limit was raised to 70 (by what mechanism or for what reason I'll always wonder – she had a lot of influence in the district, but was she *that* powerful?). She continued in her profession until just before her seventieth birthday.

Meantime, she had decided to divorce Dad after 40 years of marriage. The huge Christmas bouquet of long-stemmed yellow roses, one for every year of marriage, had become a vacant symbol. She wanted to travel and he didn't. She needed a change.

My private theory today is that by that point, both her career and her seemingly empty marriage were actually necessary to her sense of meaning in life. Her attempts to travel were interrupted or tarnished by one physical problem after another. Without her work as a conversation topic, she had trouble reaching out to new people, and I sensed her loneliness.

She had a hip replacement and was sent home alone to her apartment. Not wanting to appear weak, she didn't ask her adult children for help in the recuperation period. It didn't go well, but we were out of the loop – she put on a very convincing, stolid front. Had she shared openly, or had we been more perceptive, we might have realized that she was in more pain than was normal; we might have insisted the doctor take action. As it was, a blood clot formed at the surgery site and traveled to her lung. She was hospitalized for her final three days, and the embolism was not diagnosed until the autopsy. We were shocked and dismayed when she died, less than three years after retiring.

When she first came across Richard Bach's book *Jonathan Livingston Seagull* in 1970, Mother had deeply connected with the story. The book tells of a special seagull who tires of squabbling over food scraps and reinvents himself. He is scorned by his tribe for his daring flight experiments, but eventually soars beyond their known world and enters a "higher plane of existence" which is not heaven, but is accessed through knowledge. He becomes a master teacher for other young experimenters like himself.

Looking over Mother's life, I see that she was very Jonathan-like. Increasing her knowledge and understanding was essential. She could never "let well enough alone" – it was her nature to move forward, outward, upward. She pushed past obstacles of all kinds to continually develop her capabilities. She soared to exceptional achievements in community and career, but not without the risks and failures that are intrinsic to bold experimentation. She weathered scorn from many traditionalists who felt she was overreaching her assigned roles. Despite my own reactions as a child, as an adult I'm filled with admiration for her initiative and courage.

Today, I'm fortunate enough to live at the top of a hill again. Once in a while a single seagull flies past my window at very close range. Whatever I'm thinking about at the time, I try to consider what Mother might contribute to my situation if she were here. I hope that she, like Jonathan, exists on a higher plane.

Ch-ch-ch-ch-changes,
turn and face the strange*

Novels describe pre-teen girls chattering about which of their friends have started their periods. I'll always wonder if I knew anyone who had those conversations. In my world, these things were private, and were meant to be kept secret.

In the sixth grade, our teacher was Mr. Creighton. One day he announced that he and all the boys would be going to a different classroom for an hour, so we girls could see a special film. For the most part we were naïve – eleven- and twelve-year-olds perhaps equivalent to today's eight- or nine-year-olds. We buzzed with curiosity, and there were a few titters from the more sophisticated students, who were sure that the subject would be... sex.

It was quite an event in our day-to-day life. The school nurse came in, introduced herself, and showed the film. Its star was a little boy being given a bath by his mother. Upon seeing his nude body, many of the girls in the room gasped or gaped in shock.

I had seen this kind of excitement before. When we were seven or eight, my playmate Laurie had led me on an adventure in the woods beside her house. I wasn't a daring youngster, and to me, just about everything at Laurie's house was already an adventure. Her mother collected fragile, graceful ceramic figurines of dancers, which I was warned several times not to touch. Beautiful as they were, I couldn't imagine why I'd want to touch them. Mrs. Weston also smoked cigarettes and mixed herself a drink every day at happy hour, which made her truly exotic in my eyes. Laurie's older brother was very

*Lyric from "Changes," David Bowie, 1971

big and made it clear that he hated us. His comments were unlike anything I heard at home. I was edgy when he was around, but in fact he couldn't get away with hitting girls, and his mental weapons weren't sharp enough to pierce our feelings. In the midst of all this novelty, when Laurie asked if I wanted to see something really wild, I was ready to advance to an even more exciting level of experience.

The neighbors' house was less than 30 yards away. It was dusk as we crept through the woods and positioned ourselves in the wild undergrowth facing a large window. "Just watch," said Laurie. A woman and a small boy came into sight behind the window, in what turned out to be a bathroom. (Who builds a house with a floor-to-ceiling bathroom window?) The woman undressed the boy, and as he was lifted into the tub, we glimpsed his tiny genitals. Laurie was nearly breathless with the thrill of it all. "See? Did you see?"

I was underwhelmed. My brother was just over a year older than I was, and the two of us had bathed together dozens or hundreds of times, until we were four or so. There was nothing unusual to me about a naked toddler. That afternoon, even with my low standards for adventure, I was disappointed and a little ashamed to find myself crouching in the woods to peep at the penis of a two-year-old.

But now I was in sixth grade. This was school, a school movie. There must be some kind of meaningful purpose to showing us this child. I waited and watched. As it turned out, my female classmates and I didn't even get treated to the full mini-Monty — we saw only the boy's cupid-like little backside. The lesson I took away from the film was delivered in the final scene, where the mother used the towel to thoroughly dry between the child's toes. "Always pay careful attention to washing and drying every part of your body." I'm sure we were expected to extrapolate from the veiled reference to "every part of our bodies," but that was a gamble the producers took. I, for one, was very literal-minded. I saw toes, and thought only about toes.

Our much-anticipated "special" movie wasn't about sex, it was about hygiene. Alas, there was no sex movie, no introduction to the unimaginable physical changes that were about to take over our bodies, nor to the hormone-related emotional chaos that was waiting in the wings.

Menstruation would have come as a complete shock that same year, if my mother – perhaps inspired by the Girl Scouts of America – hadn't quietly handed me a pamphlet just in the nick of time. I read it and did my best to understand what was happening, studying the curving lines on the curious drawings. But the important, easy-to-remember message was that blood was going to come out of my body. And I wasn't supposed to let that bother me.

We were all at a family gathering down the hill at my grandparents' house when it happened. After the Sunday afternoon meal, we cousins entertained ourselves in one room, the uncles in another, and my mom and two aunts would gossip as they helped Grandma clean up the kitchen. I came out of the bathroom feeling quite befuddled, and sought out Mother. When I was able to get her attention, I whispered in her ear, "I think I've started to men-stroo-ate." I had only seen the word in print, never heard it pronounced.

"What??" A puzzled frown on her face.

How could she not have heard me? Did I really have to repeat myself? "Men-stroo-ate, I think I've started." She turned to the other women and quietly said something to them, one aunt let out her trademark sharp, scornful cackle, and the others smiled. I was so embarrassed.

To her credit, Mother walked me home. There she presented me with a "sanitary belt," a contraption configured from elastic strips and tiny, unwieldy metal clips. Next, Mom showed me where the Kotex were kept. Did she instruct me to keep my periods a secret, or did I invent the rule that my dad and brother should never, never know?

My relationship with my mother was, to put it mildly, complicated. I'd say I was in awe of her. By that I mean that (1) what she told me was the absolute truth and (2) what she didn't tell me, I didn't dare ask.

A bolder child might have said, "Why do we keep the supplies in Mother's hall closet, where anyone in the house could see me fetching

one? Could we keep some near my bed, or in the bathroom?" A
more observant child might have said, "There's a dispensing machine
in the school rest rooms. Will you give me an allowance, or at least
some nickels so I can buy pads instead of carrying them with me?"
Also, I didn't know that tampons existed. Either Mother was equally
unaware, or she had fallen for the line that they would cause harm
to young vaginas. In any case, they were never mentioned at home.
I struggled for three years with carrying the bulky Kotex to junior
high school, until finally in high school my best friend asked me why
I didn't just put one or two Tampax in my purse. I bought a package
and followed the instructions on the box to learn to use them. Oh, the
marvelous freedom!

In junior high we didn't carry book bags or backpacks to school.
Girls carried a purse, and pressed their books and notebooks to their
chests while walking. Stylish purses were quite small at the time, and
sanitary pads were large. Most likely today, even those young women
who use pads rather than tampons don't realize that the development
of space-age materials such as super-absorbent fibers and safe
adhesives have totally transformed feminine products so that you can
now slip "maxi-thin" protection into a billfold. Every month I carried
a paper bag to school, in addition to my books and purse. Once,
between classes, a trio of boys grabbed my paper bag containing three
fat sanitary pads and played catch with it, keeping it out of my reach
for several minutes. I broke down in tears. I still recall this as one of
the most intensely humiliating moments of my life – for whatever
mistaken reasons, I believed menstruation MUST be kept secret
from the male of the species, and I had no way of recognizing the
reality that secrecy was not only impossible but unnecessary.

My periods were painful. I had severe abdominal cramping for
one or two days each month, and the bleeding usually continued
for at least a week. I was also seriously depressed from age 12 to
15, but never diagnosed. I suspect that a large part of my monthly
misery was caused by an extreme resistance to growing up. I had
been a pampered child, and as I looked at the adult women around

me, I didn't see any of them being pampered. Their lot seemed hard. I would have chosen to stay eleven years old if I'd had my druthers. Menstruation became the focus of all these feelings.

In a sad way, my periods became occasions to receive the pampering I was beginning to miss already. "I have cramps," I'd say to the teacher. "Well, go to the nurse's office and lie down." I wasn't faking the pain, but had I not been homesick for childhood, my mother's advice might have worked just fine. She was a woman of action, and usually said briskly, "You'll forget about it if you get up and get busy." I didn't get up and get busy, because distraction from the pain wasn't what I wanted.

Only in high school did I consciously use menstruation to manipulate a situation. What was my motivation for this crime? Physical education, or PE as we called it, was an unsolvable problem for me. It was a required daily class, and I must have been the least physically educated girl in the school. I had never learned a single sport, and we were required to play kickball, volleyball, dodge-'em, basketball, and worst of all, baseball. Never were the rules of a game presented before play began, and there was no guidebook. Rules were only mentioned when there was a mistake or a dispute, so I operated in a deep fog of ignorance compared to most other suburban teens, who had years of experience with these activities.

I think there's a term for the way your teammates intimidate and insult you during a baseball game, but for me it was just brutality. I didn't know what a base *was*, much less what to do when I met one. "Easy out, easy out!" The first – perhaps only – time I managed to somehow hit the ball, I stood there with the bat in my hand, feeling relieved that I'd done something right. "Run, stupid!" was shouted by at least 4 players. "That way!" Then, "Drop the bat, dummy!"

Miss Mackel was a dyed-in-the-wool jock. She liked the athletic kids and had little time for the rest of us. She never stepped in to stop the insults. But under that neat, pressed button-front shirt beat a human heart, and I think in her crusty way she recognized that I couldn't stand a full course of PE. The rule was that whenever a girl had her period, she could be excused from class for a few days. My periods began to extend to twelve or fourteen days, especially in baseball season, giving me an officially approved reason to sit on the sidelines, other than the usual reason that nobody wanted me on their team. In the end I became rather fond of her and started calling her "Macky" like the coordinated girls did. In our senior year we were allowed to choose a non-team sport, and I chose tennis. It was completely new to me, and to my astonishment, I actually enjoyed it. My final grade for PE that term was a C+. In the comments section was written, "Barbara tries too hard." I laughed at the irony and graduated happy, my grade average only dragged down to a 3.7 by dear old Macky.

Once I married, of course, menstruation was an open topic between us. I recall with gratitude a moment when, during a trip to the Soviet Union in 1988, my husband provided exactly the help I needed. I was 42 and in menopause; I hadn't had a period for a year. But, out at the end of a five-hour bus ride, in the ancient city of Samarkand, I started bleeding. In the city's only hotel we found an English-speaking staff member and, somewhat embarrassed, asked him about supplies. Without missing a beat, he led us to a *glass-topped cabinet* in the center of the lobby. Arrayed under the glass like precious jewelry was a display of pads and tampons! Somehow the remoteness of the location – and the dusty display – gave me the feeling the tampons might not have been manufactured in conditions sterile enough for internal use, so I elected to buy a pad. This object was two inches thick, three inches wide, and nine inches long in the old-fashioned shape with a tail at each end (no peel-and-stick option).

Fortunately, I always traveled with safety pins. Our bus should have left half an hour earlier, and our fellow travelers were impatiently thinking we were out lollygagging somewhere, so we dashed back to the bus. My spouse helped me find a back seat, and arranged himself and his jacket to create the privacy needed while I pinned this bicycle saddle into my clothing. I rode out my final menstrual period with equipment nearly identical to my first one thirty years earlier.

It's a blessing that people are now freer to talk about formerly taboo subjects, and I'm especially touched when I hear of mothers and fathers explaining puberty to their daughters and sons, and celebrating their children's coming of age. Adolescents have enough cause for confusion without being left in the dark about their own bodies.

In closing, a final salute to American public education in the baby-boom era. To this day, after bathing I always pay special attention to toweling off my toes. I hope you do too, dear reader.

Some think it well
to be all melancholic*

It began subtly. Mother started taking evening courses toward a new master's degree. That was okay with me – she was still available to listen to all my day's happenings when I came in from school. I was ten, and except for Brownie meetings, the center of my afternoons consisted of bonding with Mom. My evenings were for homework or reading while she was in class, and she returned home in time to maintain most of our bedtime rituals.

Two cosmic forces ruled my life at that time – Mother and school. The next fall, everything I knew about going to school was overturned. The shock was caused by the district's failure to finish renovations in time for my age-group to start junior high school in the former Edmonds High School building. I'd been inside several times, and it had the familiar shape of a traditional school, like Edmonds Elementary. Our grade school, built in 1928, was a three-story edifice with straight hallways connecting evenly spaced classrooms. Moreover, the vast majority of my fellow students had been with me since we were six. We knew each other. We spent the day with a single teacher. The old high school was only a few blocks away from the elementary, and I looked forward to commuting to downtown Edmonds daily, as always.

Instead, we rode the school bus three or four miles in the opposite direction, to Lynnwood Junior High. There, we "double shifted" with the regular Lynnwood students. I don't remember exactly how the schedules were set up – I believe the Edmonds kids started their day

* Lyric (translated) from "Funiculi Funicula," Luigi Denza and Peppino Turco, 1880

in the afternoon, but the Lynnwood students were still there. During the overlap, the halls bulged with twice their intended population. I was eleven, younger than most, having started first grade at five. I found the Lynnwood kids tougher and scrappier than the children I'd known, and they seemed resentful of our invasion. The bumping and shoving alarmed me. Lynnwood JH was a modern, spread-out, single-story building, and I was always disoriented and often harassed by other students for being lost or late to class. The kids I knew were no longer my main companions, since each of the junior high schools pulled from wider areas than the elementaries.

I had anticipated the change from a single teacher to several. I hadn't applied my imagination to the difference, from a teacher's point of view, between getting to know thirty students for several hours each day and trying to cram subject matter into 120 to 150 pupils seen for, at most, an hour and a half. They didn't *care* about us in the way last year's teachers had – we were supposed to be old enough not to need that. And they, too, found themselves in a hostile – or at least difficult – situation, sharing classrooms with other instructors who weren't really members of their team. Discontent was pervasive.

I was overwhelmed, and muddled through the season in a daze. Eventually, with great relief, our entire cohort made the longed-for move to the four-story concrete structure that was to be our home through ninth grade. But my brain was still fuzzy.

There was a big auditorium. I was a member of the school chorus, and we were scheduled to perform at an all-school assembly. Fresh in my mind today is the intense disappointment of failing to show up to sing in the concert because I couldn't find my way to the backstage entrance. I watched standing in a doorway behind the audience, mouthing all the songs I knew so well and mourning the opportunity I had witlessly forfeited.

The summer I was twelve, I started my menstrual periods, and coincidentally had my first incident of being touched sexually by a grown man. Mother helped a little with the first, but she was no use with the second. Instead of comforting me or asking for more information, she literally turned her back and gave her attention to whatever was simmering on the stove. The ground fell away under my feet. Decades later, when at last I realized she was probably torn between her loyalty to me and her complex connection with the adult in the situation, I did forgive her. Today I can even smile as I remember how Mother always knew what to say, and that may have been the only time I ever saw her speechless.

Just one thing changed after our one-sided talk – if I ever told her that a man we met gave me the creeps, she no longer pooh-poohed my observation. I noticed this difference and appreciated it as a hungry dog appreciates a single morsel of kibble. It isn't a meal, but it's better to taste something than nothing.

The next fall, Mother was teaching school full-time. She often had team meetings or other preparations that kept her there until it was time to come home and fix dinner. Gone were our daily discussions. I was confused and floundering, and yearned for the sturdy tree trunk I had always leaned on. But a new and vibrant sapling was rooted in her heart, and after dreaming of it for so long, she had to nurture this budding life into bloom. She didn't belong to me.

Eighth grade was one of the most painful times of my life. That was the year I instigated my pointless power struggle with Mr. Lyons in English class. The year I found Mr. Banty Rooster, my math teacher, so unbearably condescending that I furiously made every assignment letter-perfect, aiming to prove I was as smart as he was. The year I just about stopped talking to my mom.

This wasn't a mood. In fact, unpredictable moods came and went, and two or three times I even wrote in my diary, "I'm so happy! The world is so beautiful! How can anyone bear to be this happy?" But I was like a river whose surface ripples reveal little of the strong dark current and dangerous boulders deep below. No matter how elated I was, within moments my effervescent happiness was immersed again.

When I say I sank into depression, I mean I lost hope that the future could be any different than the miserable present. There was no way to return to the child I wanted to be, and there was no evidence that I could become the person I was supposed to be. I was frightened and enraged by the facts of life, and I acted out my wretchedness in sulking rebellion. My hair hung lank and oily, my face was a mountain range of acne, two weeks might go by between showers. I changed clothes every day because Mother still supervised what I wore. She continued to do all our laundry, so the clothes were clean. I contributed nothing.

I felt near drowning for all three junior high years. Thankfully, I never seriously considered suicide, possibly because that would have required initiative and I had none. I survived the long bout of despair mostly thanks to Cynthia. We met in seventh grade and immediately fell into hours of conversation consisting largely of expressions of rage at our parents. We also debriefed at the end of each school day, providing a forum for feelings that Mother didn't have time – or didn't want – to hear. With Cynthia it was okay to be angry, and okay to need a friend.

Fortunately for me, high school came along in the ordinary sequence of things. I continued to resist growing up and didn't have a very easy time of it, but high school brought a different learning environment, a few close friendships, and the simple passage of time, which gradually lifted my hopelessness. I'm still grateful to those friends and teachers, along with my own maturing process, for the badly needed improvement in my outlook.

All I really want to do is,
baby, be friends with you*

W ho can say for certain what drew us together? We were
instant friends.

During our seventh-grade year, Cynthia showed up on my school
bus. She had just moved to Edmonds from California. It seems to me
that on the very first afternoon we walked up the hill toward home
from the bus stop, I sensed she was exactly the person I needed in
my life. She was smarter than I was, and more informed about world
events, but I knew the ways of Edmonds. We had something in
common that I couldn't see at the time, but I'm sure I felt it below the
level of awareness – an underlying unhappiness that each of us had
buried deep within our own personalities.

She lived a little farther up the hill than I did, but we were
equidistant from the intersection where our routes divided, so by the
time I arrived home, I could call her to continue the discussion that
had started on the bus and had progressed as we trudged up the slope.
(My mother's comment as she heard the ratcheting clicks of our phone's
rotary dial: "Didn't you *just* spend an hour with her?") On weekends, we
were near enough to hike or bicycle over, and we got acquainted with
each other's families. We went for long walks, talking, always talking.

Topics ranged widely. Her family watched Walter Cronkite every
evening on the CBS news. My parents changed the channel whenever
a news program came on. So Cynthia would update me on the
goings-on of the planet beyond my home town. We would compare
notes on teachers and classes, and gossip about our fellow students,

* Lyric from "All I Really Want to Do," Bob Dylan, 1964

both during the painful transitions of junior high and as we passed through the forbidding entry gates of cliquish Edmonds High School. But the most frequent and consistent targets of our grumbling were our parents.

I had reached adolescence, and the bubble of my childish enmeshment with my mother and dad had sprung its first leaks. I needed to talk out my criticisms of them with someone who would listen. Cynthia, too, had longstanding family difficulties and often offered similar points of view, along with occasional insights.

In tenth grade, the first year of high school, the schedulers implemented a covert policy of placing us in separate classes. With 1300 students in the building, even lunch times were staggered, based on the student's third- and fourth-period class assignments. At first, I assumed our separation was random, and was sad not to see Cynthia at all over the course of the whole day. We had a lot of catching up to do on the trip home, and much of our spare time was still spent together.

Apparently this was worrisome to Cynthia's parents. One day my mother found a private moment and told me that Cynthia's mother felt I was a *bad influence* on my friend. I laughed out loud, and was shocked to see that Mom did not smile. "What did you say to her?"

"I asked her what she meant by *bad influence*. She couldn't seem to explain." Mom was an expert side-stepper, and my real query – Was there something wrong with me? – went unanswered.

The next day Cynthia told me that her mother had also had a chat with her, hissing out through clenched teeth her fear that we were going to make each other *ho-mo-sex-ual*. I was insulted by her paranoia, and saw this notion as yet another injury inflicted by the adults. It was unfair that we were even answerable to these obsolete relics of another era!

Investigating further, I returned to Mother to ask if she – who was on a first-name basis with everyone in school district operations – had arranged the divergence in our course schedules. She admitted that she had *made suggestions*. To Cynthia, I thundered, "Grownups are so *stupid*!"

As we entered our junior year and registered for college-prep classes, there weren't enough sections of each course that we could be kept apart, which pleased me, and for one reason or another, our parents dropped the issue. Cynthia started participating in after-school sports, and in the summers she became a camp counselor. Both activities appealed to me as much as a bad case of rabies, and I admit that as an introvert, I was envious of her broader social contacts. We each followed our own inclinations and grew in our own directions, and the friendship continued.

That was 1961. Today much more is known about the nature of homosexuality, and the nature of human relations in general. The Tao tells us that every person has masculine and feminine aspects, and a number of lesbian, gay and bi friends have confirmed to me that for them, sexual identity is a spectrum, not an either/or divide. As early as the 1970s, a psychiatrist assured me that many close same-sex friendships contain elements of attraction that are similar to romantic feelings. It's likely that some of those elements were present, but in our case, Cynthia and I had no interest in any physical contact, and even during the two years we shared a one-bedroom apartment, we turned our backs to change clothes.

We were the kind of roommates who walked to classes together, drove to work together, and had separate social lives, which we described to each other in summary. I knew who she was dating and where they went, and she knew the same about me, without too much focus on details. Our diverse erotic activities were sometimes foolish, sometimes risky, but all with men. From what I know of that experimental time, I conclude that we didn't cause each other to become *ho-mo-sex-ual*.

What if one or both of us had been lesbian? I'm sure it would have been a much different and almost certainly more difficult life journey. But by now it's been proven many times over that, if given the freedom to express that identity fully and not be forced to live a lie, we could have contributed to the world at least as much as we have in our heterosexual identities.

No flounces, no feathers,
no frills and furbelows*

"Are you going to the dance?"

"No way!" Cynthia answered definitively.

"Kelly?"

"Why would I go? I don't know how to dance."

"Bonnie?"

"I have to babysit. My mother and stepfather are going out."

It was the ninth-grade party. None of us had attended any earlier school dances, other than one or two "sock hops" at three in the afternoon. I was determined to go, but as a devout introvert, I was nervous. Among other things, I didn't have the first clue what to wear.

For Mother, on the other hand, it was as if she'd been waiting all of my fourteen years for this occasion. She relished putting me in costume. She brought out a gorgeous satin dress that had been given to us by a family friend. It was my very favorite color, indigo blue, and I fell in love with it. She tailored it to show off my curves. At the final fitting I realized the sweetheart neckline was cut embarrassingly low. Suddenly I was terrified to go out in it.

"Don't be silly. You look just beautiful. All the boys are going to want to dance with you," Mother assured me. This was the same woman who had told me many times that I'd have a better social life if I would "bat my eyes at the boys." Her ideas about gender relations were from a different world. But I was naive, and took her at her word.

* Lyric from "It's a Fine Life," Lionel Bart, 1968

The result was disastrous. Other girls were in simple skirts and blouses. I was a freak. There was one boy, the nicest boy in the whole school, who danced in turn with me and the other, more normal-looking wallflowers. After that I spent most of the evening weeping in the restroom, leaving the building early to wait in shadows for Mom's car to turn into the lot.

I kept the dress in the closet for a year because it was so beautiful, but I wouldn't have been caught dead ever wearing it again.

Our parents were never extravagant, and clothing was one arena where Mother was confident she could save money. Not only did she make most of our wardrobe herself, but we wore things until they began to fall apart. And gifts of used clothing were welcome. Carolyn, with her lanky height, received good quality, cast-off items from all the tall women of our acquaintance – three or four, as I recall. These were often stylish, but not necessarily suited to a young teenager. Mom skillfully altered or redesigned selected items, and Carolyn was well turned out in her newly acquired garments. Most of the hand-me-downs I received were from Carolyn. Clothes were gender-distinct at that time. Beyond the universal norm of skirts and dresses, even girls' shorts and jeans had side zippers, and for no logical reason, shirts buttoned on the opposite side. The only items of Ken's that I remember wearing were outdoor jackets, which we all swapped around with great abandon. A favorite was Dad's World War II canvas Army jacket, which weighed almost as much as a backpack full of rocks.

Although clothes shopping was not part of our life, shoes were an exception. "You can't go wrong with good, supportive shoes," Mother intoned, "especially while your feet are still growing." At least once a year, we made an excursion to downtown Seattle to buy our shoes at Nordstrom. Dad got to know Mr. Orner, who owned the shoe store on Main Street in Edmonds, a few doors up from Dad's office. He pressed Mom to buy our shoes there, in our own home town. Our parents shared the ethic of "buying local," and one day we all trooped into Orner's. We did buy sneakers that time. But for whatever reasons, Mother did not find the products up to her standard, and soon we were again trekking downtown for our shoe needs.

I never purchased a garment until I was sixteen. It didn't much matter to me what I wore – comfort and convenience were always more important than appearance. I remember a particular pair of red corduroy pedal pushers that Mother made. I donned them every day for two or three summers, till the knees sagged like empty balloons and the nap was completely rubbed off between the knees. Finally the side zipper gave out and there wasn't enough good cloth left to attach a new one.

Mother did her best to teach us to take care of our clothes so they wouldn't wear out too quickly. I was surprised she didn't get tired of hearing herself say – each time as though she'd never said it before – "If you get undressed in front of your closet and hang things up as soon as you take them off, you'll save time." Eventually she expressed this dictum in actions as well as words.

When our parents made their final choice of bedroom, they hired Uncle Van to build a long closet at one side, with sliding doors extending from wall to wall, and inside, hanger rods and two sets of built-in drawers. Thus were created "his" and "hers" spaces. But after some time, Mother moved her clothes to a tiny closet in the hallway instead. This was a little doorless indentation next to the stairs, barely deep enough for hangers, and covered only by a fabric curtain gathered over a wooden rod. When I asked her why, she said, "Your father is using all the space for his clothes. I'm fine out here." As with most of her statements, I didn't ask further questions. Apparently Dad didn't like to get rid of old clothes and they had accumulated to fill the whole wall.

The result was that Mom, getting dressed or undressed, and obeying her own rule to hang up each garment, was in full view of the household as we passed back and forth to the bathroom or the stairs. She usually put her underwear on and took it off in the bedroom, but the bra and nylon boy-shorts provided a bare minimum of concealment. Her body was not attractive in a traditional way, more of an illustration – in the flesh – of lack of sun and exercise. As far as

I know, no one ever confronted her on her public nudity, not even to express any concern about her teenage son.

She did have an unusually casual attitude toward the human body. According to her stories, this was honed during her college drama years, when she saw every sort of actor in every stage of undress. She told me that she had once embarrassed a young man backstage by looking at him, and that was the day she learned where a blush starts: below the waist, as she put it, rising gradually to the face.

Mom was a talented designer and loved sewing. And she liked to get the jump on fashions. Other home stitchers would look over the pamphlets published by the pattern companies, choose a pattern, buy fabric, thread, buttons, and sew up a new shirt or suit. This would take at least a few weeks. My mom, on the other hand, glanced through the Simplicity and McCall's flyers to deduce the trends, and devised her own approximation of the styles. Often she had the needed fabric right there on her sewing-room shelves, having amassed quite a collection by keeping an eye on the remnant sales.

Because she took action the minute the brochures were printed, and she could complete a garment in a day, I ended up with fashions that were sometimes a whole season ahead of the popular trends. As high school began, something shifted in my thinking, and I noticed that I wasn't dressing like the other girls. I'd gone through junior high feeling deeply inferior to everyone, and now I was seeking reasons for that feeling. Appearances began to matter.

The miserable "Aha" moment came on the day I showed up in the newest garment Mother had made – Edmonds High School's first "chemise" or "sack dress." It was a jumper, worn over a white blouse, and I liked the fabric, a medium-weight grey hounds-tooth check. But from the armpits to the hem, the sides were as straight as the parallel lines we studied in geometry class. The half-grown fashionistas had never seen anything like it, and they were brutal, staring, pointing, snickering. Weeks later Mom asked me why I never wore that jumper any more, and to humor her I put it on once for a family party. But never again to school.

For my sixteenth birthday, I received a startling gift – a sweater and skirt set from Dad. He ordinarily relied on Mother to provide our gifts, and gave us a greeting card himself if he thought of it. But by my teen years he had arranged with his secretary to alert him when our birthdays were coming up. In this case, I think the secretary also selected the gift, as a favor to him. I could see that Mother was annoyed – dressing me was her bailiwick. But me? I was delighted to have these unique, ready-made garments.

Alas, the outfit was too small. (A couple of times in later years Dad bought me other clothing – always too small, as in his mind I never did grow up.) But the hidden blessing in that initial effort was that for the first time ever, I got to go to the store and choose something else. As a popular Edmonds businessman, I'm pretty sure Dad had easily arranged with the shop owner that I could pick out whatever I wanted.

What *did* I want?? I had never *wanted* a piece of clothing before. Garments were provided, I put them on, that's how it was. So trying on different items was more than a novelty – it was a thrill. Mother, of course, accompanied me to the shop, but for once she kept her advice to a minimum. I walked out glowing, carrying a dress box (a dress box!) with a new sweater and a matching gathered wool skirt in bright green with three thin rainbow stripes around the border. The kids at school neither openly insulted nor complimented my new outfit. With the narrow waistband and bulbous skirt, I suspect I looked something like a green snowman. But this lukewarm public response was good enough for me. I loved my first store-bought skirt and sweater.

The following year, my four friends and I ("the Rejects") became adventurous enough to take the bus from Edmonds to Seattle. On one occasion I went downtown with Ann, who was an honorary Reject but more fashion-conscious than the rest of us. She led me to the Best Apparel store. (Nordstrom was still exclusively a shoe store then, before the 1963 merger that created Nordstrom Best.) I had never been in such an upscale establishment and I was agog. Ann strode directly to the clearance section, where I found something so wonderful that I had to have it. This was the second clothing purchase of my life, and the first without Mother at my elbow. I still remember that short-sleeved brown shirt with the rounded collar, printed with tiny orange, yellow and green flowers.

I wore it on the exciting day when we Rejects took the bus to Volunteer Park. I felt more confident and capable in that blouse than I ever had, and we had a joyful outing, even making bus connections in the big city with no trouble. By the time we boarded the Seattle bus, we were joking and giggling loudly enough that other bus riders glared at us. For once we acted like the teenagers we were, freed from our quiet, studious, obedient home-and-school selves. We ran around the park pretending to be the wind, climbed the water tower to hear our voices echo and to gain a perspective on the land below, and oohed and aahed through the brilliantly colored vegetation of the steamy tropical conservatory.

Edmonds girls at Volunteer Park, spring, 1961. I'm on the right, my brown blouse hidden under the red "car coat" Mother had bought for me.

Recently, I saw a brown blouse printed with little flowers, and was momentarily flooded with nostalgia – partly for the shirt itself, but mostly for the bloom of independence that it epitomized.

All the way through school, I was deeply conflicted as to whether I wanted to grow up and become responsible for my life, or whether I wanted to retreat to childhood and have everything taken care of with little effort on my part. Apparel was just a small part of this raging interior battle.

As unquestioned as the law of gravity was the understanding that girls wore skirts or dresses to school. Those who needed to push the limits would shorten their skirts by rolling them up at the waist, and once in a while a teacher or administrator declared this one or that one was just too high up the thigh. There was even a dress code created: If you knelt on the floor, your hem had to touch the ground. As for me, I had no interest in hem lengths, but just wore what was in my closet.

There was another aspect of clothing that I didn't care to pay attention to, and my cavalier attitude on the topic was too much for some of my high school classmates. I did not want to start wearing nylon stockings. Stockings required a girdle or garter belt. Stockings developed runs if you looked at them sideways, and then you were stuck for the day with an ugly stripe on your leg – an oblique or zigzag stripe, if you hadn't gotten everything exactly right in the morning. You had to *buy* the darn things, a habit I didn't care to develop. But honestly, I also figured that as busy as everyone was with classes and friends, nobody was examining my legs, right? So how could it possibly matter?

The school was built on what we called the California plan – pods of classrooms connected by outdoor walkways instead of halls. One day during class, I had a hall pass to go from one room to another, and there were a couple of other girls on a walkway across the campus. One of them shouted to get my attention. "Hey, Reid!" I turned to look, but didn't recognize her. I waited. "Nice nylons!" she called. I was, of course, bare-legged. As the pair dissolved in giggles, I silently walked on, furious. What were my legs to this stranger? But the jig was up. That night Mom and I bought a garter belt and a supply of gossamer stockings and I did learn to wear them, but always against my will.

The other crisis came before a performance. The high school singing group wore choir robes, a uniform very comforting to me in its simplicity. But as the concert approached, Mr. Agers, our beloved director, casually announced, "Boys, you will wear black dress shoes and black trousers, and the girls will wear black heels."

I rushed off to find my best friend. I was irate. "I will *not* wear heels. I don't *have* any heels. I don't *wear* heels." My immediate fear, of course, was wobbling and tottering dangerously as I climbed to the third row of the risers. But that was nothing compared to my fear of having to take on adult roles in life, a deep paranoia represented by the exigencies of fashion. I repeated my absolute refusal to Mother, but, you guessed it, she and I bought a pair of one-inch black pumps at Nordstrom, and I practiced walking in them without a single mishap. The march of "progress" had the last word.

Somehow, thankfully, I escaped being imbued with the message that many women internalize, "How you look is who you are." For me, today more than ever, comfort trumps style. The frugality of hand-me-downs is also part of my DNA, and most of what I wear comes from thrift stores. I suspect that's obvious to everyone, but my true friends forgive me for looking less than chic. Every five or six years I buy a new Gore-Tex waterproof jacket and wear it all seasons, week in and week out, until the Seattle rains start soaking through. I do maintain Mom's attitude that feet deserve special treatment, and always buy my shoes new.

There are two dresses in my closet (both from used-goods stores), and I haven't worn either one since my last series of job interviews in 2007. The pantyhose in my bottom drawer probably will rot there. Since I retired and discovered loose, non-binding blue jeans, I've rarely worn any other trousers, except for weddings, funerals, or travel. For such occasions, I choose from the seven pairs of nearly identical second-hand dress pants acquired during my working years. Some women swear by a particular brand of jeans that fit their curves, but my curves have to make do with what's at the thrift store, and I'm pleased to pay eight dollars rather than the fifty to two hundred spent by stylish ladies. I'm waiting to be old enough to get away with wearing nothing but sweat suits all the time.

Don't know much
about algebra*

W ithin a block of Edmonds High School there was a Dairy
Queen drive-in. Of course leaving campus during the school
day was against the rules, but I heard rumors that students went there
to buy lunch sometimes. Why would anyone risk the kind of trouble
that could come from breaking such an important restriction? As I
daydreamed (probably during geometry class) about the possibility of
going there *after* the final bell – which would be legal – it dawned on
me that my objection wasn't about the rules at all. The truth was that
I wouldn't have had the first clue what to say or how to act, and most
likely even the way I dressed would have been ridiculed. The DQ
culture was as foreign to me as the rituals of the Japanese imperial
court.

Like most high schools, ours was full of cliques. We had the "jocks,"
closely allied with the socialites, who, in our cliquish shorthand,
we called "soshes" (with a long "o"). Athletes, choir soloists, class
officers, and cheerleaders were so attractive and worthy that they
were the ones who dated, went to parties (and the DQ), and became
homecoming queens and kings. We believed they were destined to
join fraternities and sororities in college, marry each other, and take
over Daddy's businesses. They were as far from my realm of existence
as movie stars, and I viewed them in much the same way – like
characters on a screen. I imagined what it might be like to mingle
with them, but I knew there was no reality to my imaginings.

* Lyric from "Wonderful World," Sam Cooke, 1960

At the other end of the spectrum were the "rinks." These boys wore their greased hair in the "DA" style, but my friends and I were so prudish that we called it a "DT" – we didn't want to even *abbreviate* "duck's *ass*," and renamed it "duck's *tail*." They smoked cigarettes around the hidden corners of the buildings. Their girlfriends wore long, dark, straight skirts and chewed gum. This group declared that they hated school, and dreamed of riding motorcycles into the sunset. To me, they were like grey clouds in the distance that had no effect on the weather in my world.

Among the in-between crowds were the shop boys/ AV assistants. They gained technical skills with little difficulty, but generally were not academically gifted. Unlike the other boys, they wore jeans, and they were clean-cut but often with grease under their fingernails. These boys took shop classes and did their work earnestly, mastering car engines and power tools, and operating film projectors for the teachers. They were very polite, but shy except among their own kind, where they could literally talk shop. They didn't hang out with girls.

My little group of four or five girls called ourselves "the Rejects." We were on the college-prep track, worked as hard as necessary for good grades, and didn't obsess over our looks – although I can't say we weren't a little envious of those who did. We did not have boyfriends, only because boys had no interest in us.

There were 1300 students at Edmonds High, and among them were most of the children who had attended preschool, kindergarten, and elementary school with me. The population could have been called stable – or stagnant. As far as I recall, there was no racial or ethnic diversity, if you discounted the distinction between Bruce MacBurney's ancestry and that of Tor Johannessen. In my junior year, just one dark-skinned young man named René joined our ranks when his family moved from Louisiana. Everyone talked about him, but I'm pretty sure he wasn't absorbed into any group. I was mystified as to why he kept insisting that he was Creole, not Negro – that was the level of my ignorance in 1961. He didn't come back for our senior year.

In that static, monochromatic environment we encountered Mr. Cunningham, a creative and courageous teacher who was far ahead of his time. He taught a selection of courses, but the one I remember was called simply "Humanities." For one term we studied Edith Hamilton's *Mythology*; for another, Ruth Benedict's *Patterns of Culture*; for a third, Huston Smith's *The Religions of Man* (now re-titled *The World's Religions*). Finally we wrestled with the confusing Old Testament book of Job. Mr. Cunningham was frequently in trouble with school administrators for his challenging methods of prying open our narrow, literal minds to ancient Greek world-views, the evolution of Buddhism out of Hinduism, a complex Hebrew God, Navaho and Hopi rites, and white America's attitudes toward people different from themselves.

One day we walked into the room and saw, chalked on the blackboard in letters a foot high, "I AM GOD."

One of our classmates was a fundamentalist Baptist. She knew when she was right and didn't hesitate to say so. So it was Betty whose eyes narrowed suspiciously as she asked, "What does *that* mean?"

Mr. Cunningham calmly pointed to himself and said, "I am God."

She let out a shriek that seemed propelled by near-panic: "*Mis*-ter *Cun*-ningham, *you* can't *do* that!"

"Of course I can! Once I threw a Bible at a student!" (We never heard the details of *that* story.) After receiving our initial reactions, he went on to scribble, in equally tall letters, "YOU ARE GOD. HE IS GOD. SHE IS GOD," and the battle was joined. Nearly everyone jumped in with comments, questions, arguments. The teacher's task was to manage the flow and challenge our logic here and there. It was exhilarating. Needless to say, we were required to write a paper on the subject, presenting and defending our viewpoints with consideration of the various spiritual perspectives we had studied.

One day between classes in my junior year, a few of us were in Cunningham's room discussing our schedules for the following term. I told my friends that the counselor had impressed upon me the need to take some "commercial" (secretarial) courses, so I was going to use up one or two of my electives on typing and shorthand. Cunningham bellowed, "*What??*"

"Well, all the adults say you should have those skills to fall back on."

He collected himself and patiently said, "*You* are not going to need shorthand in your life. And if *you* feel you need typing, then teach yourself to type over the summer. Don't waste your precious school time on that nonsense!"

I felt as if a ray of sunshine had briefly pierced an unnoticed fog, providing a glimpse of intriguing possibilities for my future. I wasted no time in secretarial courses. That summer I acquired a practical workbook, borrowed Dad's old manual typewriter, and learned touch typing. It wasn't hard, although I ran out of enthusiasm before mastering the top row, and to this day I have to look at the keys to locate the number 6 or the dollar sign. This was before Xerox machines, and I had wanted to collect some poems and song lyrics. Great typing practice! Today my files still contain a few of those works that I copied from books, using the instrument's only font, which consisted of capital characters in tall and short versions, and no lower-case letters.

In the years to follow, I used this self-training in a number of my careers. Before computers, I had one boss who, even though I had told him that I didn't know shorthand, wanted me to take dictation anyway. I listened and made notes as I had in college lectures, and when I handed him the typed letter, he asked, "Did I say this?"

"Not in so many words," I replied, discomfited.

"Well, it's exactly what I meant to say." He signed the letter and found my edits invaluable after that. Cunningham was right – no shorthand needed.

My closest high school friend was Cynthia Quail. At Edmonds High it was common to call each other by last names. She had sometimes been teased about her birdy moniker, but by the time we were in high school, Cynthia had learned to live very comfortably with it.

Cynthia had an incisive mind. Unlike the average high-schooler – even some of us "A" students – she wanted to fully understand what was being taught. On her own, she would probe the topic and do her best to resolve any uncertainty. Even when she was puzzled, interrupting an instructor was a last resort, and she didn't often raise her hand. But as she delved into her own brain to penetrate meanings, her face sometimes showed the effort. She would stop taking notes, ball-point pen poised above her paper. Her forehead would lower until she squinted, while her steady gaze followed the teacher in a manner that looked almost menacing.

Cunningham gained familiarity with Cynthia's pattern, and sometimes elicited her observations, which could take the whole class to a new level of comprehension. One day, his lecture was rolling along nicely when he noticed Cynthia's deep frown. He watched her for a few moments, continuing to speak and pace back and forth as usual. Suddenly, in mock annoyance, he stopped in mid-sentence, facing her, and shouted, "*Quail, you dumb cluck, what's the matter?*"

There was a moment of shocked silence, then the room exploded in laughter – laughter that caught up Cynthia as well – and when it died down, she took a deep breath, smiling, and pointed out an inconsistency in what the teacher had presented. A fascinating, free-flowing discussion ensued, which not only demonstrated for the students thinking skills that most of us hadn't developed, but also highlighted Cunningham's honest respect for our classmate, the dumb cluck.

Cunningham was quirky about his territory. There was no sound insulation between adjacent classrooms because the upper eighteen inches of each wall was formed by a steel I-beam on which the flat roof rested. Steel conducts sound. After some research, Cunningham found that pressed-cardboard egg cartons were excellent sound deadeners, and he put out a request for all of us to bring in empty cartons. Stapling them edge to edge, he attached them to the steel, creating a bumpy, but much quieter, space. Had he wanted to dampen the noise coming in, or had his neighboring colleagues complained about his occasional high-volume expressions?

The room had large south windows, and one day we arrived to find three-quarters of them covered with aluminum foil. "It gets too hot in here, and I've read some articles confirming that tin foil is a great way to reflect heat back outside." And it worked as well as the egg cartons had. Was it coincidental that we students were no longer distracted by views of people moving around the walkways and parking lot beyond the windows?

His final pet peeve was the public address system. Periodically he would find a co-conspirator to help him disconnect the classroom speakers. This gave Cunningham some respite from intrusive interruptions, until, inevitably, the sabotage was discovered and the wiring was re-installed. The repairs never lasted long. He didn't mind pushing the limits, and school administrators considered him a painful thorn in their side.

Someone at the student newspaper got the tired old notion of asking a number of teachers for their definition of a good student.

Dr. Parris: "A good student is one who studies every day and is always prepared."

Mr. Yeager: "A good student remembers dates and understands the relationships among historical events."

Mrs. Wheeler: "A good student is interested in math and quiet in class."

And finally, Mr. Cunningham: "A good student is one who agrees with me."

His dry humor was as offbeat as his instructional approach. The paper published it, enhancing his reputation immeasurably. Long story short, you couldn't finish one of Cunningham's courses without gaining a broader awareness of the vast variety of human life, belief, and expression – or without laughing.

I entered Edmonds High emotionally bruised from a thoroughly disheartening three-year stint in junior high school. The alternate teasing and dismissiveness of my fellow students had convinced me that, as a person, I wasn't worth much. I anticipated more of the same in high school. In my very first class, college-prep English,

Mrs. Beaver thrust me into an experiment that began to convince me otherwise. She selected me as Roxane. I tried to refuse, but she allowed no escape. We were to read *Cyrano de Bergerac* aloud, and she cast me in the play opposite Bob Barnes. Bob, already a socially successful high achiever, was that boy who later earned letters in three sports, captained the football team, and graduated in the top ten percent. Bob read the part of Christian. Cyrano was played by the funny and sometimes cynical Ron Stephens, a fascinating individual who hid his real self under quick-witted cleverness. I felt the two of them were quite suited to their roles – but I was no Roxane to be desired from afar!

At first, I assumed we would have new actors every day or two until the play was finished, but the three of us kept our roles. Mrs. Beaver's classroom atmosphere was insistently positive – helpful comments were welcome, and no one was allowed to insult or embarrass another pupil. Bob and Ron were respectful. Before long, on the way out of the room, a few people told me that the drama took on more meaning for them because of the way I read – with feeling. This reaction catalyzed a gentle shift in my thoughts about who I was. When I looked into the mirror of their eyes, I didn't see the clumsy, unacceptable teenager of earlier years, but someone who could become equal to those around her. I began to take a little more interest in my appearance, and a little of my shyness fell away. High school took on a different color than my recent school experience. Mrs. Beaver had an amazing knack for nurturing growth, and I'll always be deeply grateful for her high expectations and firm, gentle encouragement.

Mr. Bond was the librarian. He was ahead of his time, in a way – one of the few faculty members intent on actually helping students pursue learning on their own terms. Two of my friends and I became curious about the popular phrase "brownie points," and we asked Mr. Bond if he could help us find out where the term came from. We had looked in the big desk dictionary, but there was nothing there. He made us promise not to tell where we got the information, then opened a book that he furtively pulled out of his desk drawer. "This is a reference book, and you can't take it away from this counter." (I believe it was the *Dictionary of American Slang*, but I couldn't swear to it.) The keys in that book unlocked portals one by one until we arrived at the true origin: *brownie* back to *brown-nose* and further back to *ass-kisser*. We were thrilled! He quickly and covertly returned the book to the drawer – maybe for dramatic effect, but maybe because it could actually bring him trouble. For a few days, every time we saw Mr. Bond we flew into fits of giggles. And woe be to the person who said "brownie points" after that!

My friends and I were all pre-tested for placement in another college-prep class, a new multi-year program called "Illinois math." I hated math and was convinced I couldn't master it. I very consciously decided to do poorly on the pre-test, because the prospect of facing advanced geometry, trigonometry and calculus seemed like a terrible waste of time and effort. The tactic worked. My high school mathematical experience consisted of bonehead algebra and geometry. I sat in the back with the boys who couldn't be still, and I brought cookies to share with them. In that class, no one thought we would learn much, and we kept the bar low, becoming comrades and having a few laughs at poor Mrs. Wheeler's expense.

Some twenty-five years later I ran into a fellow who had been my brother's friend, and told him, "I had such a crush on you. After all, you were one of the athletes."

He gave me a disbelieving look and said, "Barbie, I was the *manager* of the teams. I carried buckets of water and dirty towels." He continued, "But you – you were impressive. You were one of the brains." To me, that had been a miniscule part of my fatally flawed social identity. We'd been so young, so cocooned in our own little worlds! Thank heaven most of us grow beyond the skewed perceptions of self and others that burdened us in our teen years.

Pray that there's
intelligent life*

Laurence J. Peter** wrote, "Psychiatry enables us to correct our faults by confessing our parents' shortcomings."

I cannot argue intelligently. After a thoroughly superficial study of psychology, I feel confident in my right to blame my mother.

We children never heard the culturally familiar, last-resort parental phrase, "Because I said so." When Mother made a decision affecting us, we were free to ask why, and most of the time, her explanation was so exhaustive that there was nothing left to say. She made it clear that what she wanted you to do was the one correct thing to do – whether it was making your bed every day or signing up for particular college classes.

I'm convinced that my sister, born six years before me, didn't have the same parents I had. She was the first baby, the experimental model, and Mom and Dad were young and ignorant, and maybe even still in love with each other. I suspect that when she was small, not everything was already decided, and she may even have heard our parents talking, trying to work things out between themselves. By the time my brother and I came along, the "working-out" phase of the marriage was all but abandoned, and the "putting-up-with" stage was becoming the norm. Whatever the cause, among the three of us, my sister argues best.

A typical youngest child, I was always striving to figure out what the adults wanted from me and making an earnest effort to give it to

* Lyric from "Galaxy Song," Eric Idle and John DuPrez, 1983

**Laurence J. Peter, after an erudite study of corporate behavior, identified the Peter Principle: "In a hierarchy, every employee tends to rise to his level of incompetence."

them. The trouble was, in focusing on their desires, I didn't learn what I wanted. In fact, if on occasion I did know what I wanted, it seemed too risky to put it into words. Their disapproval was my most painful punishment. Expressing myself out loud dropped to the bottom of my priority list.

There were powerful talkers in the family. My mother was a clear-witted, well-spoken achiever. Her brother, Uncle Sherman, was known for engaging unsuspecting family members in debates that didn't end until he wore down the opposition through unrelenting persuasion. Granddad, Mom's father, didn't say much, at least when I was around, but when he did speak, his comments were sharp and to the point, and his wit was acerbic. If there was ever a disagreement, each of them readily accessed facts and reasoning to achieve their aims. My sister inherited the family legacy of logic.

I was the antithesis of these verbally adept role models. Unable to provide rationale for my position, I fell back on either basic stubbornness or abject compliance. I deduced that I was brain-deficient.

To this day, when someone shares a plan or opinion divergent from my own, I feel my stomach twist like a dishrag, and my responses become less and less coherent. My gut disagrees with the person, but my brain can't translate that emotion into understandable language.

I use more profanity than my siblings, simply because I seem to lose access to my vocabulary just when I most want to clarify my side of an issue. Confronted with strife, my sister persistently presses her point; my brother leans back and speaks slowly and with authority; I gnash my teeth and make grunting sounds. It's as if we had sprung into present time from three different evolutionary eras.

There's been one change, but it's not necessarily an improvement. Today, I'm generally aware of what I want. Unfortunately, I'm likely to express it very undiplomatically. A face-to-face disagreement still means a taut solar plexus and a tongue that trips itself up. I guess I can be thankful that only a few of the many asinine, inappropriate or downright cruel things I've said in this life still come back to attack me. My regret comes too late.

This circumstance engenders a major attraction of the written word. In print, I can visually review my thoughts and catch the worst of the meanness and stupidity before they escape my private realm, potentially writing something relatively smart, slightly sensitive, or even somewhat kind. I know many admirable people who regularly achieve this feat in spoken language, on the wing as it were, but sadly, I am not among them. Listening and responding with intelligence is still a distant goal of mine.

The story is not ended, and the play is never done*

A memoir is always a work in progress, history and herstory rewriting themselves. A biography starts from a point in the past and stops at a point in the past, but the stories began much earlier than the book's beginning, and they continue in a most unruly way, defying closure. With luck, you, the reader, and I, the author, co-creating alongside Life itself, will keep on making stories, and after us, others will do the same. As advertisers used to announce:

Watch this space.
There's more to come.
Always.

Thank you for joining me on this portion of the merry spiral from seed to sapling, sprout to tree, tree to fruit, apple to seed to sprout to tree. Keep growing.

* Lyric from "The Fantasticks," Harvey Schmidt and Tom Jones, 1960

Acknowledgments

My thanks go to so many! I mention a few here. To masterful instructor/ advisors Joanne Horn and Steve Lorton, for getting me started, and for teaching and guiding me and other writers with their knowledge and encouragement. To Carol, Jan, Nancy, and Kathryn – my first writers group – for scribbling alongside me, for their energy and appreciation, and for sharing their homes and their stories. To Bill, Caryn, David, Jean, Mary Lou, Nora, Pete, Rose, Steve, Tamara, and Thomas – my second writers group – for helping me stay on task and on track, and for their ample and much-needed suggestions, critiques, and attention to the meaning and art of the written word. To insightful editor Mary Oak, the first person to read the entire manuscript, for pointing out what was missing, helping arrange the chapters, and being a thoroughly kind and gentle cheerleader. To talented artist Heidi Favour for her enthusiasm for life, and for the marvelous cover design which elegantly expresses the heart of the memoir. To Bob Lanphear for accompanying me through the labyrinthine publishing project, and for miraculously transforming my words into an actual book. To dear and trusted friends whose positive responses have kept me moving forward along the path, and to the whole fam-damily for inspiring these stories and forgiving any errors. Finally, to Ken and Carolyn for their brotherly and sisterly responses to the writing, and for always supporting me in spite of everything.

68598184R00165

Made in the USA
Lexington, KY
15 October 2017